IT Networking Labs

Thomas P. Cavaiani

Boise State University

Prentice Hall

Boston   Columbus   Indianapolis   New York   San Francisco   Upper Saddle River

Amsterdam   Cape Town   Dubai   London   Madrid   Milan   Munich   Paris   Montreal   Toronto

Delhi   Mexico City   Sao Paulo   Sydney   Hong Kong   Seoul   Singapore   Taipei   Tokyo

Editor-in-Chief: Eric Svendsen

Executive Editor: Bob Horan

Editorial Project Manager: Kelly Loftus

Production Project Manager: Debbie Ryan

Operations Specialist: Arnold Vila

---

10 9 8 7 6 5 4 3 2 1

Prentice Hall
is an imprint of

PEARSON

www.pearsonhighered.com

ISBN-13: 978-0-13-10738-5

ISBN-10: 0-13-610738-9

IT Networking Labs

by

Thomas P. Cavaiani
Boise State University

BRIEF CONTENTS

TABLE OF CONTENTS

PREFACE

IT Networking Labs provides a set of hands-on activities designed for college students majoring in information technology. The manual provides in-depth coverage of topics that are essential for developing a basic understanding of computer networks. Topics are approached from an applications point of view as opposed to a systems view. The labs in this manual make extensive use of open source software, and are designed so that students can perform them either at home on their own computer, or on-campus in a designated computer lab. A typical chapter includes concept coverage, an overview of the lab, lab procedures with numerous illustrations, and follow-up questions.

A developing trend in computing is to move standard office applications from the desktop to the World Wide Web. Numerous vendors are supporting this move. Google, for example, is providing applications, storage space, and email services to its customers via Google sites and Gmail. Other sites on the World Wide Web provide free applications for common activities, such as file transfers, remote access to servers, network monitoring, and simulating and testing network performance. The premise of this manual is to involve students in activities that provide them with an opportunity to learn about network technologies by utilizing resources that are literally at their fingertips, while keeping hardware and software costs, and preparation time, to a minimum.

The labs in this manual are designed to create an environment that provides students with the opportunity to learn through a guided discovery approach. Many of the labs require the student to access on-line resources to gain insight into the functionality of a particular program or technology. Extensive use of reputable sites on the World Wide Web is made to provide students with sources of information regarding the use of specific technologies. For example, students learn how to configure specific components of a wireless access point by consulting Cisco's on-line reference manual for one of their Aironet access points. Even though discovery is the preferred approach to learning in these labs, step-by-step instructions are included in some labs and in the appendices for basic procedures, such as downloading and installing software. Numerous screen shots are included to guide students through these procedures. Diagrams, when appropriate, are also included to illustrate network configurations and directory structures.

This manual focuses primarily on developing a basic understanding of networking technologies supported by the Windows platform. It also includes basic coverage of file management in Linux, first from the command-line and then via the KDE desktop. Each lab focuses on a different topic and is preceded by a short overview of the conceptual knowledge required to complete the lab. Appendices are included that guide students through the process of locating, downloading, installing, and configuring open-source software. These appendices can be used as also be used as preliminary labs so that students may take a more active role in the lab preparation process that typically is performed by either the instructor or a lab assistant.

An added benefit for using open-source applications is that doing so reduces hardware and software costs as well as lab preparation times. The simulation software used in these labs provides a programmatic means for creating networks with an unlimited number of nodes. No physical space and furniture need to be set aside for network hardware, no actual hardware needs to be acquired and configured, and no cables need to be connected. Typically downloading and installing a given open-source application used in one of the labs takes between 10 to 15 minutes. This of course amounts to a huge savings in preparation time for those responsible for installing and configuring the hardware and software used in the laboratory.

AUDIENCE

This manual is intended for students enrolled in an introductory college-level computer networking and telecommunications course. It is assumed that these students are typically sophomores or juniors with some previous knowledge of, or exposure to, operating systems fundamentals and common desktop applications such as word processors, spreadsheets, and presentation graphics applications.

LAB ORIGINS

Originally these labs were created as on-line activities for a university-level laboratory course designed to supplement an introductory lecture course on business telecommunications and networking essentials. Five sections of the lab course were offered and completed before the labs were converted into book form. Approximately 150 students have completed the course and have reviewed the labs. The feedback provided by these students has proved to be extremely helpful in locating and eliminate errors found in the early versions of the labs and to increase the clarity of the included instructions and explanations.

LAB OVERVIEW

IT Networking Labs consists of 16 labs as shown in Table 1. Each lab covers different topics related to accessing or managing information on a computer network. Coverage ranges from network authentication to analyzing network performance. Each lab has been designed so that a minimal amount of pre-requisite knowledge is needed to complete the lab. Basic topics are discussed in the first few labs with more advanced topics covered later in the manual. Descriptions of each lab follow Table 1.

Table 1: An outline of the labs included in this manual

Lab Number	Lab Title
One	Accessing Network Files and Applications
Two	File Transfers
Three	Selected Networking Features in Windows
Four	Computer Hardware
Five	The HyperText Markup Language (HTML)
Six	Constructing a Network Cable
Seven	Local Area Networks Fundamentals
Eight	Designing a Local Area Network
Nine	Configuring a Wireless LAN Access Point
Ten	The Linux Command Line Interface
Eleven	The Linux Desktop
Twelve	Packet Capture and Analysis
Thirteen	Analyzing Transport Layer Protocols
Fourteen	Security Policies
Fifteen	Evaluating Network Performance
Sixteen	Electronic Mail and SMTP

LAB DESCRIPTIONS

1. **Accessing Network Files and Applications** – This lab covers the authentication procedures that are used to access a networked computer. Procedures for authenticating to both Windows and Linux computers are covered. The use of remote access software is discussed for accessing Linux computer systems. Creating and accessing a site on the World Wide Web is discussed. Students create a Google site for storing the reports that they will create in future labs. A brief discussion regarding security differences between standalone and networked computer file systems is included. The role a network administrator plays in securing user accounts while providing access to file systems and web space is discussed.

2. **File Transfers -** This lab discusses how to use an open-source client-side file transfer program to upload files to a remote computer. The student gets actual hands-on experience by performing a secure (encrypted) file transfer from a Windows computer to a Linux computer as well as a non-secure file transfer from one Windows computer to another.

3. **Selected Networking Features in Windows** - This lab covers a subset of the network-related features supported by Microsoft Windows. Students learn how to add the Run option to the Windows Start menu, how to use basic network utilities such as ping, tracert, ipconfig, and netstat, how to map a network drive, how to search for and locate a computer on the network, how to change the computer's network name, how to join a workgroup or domain, and how to change the IP address associated with a network adapter. A use of a trace route gateway is discussed as an alternative to using the tracert command.

4. **Computer Hardware** – Students perform basic research on the World Wide Web to learn more about computer hardware so that they can design a computer workstation to meet the needs of office workers employed by the IT department of a large fictional corporation. Input, process, output, storage, and communications (network) hardware are investigated. Students obtain actual price quotes for their computer system designs from two different on-line vendors of computer hardware.

5. **The HyperText Markup Language (HTML)** - This lab is a based upon an on-line tutorial designed to introduce students the HyperText Markup Language. Students create and test web pages using instructions provided by an introductory tutorial available at the W3 Schools site on the World Wide Web. The topics range from basic text formatting to adding tables, forms, and graphics to web pages.

6. **Constructing a Network Cable** – Students perform basic research on the World Wide Web to learn more about the TIA/EIA cable standards that are used when construction network patch cables. After completing their research, students build a patch cable using a piece of CAT 5 unshielded twisted pair cable, RJ 45 connectors, and the a crimping tool. Students also test the cable using a cable tester to determine if the cable has been properly constructed. Materials for this lab are fairly inexpensive and students gain an appreciation for the demands of building functional cables.

7. **Local Area Network Fundamentals** - Students perform some basic research on the World Wide Web to learn more about the physical and logical topologies of local area networks. Students also investigate different media access methods, such as CSMA/CD, as well as the two most popular security models (peer-to-peer and client/server) used in LANs. VLANs are also investigated. Students create a report based upon their findings.

8. **Designing a Local Area Network** - In this lab students apply the information collected in Lab 7 to designing a Local Area Network for a fictional organization. A site on the World Wide Web is used that provides students with a virtual environment for designing and building their networks. The site also provides numerous scenarios that students can review and use as a basis for learning how to design their own networks.

9. **Configuring a Wireless Access Point** – In this lab students learn how a wireless access point (WAP) is configured via the Cisco command line interface (CLI) by investigating selected sections of an on-line Cisco WAP reference manual. Commands for setting the IP address of the WAP, enabling the WAP radio, and securing the WAP are covered. An optional exercise allows students to apply what they learned from the reference manual by configuring an actual Cisco Aironet WAP.

10. **Using the Linux Command Line Interface** – Students issue Linux file and directory commands to help them gain a basic understanding of file management techniques on computers using the Linux operating system. Students learn how to create and delete directories and files, how to view the contents of a file, how to copy files from one directory to another, how to change the permissions of a file, and how to use the grep command for searching for substrings in a file. Two versions of this lab are included in the manual. One version is based upon the Suse Linux distribution and the other is based upon the Knoppix distribution. The Suse lab also discusses access to a remote Linux system using the puTTY terminal emulator. The Knoppix version includes discussion of how to run Linux from a bootable CD-ROM and troubleshoot common problems that may arise as files are loaded from the CD-ROM into computer memory.

11. **Using a Linux Graphical User Interface** – Students learn how to use public domain viewer software to connect to a Linux computer and access the KDE desktop. Students perform a set of activities that helps them learn various file management techniques using the KDE desktop tools. The Knoppix bootable CD-ROM distribution of Linux can be used for this exercise if network access to a remote Linux computer is not available.

12. **Packet Capture and Analysis** - Students capture packets sent over a network using *Wireshark*, an open source protocol analyzer. Once packets are captured students analyze the results. Students learn how to creating capture filters to simplify data analysis. An extensive discussion regarding how to use the Wireshark software is included. An appendix provides step-by-step instructions for downloading and installing the Wireshark software.

13. **Analyzing Transport Layer Protocols** – Students used techniques learned in Lab 12 to capture packets that are transferred during the download of a large data file from two different types of servers. Specifically *Wireshark* is used to capture packets downloaded from FTP and TFTP servers. Students then apply filtering techniques to simplify the analysis of the data. Data related to the Internet transfer layer protocols, TCP (*Transmission Control Protocol*) and UDP (*User Datagram Protocol*) are investigated to gain a better understanding of the performance differences of the two protocols.

14. **Security Policies** - This lab provide students with an opportunity to gain a basic understanding of the components of a security policy and how to customize a security policy template to fit the needs of a fictional organization. Students download a security password policy template from SANs.org and modify it to meet the needs of the fictional organization.

15. **System and Network Management** – Students work through a tutorial to create a scenario using the IT Guru Academic Edition network simulation software that measures and compares *load* and *delay* on baseline and expanded versions of a simulated network. The simulation captures traffic data on the individual networks, and provides tools for students to create graphs that display

performance measures in a meaningful way. An appendix provides step-by-step instructions that students can use to download and install the software on their own computers. Instructions for registering the software are also included.

16. **Electronic Mail and SMTP**- In this lab students use telnet to connect to an SMTP server and then manually send a message to the server using SMTP commands. Students learn the limitations of SMTP as well as how to use these commands for troubleshooting file transfers to an SMTP server.

NOTES FOR THE INSTRUCTOR

Most of us associate a computer lab course with a considerable investment in computer hardware and software to support such a course. This assumption was not made during the development of this lab manual. A different approach was considered as a result of emerging trends based upon the ubiquity and proliferation of Internet access and computer hardware, specifically laptop computers. Since most students now own or have access to either a desktop or laptop computer these labs have been designed to take advantage of that fact to minimize, if not eliminate, the need for a special purpose computer lab for conducting the lab sessions. Additionally free wireless Internet access is readily available almost anywhere on most campuses, at most, if not all, public libraries, and nearly all coffee houses. Most students also have broadband Internet access in their homes. Therefore a concerted effort was made to design each lab so that the student could perform the lab on their own computer anywhere they had access to the Internet. For example, instead of requiring a substantial investment in hardware and proprietary software to support these labs, open-source simulation software is used instead. Also sites on the Internet are used to provide access to open-source software that can be used to provide common network services.

Hardware and Software Requirements

Table 1 breaks down hardware and software requirements by lab. As you can see, 12 of the labs require nothing more than a computer with Internet access only. Students can use information in the appendices to download the open source software and install it on their own computers or in the case of the Linux labs create a bootable CD to run the software on their computer. The remaining four labs require at least network access to a Windows server that supports Active Directory, FTP, TFTP, SMTP, and web services. A Linux server that supports a similar set of services could be used either in lieu of or in conjunction with the Windows server, depending upon whether or not you want students to experience the differences in these two platforms from an end user perspective.

Minimal Computer Laboratory Configuration

If you decide to set up a computer laboratory for students, the minimum lab configuration would require a Windows server connected to a network that students could access with their own laptop computers via either a wired or wireless connection. To minimize setup times, students could install the necessary open-source applications on their laptops. The Windows server would preferably run the Windows 2003 Server operating system. This server would be configured as a domain controller to provide Active Directory services for creating student accounts. It would also have *Internet Information Services* configured to provide students with access to FTP, SMTP, and web services. TFTP services are also required. An open-source TFTP server is available from SolarWinds that could be installed to provide these services. Instructions for installing the SolarWinds TFTP server are available on the Instructor Web site. Instead of using IIS, *Apache Server for Windows* could be used to provide web services. Since access to a Linux server is not provided by this configuration, student could not perform *Part two* of Lab 1, nor could they perform the *secure file transfer activity* in Lab 2.

Modest Computer Laboratory Configuration

This configuration adds a Linux server to the minimum configuration. FTP, TFTP, and SSH services would need to be running on the Linux server. Apache Server could be used to provide web services. Student accounts would also need to be created on this server. Installation of a graphical user interface, such as KDE or Gnome, is recommended, but not required, because it would allow configuration of services via a menu system instead of from a command-line interface. With this addition students can perform all parts of all labs. It should be mentioned once again that this server is only needed for *Part two* of Lab 1 and the *secure file transfer activity* in Lab 2.

Complete Laboratory Configuration

This configuration builds provides students with a physical location to perform the labs. This location fully-equipped with a number of Windows desktop computers connected to your lab network and the Internet. The software is preloaded on the computers. The servers would be configured as mentioned above and connected to this network.

Remote access to your network could also be provided. Students could then work on the labs outside of class if necessary. Security becomes a major concern if this option is added. Remote Access Services would need to be configured on the Windows server. If you have a firewall configured to block external access to your network, then reconfiguration of the firewall would be necessary. The appendices of the lab manual include instructions so that students can install and configure Cisco VPN client software on their computers. If this is not the appropriate client for your environment then you will need to supply instructions and software to your students for accessing your network via VPN.

Alternatives

If your institution cannot support a computer laboratory for students, an alternative is to have your students set up their own networks. A minimal network could be setup with two computers with network adaptors, one to act as a server and one as a client. Students could install the Windows 2003 server operating system and configure the services described above on one of he machines. They could connect the other machine to the server with a cross-over cable. Adding a switch or hub and connecting the computers with patch cables would allow this small network to be connected to the World Wide Web via a broadband connection. All Linux labs could be run from a Knoppix bootable CD. If you would like to use this approach, you can provide students with the instructions for configuring the servers that are available on the Instructor web site.

Other Equipment

Lab 6 includes a cable building exercise. Cabling, terminators, a crimping tool, and cable testers are required to build a cable. This exercise may be made optional if you choose not to invest in the required equipment and materials.

Lab 9 includes an exercise for configuring a Cisco Aironet wireless access point. If you choose not to invest in one or more access points you skip this part of the lab.

Both labs 6 and 9 provide the student with an opportunity to learn more about the topics discussed by completing preliminary exercises that will prove beneficial even without the hands-on component of the lab.

Table 2: Hardware and Software Requirement broken down by lab. An * denotes open-source software.

Lab	Title	Hardware Required	Software Required	Network Access?	Internet Access?
1	Accessing Network Files and Applications	Windows and Linux servers	Active Directory, web services	yes	yes
2	File Transfers	Same as 1	Same as 1, WinSCP*	yes	no
3	Selected Networking Features in Windows	Windows server	none	yes	yes
4	Computer Hardware	none	none	no	yes
5	The HyperText Markup Language (HTML)	none	none	no	yes
6	Constructing a Network Cable	cabling, crimping tool, and cable tester	none	no	yes
7	Local Area Networks Fundamentals	none	none	no	yes
8	Designing a Local Area Network	none	none	no	yes
9	Configuring a Wireless LAN Access Point	Cisco WAP (optional)	none	optional	yes
10	The Linux Command Line Interface	none or Linux Server	Knoppix bootable CD*	no	yes
11	The Linux Desktop	none or Linux Server	Knoppix bootable CD*	no	yes
12	Packet Capture and Analysis	none	Wireshark*	no	yes
13	Analyzing Transport Layer Protocols	Linux or Windows Server	FTP and TFTP services	yes	no
14	Security Policies	none	none	no	yes
15	Evaluating Network Performance	none	IT Guru Academic Edition*	no	yes
16	Electronic Mail and SMTP	Windows server	SMTP services	yes	no

USING THE LABS WITH YOUR TEXT

Table 3 provides suggestions for how you might map of the labs in this manual with the chapters in three of the most popular data communications textbooks currently available. It should be noted that the textbooks listed in the table do not include specific coverage of Linux. It is suggested that the Linux labs (labs 10, 11) be included in your schedules as time permits.

Table 3: Suggested lab to chapter mappings.

Chapter	FitzGerald and Dennis	Panko	White
1	Lab 1	Lab 1, Lab 2	Lab 1
1a*		Labs 4, 8	
2	Lab 2	Lab 5	Lab 6
3	Lab 6		Lab 9
3a*		Lab 6	
4	Lab 12	Lab 7	Lab 2
5		Lab 9	
6	Lab 7		
7	Lab 9		Lab 7
8			Labs 8, 10, 11
8a*		Lab 13	
9		Lab 14	Lab 2 using VPN
10	Lab 5	Lab 15	Labs 5,16
10a*		Labs 3, 12	
11	Lab 14	Lab 16	Lab 13
12	Lab 8		Lab 14
13	Lab 15		Lab 15

* These chapter designations are specific to the Panko text only.

Complete Textbook Information

Business Data Networks and Telecommunications, 7th Edition (Pearson)
Raymond Panko
ISBN-13: 9780136153405
© 2009
624 Pages

Data Communications and Computer Networks: A Business User's Approach, 5th Edition (Cengage)
Curt White
ISBN-13: 9781423903031
© 2009
528 Pages

Business Data Communications and Networking, 10th Edition (Wiley)
Jerry FitzGerald, Jerry FitzGerald and Associates.
Alan Dennis, University of Indiana.
ISBN-13: 978-0-470-05575-5
©2009
608 pages

SUPPLEMENTS

1. **An on-line Instructor's Manual:** The instructor's manual is available at
   http://www.pearsonhighered.com/cavaiani. It provides answers to the questions and exercises
   included in the labs. Instructions for installing and configuring the server-side software are also
   provided, as well as known issues regarding problems that might arise while students are working on
   the labs.
2. **E-mail the author:** E-mail from faculty using the lab manual is encouraged. Any questions or
   suggestions for improving the manual will be considered.
3. **Updates**: Updates, posted periodically, will contain information regarding changes and corrections to
   the manual, especially changes to the open-source software used in the labs.

ACKNOWLEDGEMENTS

This book could not have been completed without the contributions of many people. I would first like to
thank my editor, Robert Horan, for his efforts in providing guidance and support for this project from its
inception to its completion. I would also like to acknowledge the support provided by Kelly Loftus
throughout the review and revision process. The Prentice-Hall production team of Judy Leale, Senior
Managing Editor, and Debbie Ryan, Production Project Manager, also deserves a special mention for its
commitment and dedication to this project. I would also like to thank Charles Morris, Manager: Rights
and Permissions, for his efforts in identifying copyright issues pertaining to the numerous screen shots
included in the manual.

I would like thank the following individuals for their help in securing permission to reprint selected
images of their organization's products and/or web site pages:

Amy Knueppel, *Dell*

Caren Neydavoud and Alice Vu, *Cisco*

Kent Walker, *Google*

Sue Goodwill, *Novell*

Diane Sardi, *the SANs Institute*

Constantin Kaplinsky, *TightVNC*

Hege Refsnes, *W3 Schools*

Gerald Combs, *Wireshark*

Martin Prikryl, *WinSCP*

Keron, Smith, *WinZip*

I would also like to thank Krassie Petrova and Nurul Sarkar, program leaders and owners of the WebLan-
Designer simulation software for allowing me to include selected images from the Auckland University of
Technology WebLan-Designer website in this manual.

A special thanks to Dr. Emerson Maxson for his invaluable suggestions regarding the structure, syntax,
and content of the manual. I would also like to thank Alan Bonde for his support in configuring and

testing both local and remote access to the lab network so that the procedures outlined in this manual could be tested for accuracy.

Many individuals were involved in reviewing the text as it was being developed. I would like to thank them sincerely for taking the time from their busy schedules to review my manuscript. Their devotion to assessing the preliminary versions of the chapters provided valuable suggestions that led to significant improvements in the final versions of these chapters.

Hans-Joachim Adler, *University of Texas at Dallas*

Jongbok Byun, *Point Loma Nazarene University*

Michael A. Chilton, *Kansas State University*

Angela M. Clark, *University of South Alabama*

Biswadip Ghosh, *Metropolitan State College of Denver*

Shaoyi He, *California State University- San Marcos*

Carmen Lewis, *Florida State University*

Harry Rief, *James Madison University*

Mario Spina, *George Washington University*

Dwayne Whitten, *Texas A&M University*

Judy Wynekoop, *Florida Gulf Coast University*

ABOUT THE AUTHOR

Thomas P. Cavaiani is a Special Lecturer at Boise State University in Boise, Idaho. From 1997 until 2000 he developed and refined the curriculum and taught the first courses in the Computer Network Support Program in the Larry Selland College of Applied Technology at Boise State University. In the fall of 2000 he began teaching computer networking and Java programming courses in the College of Business and Economics at Boise State University. He has developed curriculum for a number of the networking courses that he has taught during his tenure in the College of Business and Economics.

His industry experience includes a working as a systems administrator at Hewlett-Packard Corporation and private consulting. While at Hewlett-Packard he developed and taught numerous courses on proprietary HP software as well as many popular Microsoft Office applications. He also supported three on-site classroom training facilities, and developed an on-line course evaluation system. As a consultant he developed software solutions, developed and published training materials, and provided computer applications training for a number of companies and state agencies in the Boise area.

Dr. Cavaiani received a Ph.D. in Mathematics and Computer Science Education from Oregon State University in 1989. He has bachelors' degrees in mathematics and Mathematics Education, as well as a Masters degree in Mathematics Education. He has published in the *American Technical Education Association Journal*, the *Journal of Research on Computing in Education,* and the *Journal of Information Systems Education*. He holds or has held numerous Microsoft and Novell certifications, including Microsoft Certified Trainer and Certified Novell Instructor.

LAB 1: ACCESSING NETWORK FILES AND APPLICATIONS

OBJECTIVES

After completing this lab you should be able to do the following:

- ✓ Authenticate to a networked Windows computer

- ✓ Connect to a remote Linux computer using terminal emulation software

- ✓ Authenticate to a remote Linux computer

- ✓ Create a Gmail account

- ✓ Create a Google site

CONTENTS

HARDWARE, SOFTWARE, AND COMMUNICATIONS REQUIREMENTS FOR THIS LAB

- ➢ A Windows-based computer

- ➢ Access to the Internet

- ➢ An Active Directory end-user account

- ➢ A Linux end-user account

USEFUL LINKS

- ➢ **http://www.google.com/sites**

LAB 1

Introduction

A file is any collection of zero or more data items. One of the many aspects of a computer system is its capability to store and process files. Files typically contain valuable information that needs to be protected. Security is a major concern for those managing computer systems and networks. Various forms of security exist to protect files stored on computers. Examples include physical security (limiting access by restricting physical access to the computer itself), password protected user accounts, and restricting who can view and change files that are stored on the network. When working on your own standalone computer, you have access to the computer as well as all parts of its file system. Your files are secure unless you allow others to access your computer.

Connecting standalone computers to a network provides numerous advantages with regard to file access. For example, you may decide to connect your computer to the Internet to gain access to the numerous sources of shared information that are available. Another advantage is that you can access your files regardless of your physical location. But there are also drawbacks. If your files are not properly secured, they may be accessible to others who could potentially modify the file content. You probably are willing to allow others to view certain files stored on your computer, but you do not want them to make changes to these or other files. Therefore, certain restrictions to file access are essential. Restricting access to files is accomplished by identifying who can login (authenticate) to the network, as well as who is authorized to view and/or modify files that are accessible. For standalone computers or computers connected to a peer-to-peer network these duties are the responsibility of the owner of the computer.

In corporate computing environments, a systems administrator is responsible for configuring user accounts. The administrator provides security for system resources by implementing policies to limit access to the system and its files. Usually a network administrator determines which restrictions will be placed on user accounts by consulting the corporate security policy. The administrator creates a system of user names and passwords so that users can authenticate (login) to the network. The administrator also configures user accounts so users can work on only those network files that they have privileges to access and modify. The administrator may also provide users with web space on the corporate intranet, so they can share files with co-workers. In the following lab you will compare the authentication procedures used by the two more popular operating systems currently used on Intel-based desktop computers.

Part One: Authenticating to a Networked Windows Computer

Note: This section assumes that you are logging into a Windows computer that is directly connected to your organization's network. It also assumes that a network administrator has created an *Active Directory* account for you. If you are working on a Windows computer from a remote location you will need to ask your network administrator if you have access to the network from your remote location. Your network administrator may have configured a virtual private network (VPN) over the Internet that will allow remote users to access the campus network. If this is the case then you will first need to run the VPN client software on your computer to establish a VPN connection to your campus network. Once you have done this you can then run the *Remote Desktop Connection* software available as an accessory in Windows to connect to a specific server and authenticate to the network. See Appendix A for instructions on how to install and configure the *Cisco VPN client* software and access and run the *Remote Desktop Connection* software.

Let's begin by investigating authentication techniques. Start your computer, if necessary. The steps outlined on the next page describe the procedures you must follow to log into a Windows server.

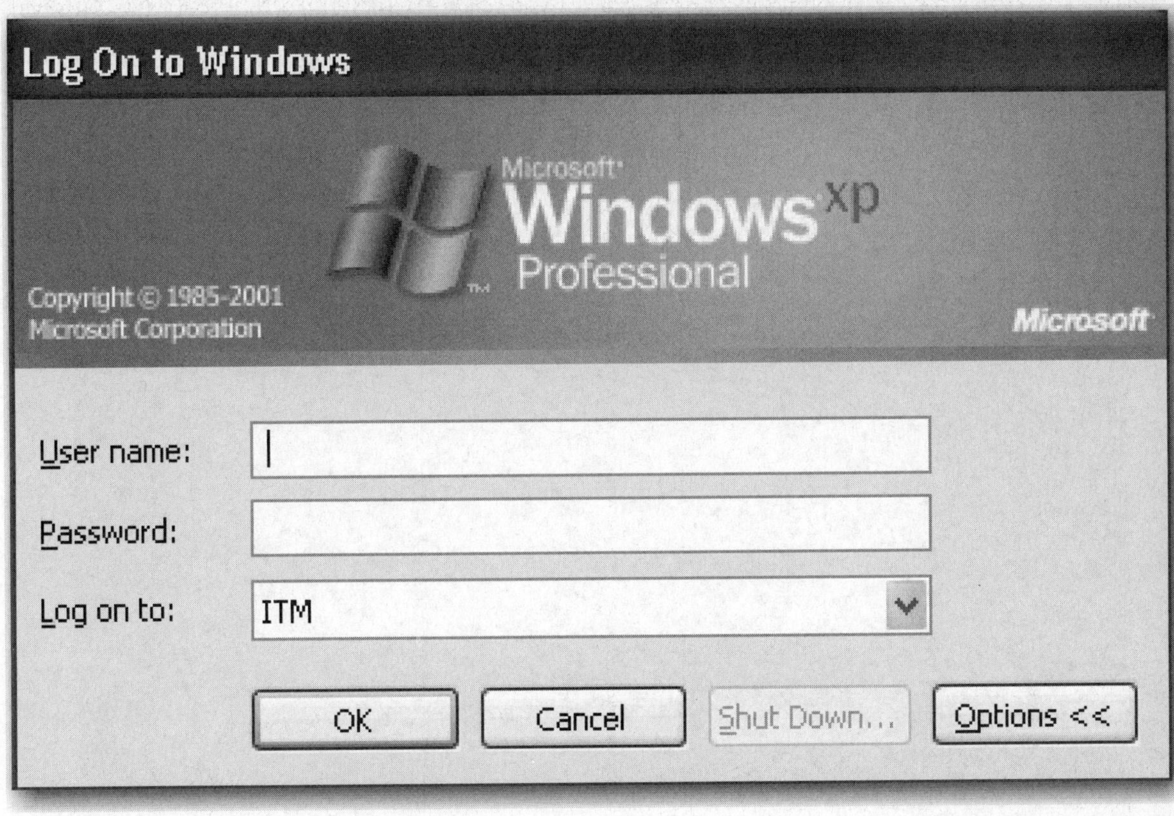

Figure 1: The Windows XP Professional *Log On to Windows* dialog box. This dialog box provides an interface that you can use to authenticate or login to the network to which your computer is connected.

1. After your computer has completed its startup procedures, a Windows logon dialog box, similar to that shown in Figure 1, appears. Before you can access the network, you must *login* to prove that you are authorized to use its resources. If your computer is currently running, but the Windows login dialog box is not displayed, press the **CTRL**, **ALT**, and **DEL** keys, all at the same time, to display it.

2. Type your **username** (typically your first name or first initial followed by your last name and perhaps a number) and temporary **password** (provided by your instructor) into the *User name* and *Password* text boxes respectively (Figure 1). A *default domain name* will also be displayed on this screen. If necessary your instructor will provide an ***alternative domain name*** that you can type into the *Log on to:* text box to replace the default value. Click the **OK** Button to login to the network.

3. Your account may have been created with the restriction that you must change your password the first time your login to the network. If so, a dialog box requesting that you enter a new password will appear. You will need to enter the current password as well as your new password. Your new password must include a capital letter, at least one special symbol, at least one numeric character and be at least 6 characters long to meet the standards for a *strong* password. Click the **OK** button to change your password.

4. If your new password fails to meet the criteria for a strong password, a dialog box outlining the requirements for a strong password will appear. Enter a password that meets the password criteria and click the **OK** button to continue. Once you have successfully created a strong password, the Windows desktop will appear (Figure 2).

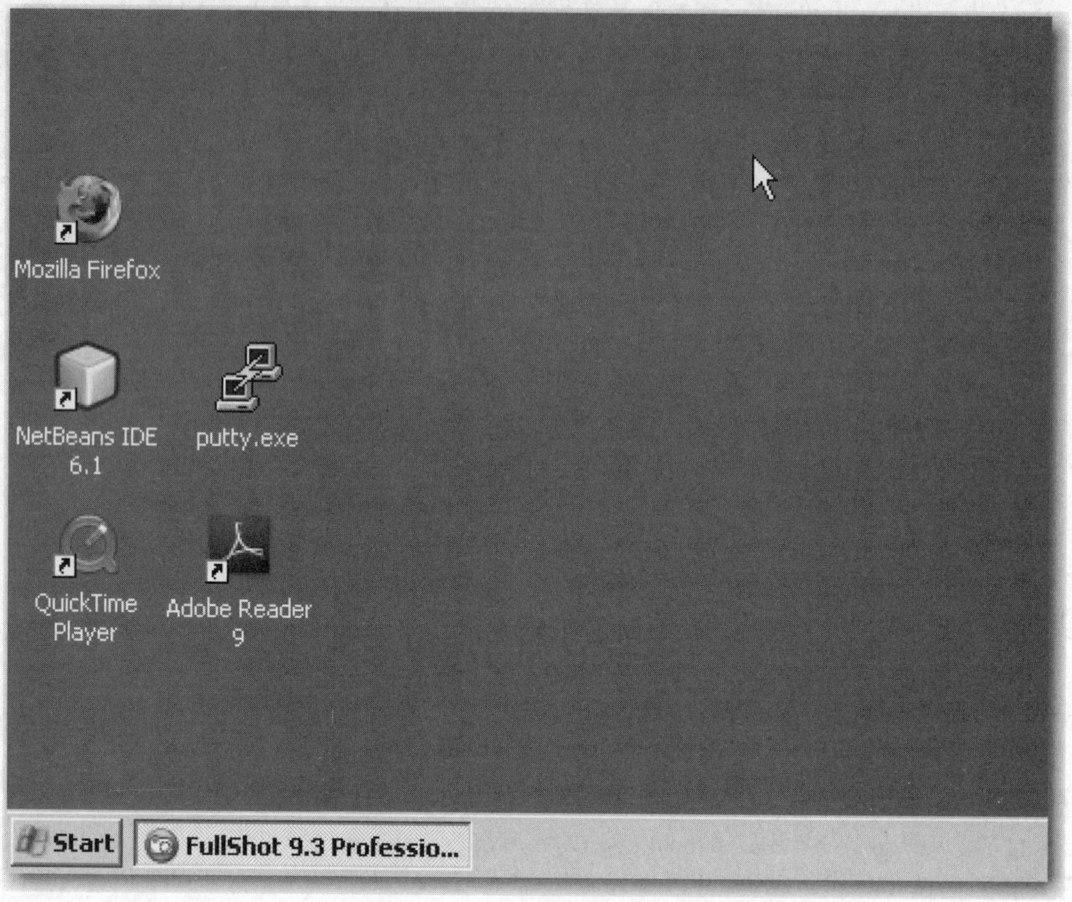

Figure 2: The Windows Desktop showing the *Start* button on the Windows *Task Bar* and some program icons

Part Two: Authenticating to a Linux Computer

The Linux operating system is based upon the UNIX operating system. UNIX and Linux were both designed to be a multi-user operating system. In the past users connected to a UNIX computer system using devices called *terminals*. Today a remote Linux computer can be accessed using a desktop computer programmed to emulate a terminal. This lab discusses how to use *puTTY*, an open-source terminal emulation program, to access a remote Linux computer via a Windows computer sharing a network connection with the Linux computer.

Note: In this section it is assumed that you are logged into a Windows computer connected to your organization's network. It also assumes that the remote Linux computer is connected to this network. If you are working on a Windows computer from a remote location you will need to ask your network administrator if you have access to the network from your remote location. Your network administrator may have configured a virtual private network (VPN) over the Internet that will allow remote users to access the campus network. If this is the case then you will first need to run the VPN client software on your computer to establish a VPN connection to your campus network. See Appendix A for instructions on how to install, configure, and run the *Cisco VPN client* software.

To connect to and authenticate to a Linux computer from a Windows computer connected to your network, perform the following steps:

1. Locate the **puTTY** icon on your Windows desktop. If there is no puTTY icon displayed, refer to the instructions in Appendix F to download and install the puTTY software onto your computer.

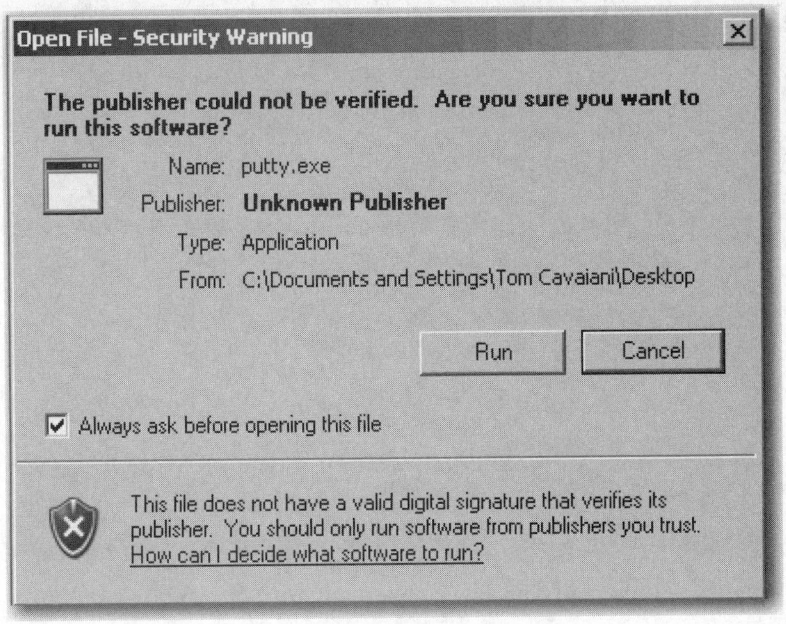

Figure 3: The *Security Warning* dialog box displayed after starting puTTY

2. Double-click the **puTTY** icon to start the application. The first time you run puTTY a dialog box displaying a security warning appears (Figure 3). If you do not want this dialog box to be displayed again click the **checkbox** labeled **Always ask before opening this file**. Click the **Run** button to continue. The *PuTTY Configuration* dialog box appears (Figure 4).

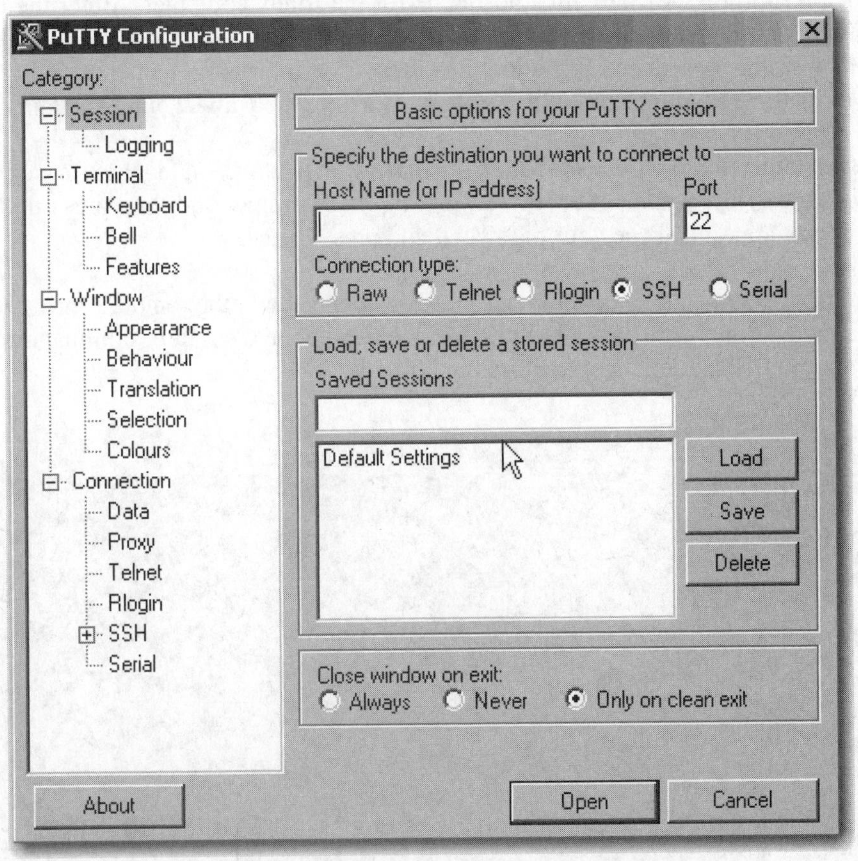

Figure 4: The *PuTTY Configuration* dialog box

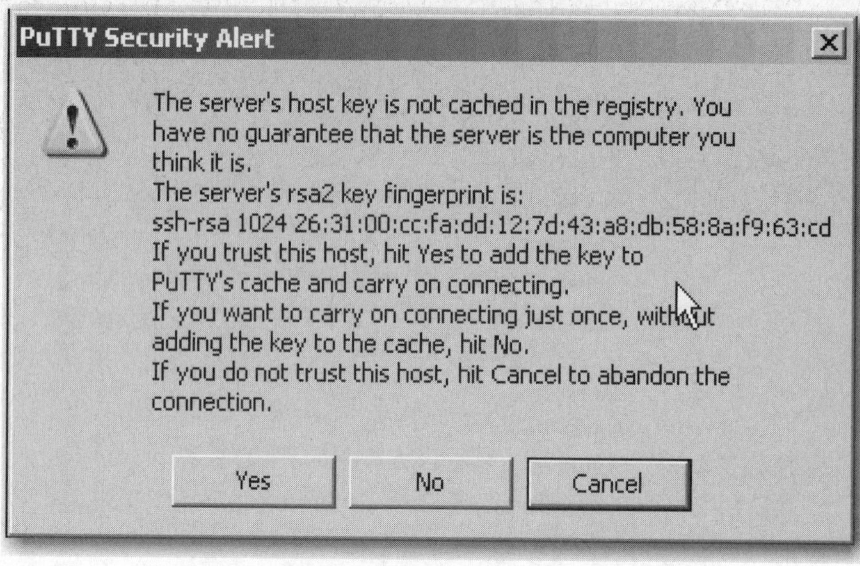

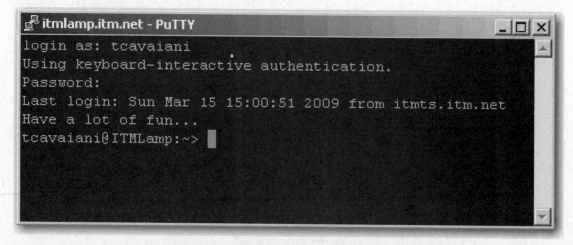

Figure 5: The *PuTTY Security Alert* dialog box

3. PuTTY provides numerous remote *Connection Type* options. It can be used as a *telnet client* for accessing a remote computer, an *SSH client* for secure file transfers or remote access, or to establish a *serial* connection to a remote computer. You may need to change the *Connection type* and *Port number* depending upon the type of connection you need. For this lab we will use the default settings of **SSH** for Connection type and **22** for the Port number.

4. Your instructor will provide you with a hostname for the Linux computer. Enter the **host name** into the **Host Name** text box and click the **Open** button to connect. The first time you connect a *PuTTY Security Alert* dialog box appears (Figure 5). Read the information in the dialog box to decide whether to click the **Yes** or **No** button to continue. Clicking the **Cancel** button terminates the process.

5. After clicking either the **Yes** or **No** button in the *Security Alert* dialog box, a command window appears (Figure 6). Type your **username** at the *login as:* prompt and then press the **Enter** key. A *password* prompt appears. Type your **password** and press **Enter**.

6. A command prompt appears. You have successfully connected to the remote Linux computer and are ready to begin working with it. You will learn more about the Linux command set and how to perform basic Linux file administration tasks in Lab 10.

Figure 6: The *PuTTY* command window

Part Three: Accessing your Web Space

Your network administrator has probably configured your account to provide you with file space on a *web server*. Adding information to the pages on your web site is a convenient way to share information with those who have access to your network. In this part of the lab you will use *Internet Explorer* to view the default home page associated with your web site. Later in this manual we will discuss how to use applications that are designed to change the content of your default page and allow you to add additional pages to your web site.

Note: This section assumes that you are logged onto a Windows computer and that your network administrator has configured your web site so that it is accessible from the World Wide Web.

To access the default home page on your web site perform the following steps:

1. Double-click the **Internet Explorer** icon located on the Windows desktop to open the Internet Explorer browser.

2. Type your **URL** for your *web site* (provided by your instructor) into the *Locator* text box near the top of the browser dialog box (Figure 7). Click the **Go to** button to the right of the Locator text box or press the **Enter** key.

3. The default home page associated with your account appears. It may contain a simple message indicating that this is the home page for your web site or it may simply be blank. Procedures presented later in this manual will describe how you can modify your home page and add additional pages to it.

Figure 7: The Windows Internet Explorer. The *Locator* text box is located directly beneath the title bar at the top of the window.

Part Four: Cloud Computing

Typically the content of files changes over time. Files must be modified as new developments occur. Files are modified by computer programs, such as word processors and spreadsheet programs, designed to manipulate the data contained in the file. You probably have a suite of applications on your computer that allows you to create and/or modify files of different types, such as text-based documents, spreadsheets, and presentations. Internet providers recently began making file processing applications available on the World Wide Web so that users can conveniently modify their files using any computer connected to the Internet. Using web-based applications provides organizations an alternative to maintaining these applications on their own computer systems. It also provides a convenient and cost-effective alternative for end-user file processing, since cloud-based application suites can be accessed not only from the office, but from anywhere the Internet is accessible to the user. This alternative is especially useful to organizations that have a traveling sales force or other remote users that require word processing or spreadsheet software on their laptop computers. The job of maintaining this software can be either minimized or eliminated all together by using cloud-based application software. In Part Two of this lab you will investigate the network file processing applications available from *Google Apps*.

Certain applications must be made available so you can modify the content of your web pages. Considerable expense and support is required to maintain file space and these applications. With the advent of Internet "cloud computing", organizations now have an alternative to maintaining file space on their own servers. Google provides file space and access to applications for any user who signs up for a Google email account. This part of this lab describes how you can create a Google site for storing your files, and how to modify your files using the Google applications.

To store your files and gain access to Google Apps you must create a Google site. Think of a Google site as a project or class notebook that can be accessed from the World Wide Web. Such a site provides an always accessible location for you to view, store, and retrieve your files. You can add new pages to your Google site at any time. For example, you could add weekly class reports that you can share with your instructor or other students. Google provides all the tools needed for uploading and saving your files, copying and pasting data, inserting graphics, and attaching files to your site. This section describes how to create a Google site and share it with your instructor. A short video that describes these procedures is available at **http://www.google.com/sites/help/intl/en/video/sites_overview_video.html** .

You will need a *Gmail* account to create a Google site. If you do not already have a Gmail account refer to Appendix H for step-by-step instructions describing how to create one.

To create a Google web site proceed as follows:

1. Double-click the **Internet Explorer** icon located on the Windows desktop to open the Internet Explorer browser.

2. Enter the URL, **http://www.google.com,** into the *Locator* text box near the top of the browser dialog box (Figure 7). Click the **Go to** button located to the right of the Locator text box or press the **Enter** key.

3. The *Google* home page appears. Click the **Gmail** link located directly above the Google Logo to open the *Gmail* home page (Figure 8).

4. Sign in to your account by entering your **Username** and **Password** in text boxes provided. Click the **Sign in** button.

Figure 8: The Gmail home page showing the *Sign in* text boxes

5. Your *Gmail inbox* page appears (Figure 9). Locate the **_more_** link (near the top center of the dialog box) and click it to display a list of choices. Click the **Sites** choice.

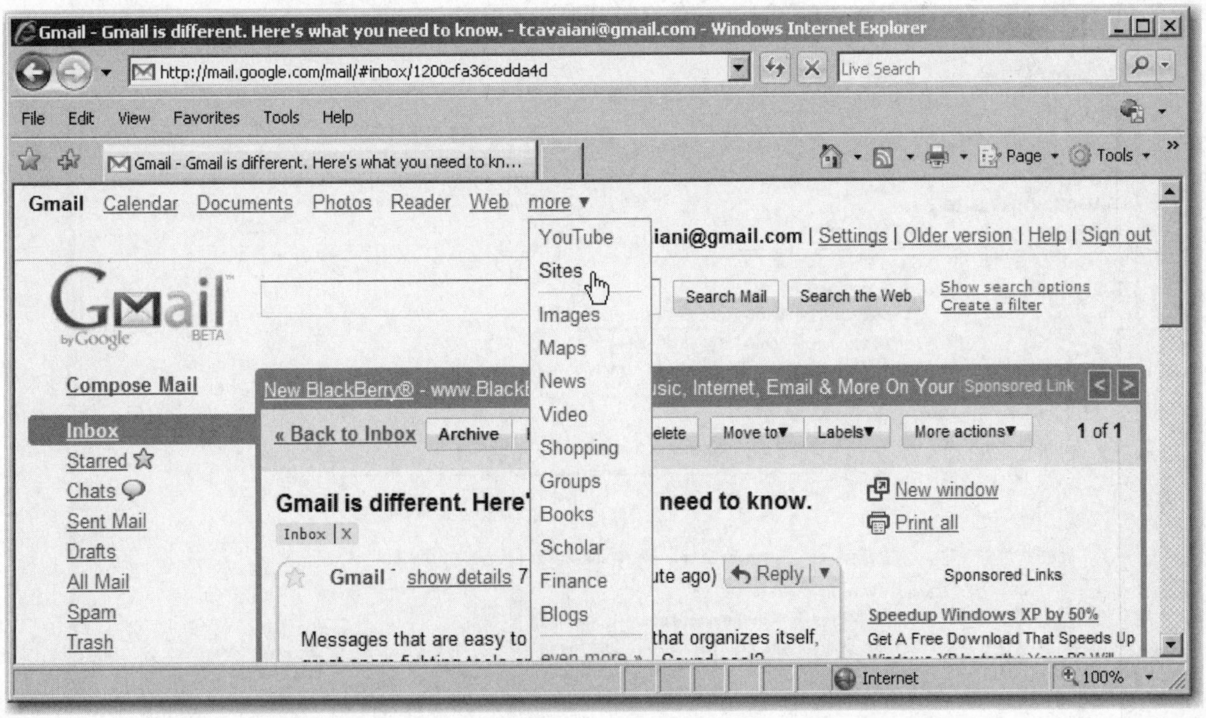

Figure 9: The *more* link menu with the *Sites* choice selected

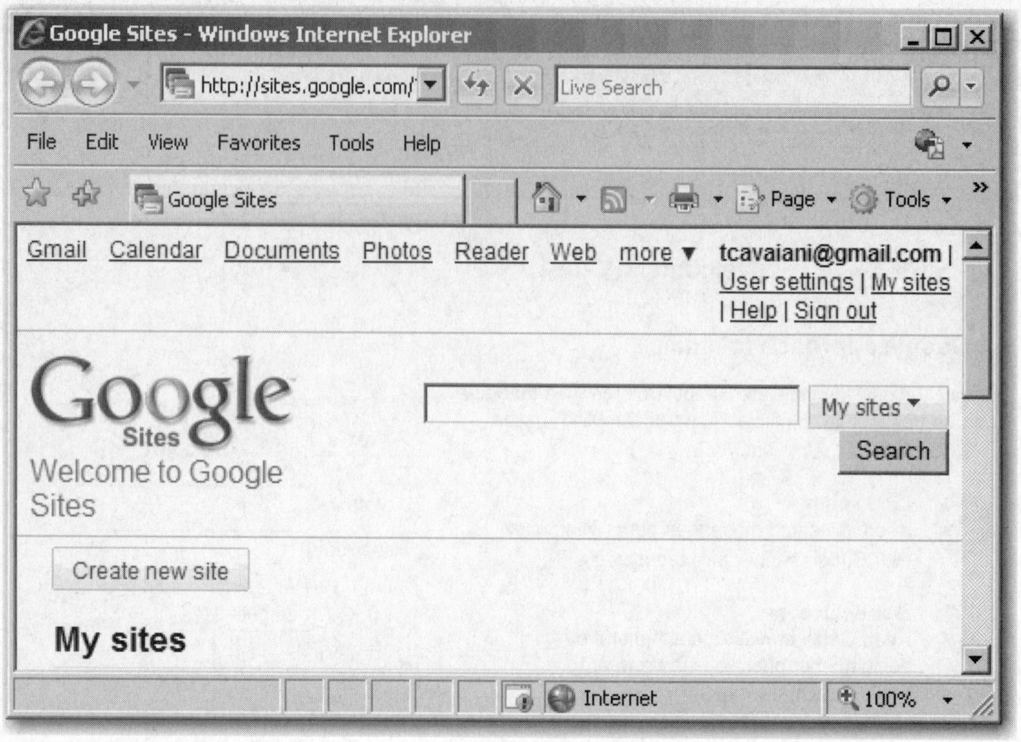

Figure 10: The *Google Sites* page showing the *Create new site* button

6. The *Google sites* page appears. Click the "**Create new site**" button (Figure 10).

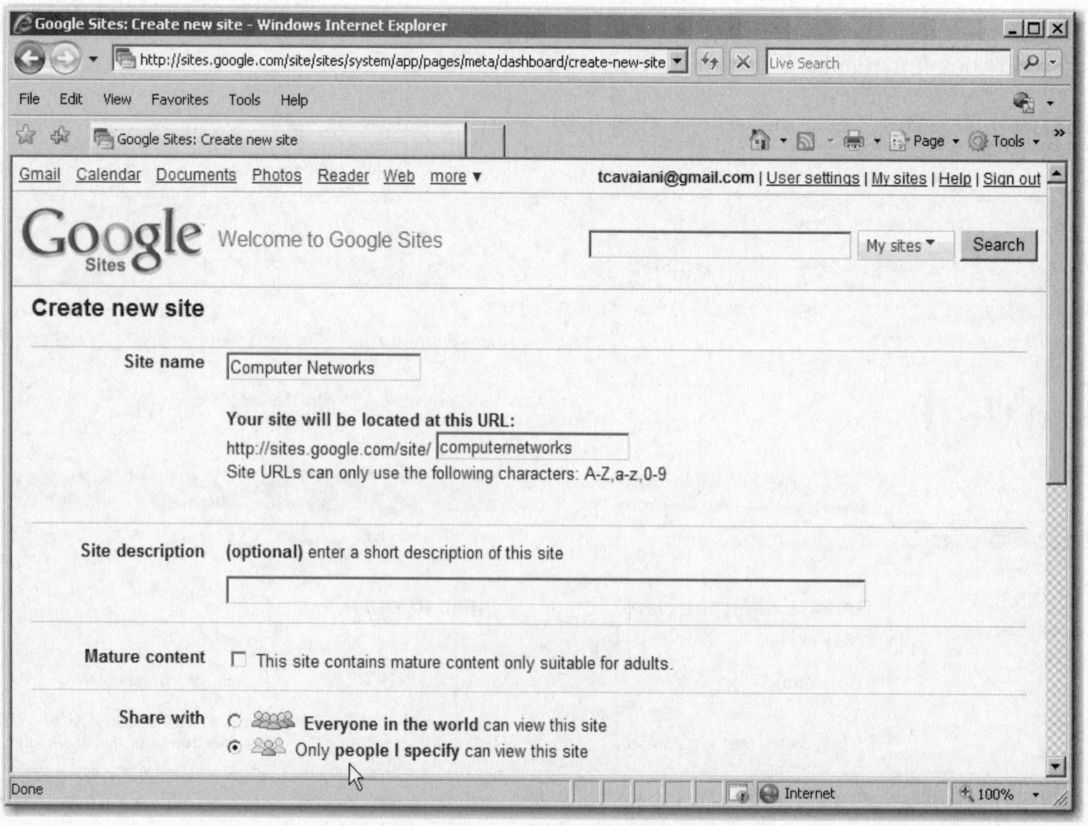

Figure 11: The *Create new site* page

7. The *Create new site* page appears (Figure 11). Enter a ***Site name*** and ***description***. Click the "*Only people I specify can view this site*" option button of the **Share with** choices.

8. Scroll down the page to see the *site theme* options and the *Create site* button (Figure 12). Select a theme for your site from the existing choices. Click the *More themes* link to see more theme options.

9. Type the **code shown** in the text box provided (Figure 12).

10. Click the **Create site** button at the bottom of the page to create your site (Figure 12).

11. A home page similar to that shown in Figure 13 appears. Notice the *Edit page* button near the top of the page. Clicking this button will put your home page into "edit mode" so that you can make changes to it.

12. Google Apps are available for modifying your home page. These applications are similar to the tools found in many word processors that are designed for formatting and otherwise modifying text files. You will get a chance to practice with these tools later in the Exercises.

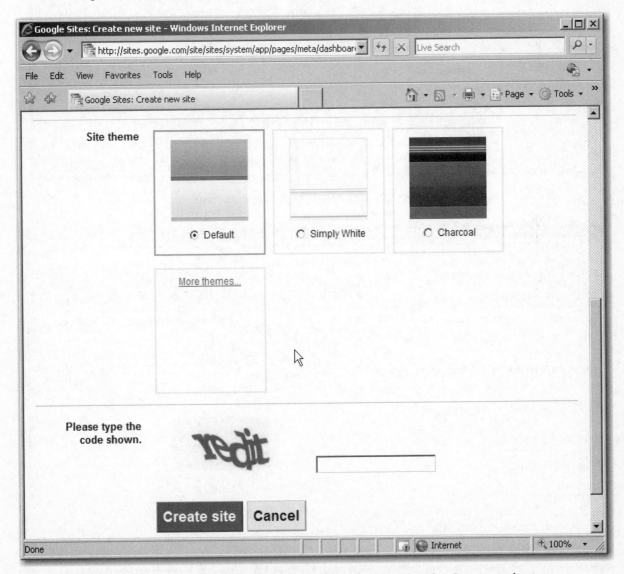

Figure 12: The lower portion *Create New Site* page showing the *Create site* button

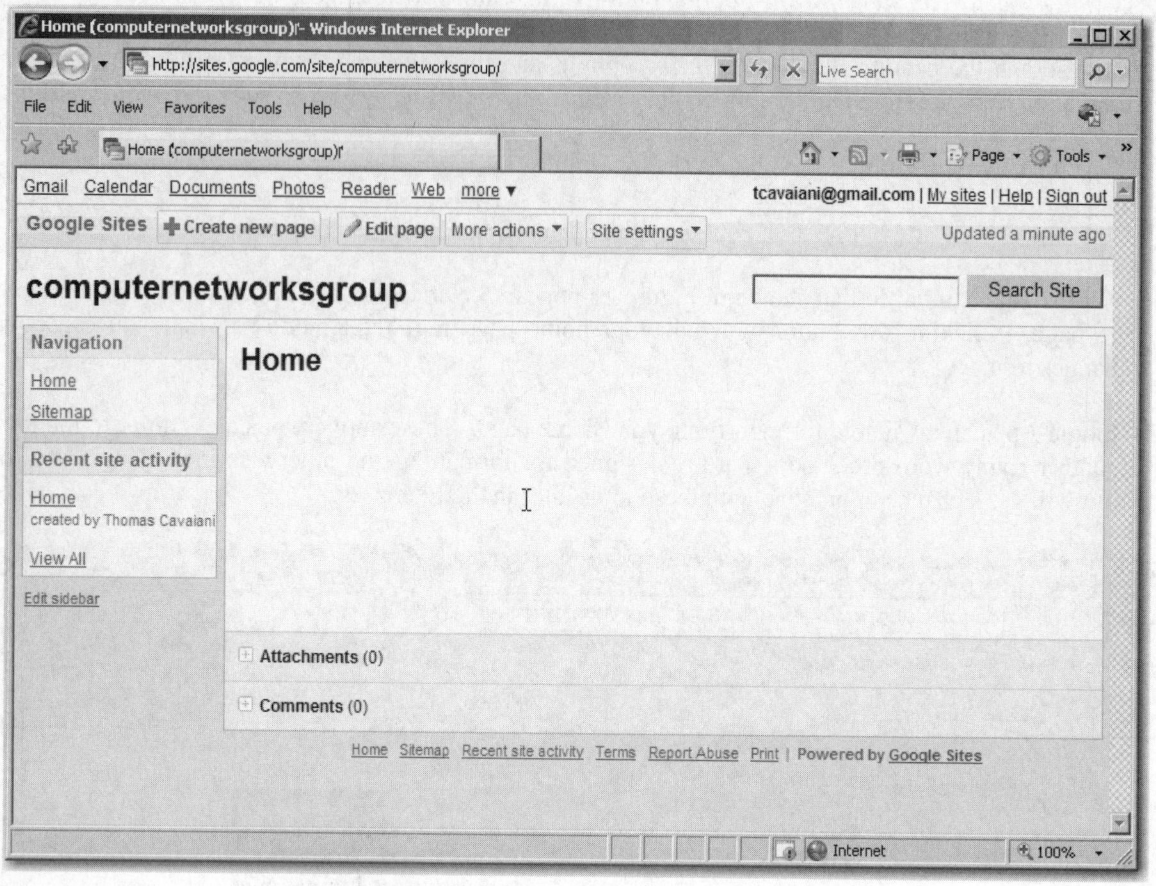

Figure 13: A sample Google site *home* page

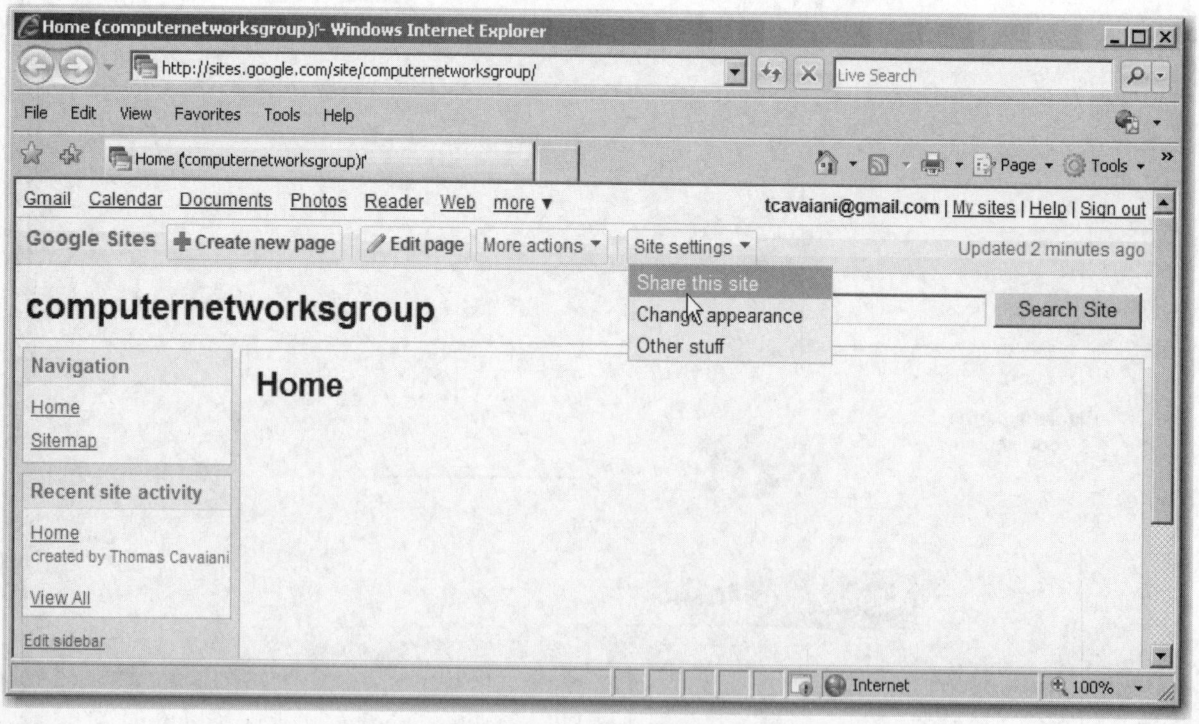

Figure 14: A sample Google site home page showing the *Share this site* choice in the *Site settings* menu

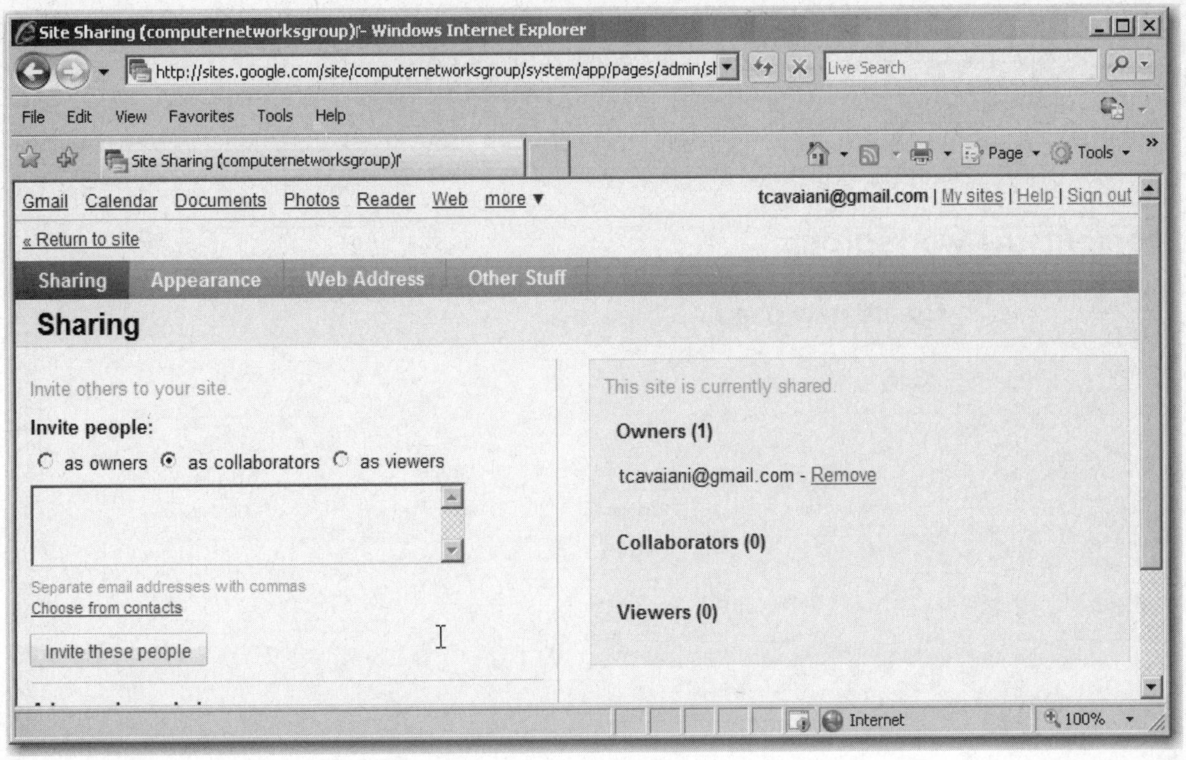

Figure 15: The Google *Site Sharing* page

Sharing your Site

To allow others to view the contents of your Google site perform the following steps:

1. Click on the **Site settings** button of your Google site home page (Figure 14) to display a list of choices. Click the **Share this site** choice.

2. The Google *Site Sharing* page appears (Figure 15). Under the *Invite people* heading there are three option buttons. Click the **as owners** button.

3. Type the first few letters of your **instructor's name** in the *text area* below the option buttons. A drop-down list of names appears. Your instructor's name should appear in the list. Click on your **instructor's name** to add it to your list of *Invitees*.

4. Click the **Invite these people** button to send an email invitation to your instructor.

5. Click the **Return to site** button (located above the *Sharing* label) to return to your Google site home page.

Adding Additional Pages

To add additional pages to your Google site perform the following steps:

1. Click the **Create new page** button on your Google site home page (Figure 13).

2. The *Create new page* page appears. Numerous page templates are shown (Figure 16).

3. Select the appropriate page template and name the page. Scroll down the page to display the *Create page* button (not shown). Click the **Create page** button to create the new page.

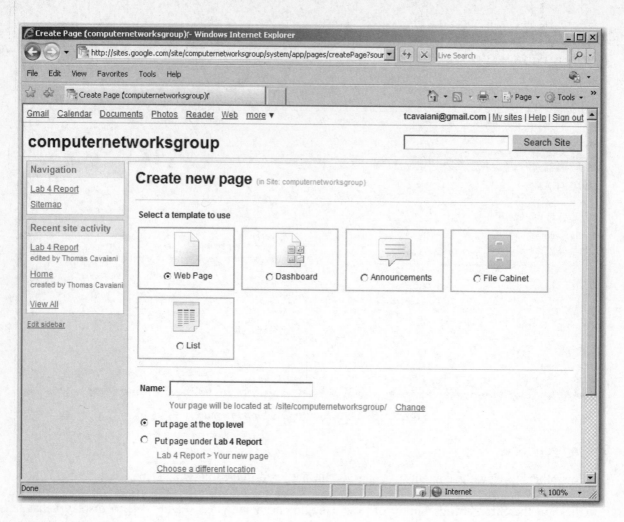

Figure 16: The *Create new page* page showing icons that represent the different page-type options

Exercises

Modifying your Google Site Home Page

1. Add your name to your home page.

2. Enter your *course name* and *section number* on a new line beneath your home page name.

3. On the next line describe any experience you may have had in telecommunications, data communications, and/or networking.

4. On the next line describe your current job (if you are working).

5. On the next line describe your career aspirations.

6. Add a picture to your home page.

Adding Pages to your Google Site Home Page

7. In the *Page Name* text box type *Lab One*.

8. Select *Webpage* for the *Type of page to create*.

9. Select the option *Put page under Home* (not shown) and click the **Create Page** button (also not shown; you may need to scroll the page to see these choices).The newly created webpage will open up in edit mode.

10. **Sign out** to close your Google site. You will also need to **Sign out** to close your Gmail home page. The *Sign out* button is in the upper-right hand corner of these pages (Figures 9 and 12).

Questions

1. Do you have an *Applications* folder on your desktop?
2. If so, which applications are stored in this folder?
3. If you do not have an Applications folder, which applications appear on your desktop (List names of at least three applications)?
4. Locate the prompt in the Linux command window. Can you determine what the first part of the prompt represents?
5. What do you think the second part of the prompt represents (*Hint*: Do a Google search for Bash prompt components)?
6. If a class web site was assigned to you, is there a message printed on the home page associated with this site?
7. If so, what is it?

Obtaining Credit for Lab One

Your instructor will review your Google site after the lab session has ended. Make sure you have completed all page modifications described in the lab procedures and have copied the answers to the lab questions to your Google site home page.

LAB 2: FILE TRANSFERS

OBJECTIVES

After completing this lab you should be able to do the following:

- ✓ Use WinSCP to perform a secure file transfer to a remote computer

- ✓ Use WinSCP to perform a non-secure file transfer to a remote computer

CONTENTS

HARDWARE, SOFTWARE, AND COMMUNICATIONS REQUIREMENTS FOR THIS LAB

- ➢ A Windows-based computer with Local Area Network access

- ➢ Access to the Internet

- ➢ An Active Directory end-user account

- ➢ Web space on a Windows server

- ➢ Remote access to a Linux computer

- ➢ A Linux end-user account

- ➢ Web space on a Linux computer

USEFUL LINKS

- ➢ **http://winscp.net/eng/docs/introduction**

LAB 2

Introduction

This lab discusses how to use an open-source file transfer program to upload files to a remote computer. If you are interested in sharing files with others by placing them on a file server or web server then learning to use a file transfer program is a must.

WinSCP is the file transfer program that has been selected for discussion in this lab. WinSCP is short for *Windows Secure Copy*. It was originally created to allow users to transfer files in a secure or encrypted fashion from a Windows computer to a Linux computer. Later WinSCP was modified to allow non-secure transfers from one Windows computer to another. If you would like to know more about the history and features of WinSCP consult the following URL: **http://winscp.net/eng/docs/introduction**. Procedures that describe how to transfer encrypted files (secure transfers) and unencrypted files (non-secure transfers) are discussed in this lab.

WinSCP is an open-source program with an intuitive graphical user interface that supports drag-and-drop transfers of both text and graphics files. It is much more convenient to use than older file transfer programs, such as FTP, which are command-oriented.

WinSCP is a client-side file transfer application. To be able to utilize WinSCP for transferring files, the server-side software that supports WinSCP must be installed on the servers before transfers can be performed. Check with you network administrator to determine if the servers on your network support the protocols used by WinSCP.

The next two sections outline the steps required to transfer files using WinSCP. Both secure and non-secure transfer procedures are discussed.

Part One: Using WinSCP for Secure File Transfers

WinSCP supports the SSH protocol for performing secure (encrypted) file transfers. Complete the following activity to learn how to use WinSCP for this type of file transfer.

1. Create a simple file using a word processor that allows you to save the file as an html document. Add your name, your class name, section number, semester, and instructor name to this file.

2. Save the file as an html document and name it *index.htm*.

3. In Windows click the **Start** button and then click on the **All Programs** choice to view the *Start* menu.

4. Locate the **WinSCP** choice (If you cannot find WinSCP consult Appendix I for instructions regarding how to download and install the software on your computer). Double-click the **WinSCP** choice to start the program. The *WinSCP Login* dialog box appears (Figure 1).

5. By default **Port number 22** is selected. This port is used for secure transfers. Notice that **SFTP** (Secure File Transport Protocol) is the protocol associated with this port.

6. Enter the **host name** provided by your instructor in the *Host name* text box.

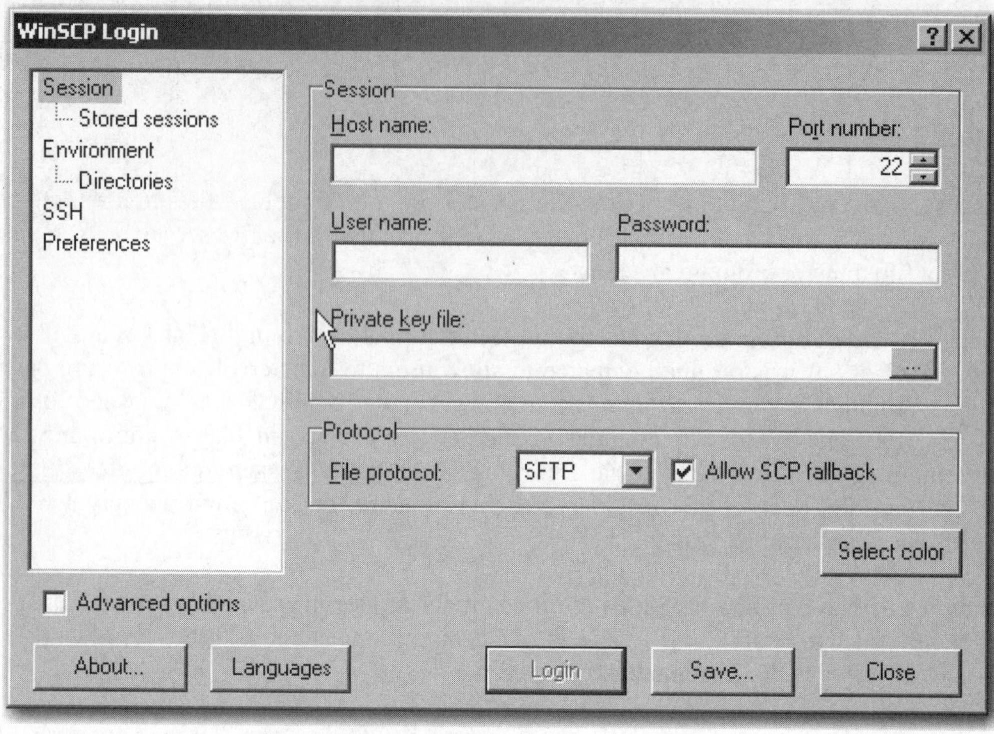

Figure 1: The *WinSCP Login* dialog box

7. Enter your **username** and **password** in the corresponding text boxes and click the **Login** button (Figure 1).

8. The WinSCP *Documents* dialog box appears (Figure 2). It has two window panes, one for local files and one for remote files.

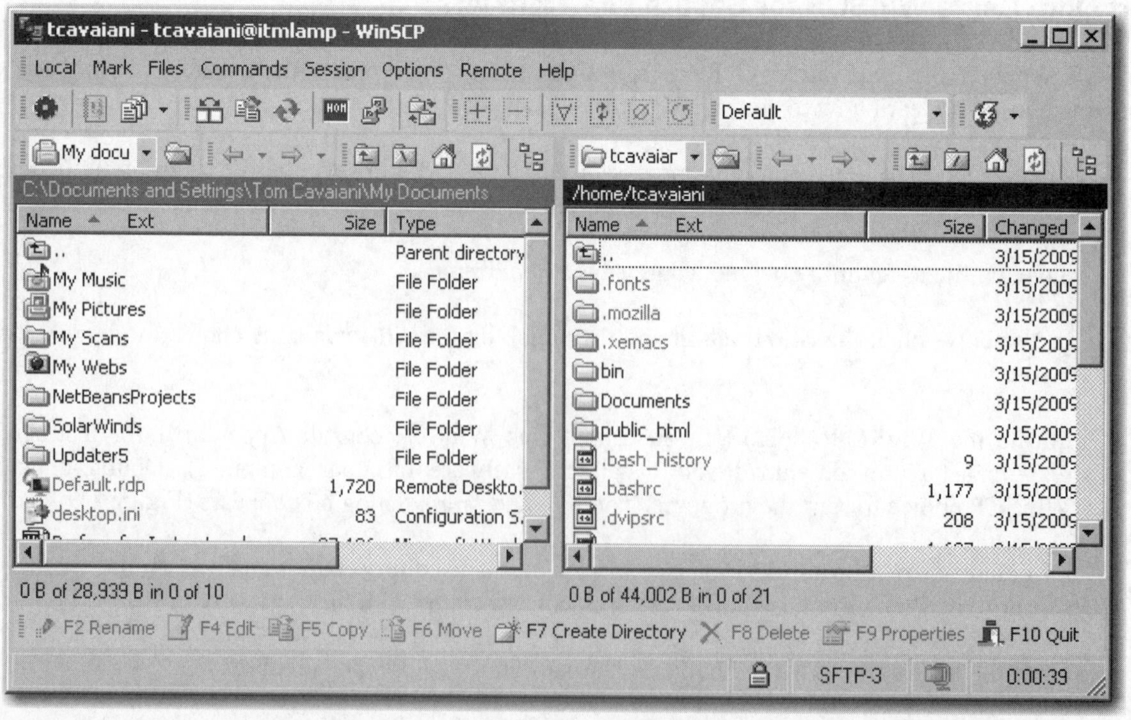

Figure 2: The *WinSCP Documents* dialog box showing local (on the left) and remote panes

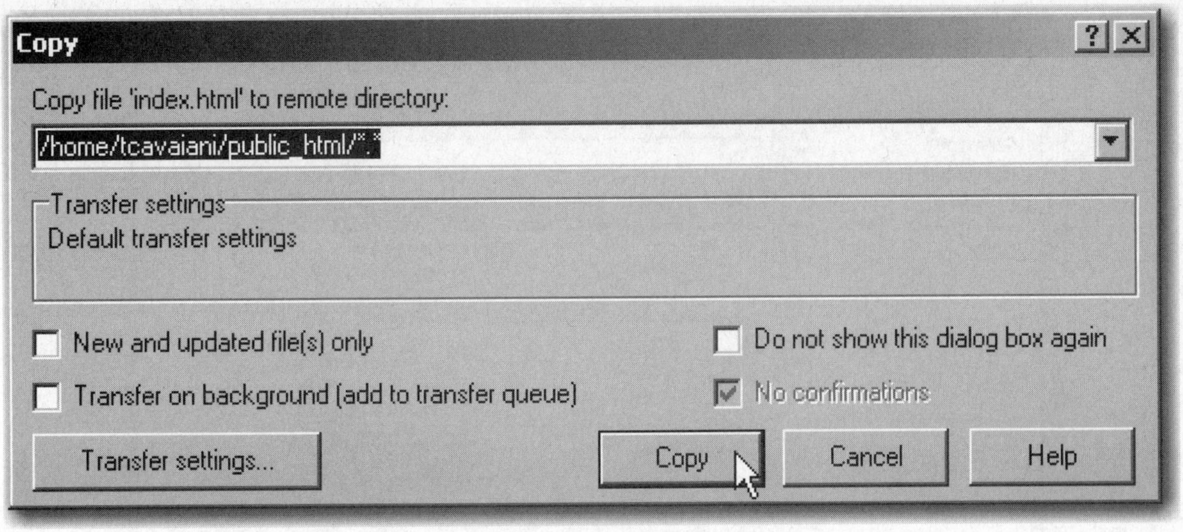

Figure 3: The *WinSCP Copy* dialog box

9. Scan the directory system in the local pane to locate the **index.htm** file you created in step 1. Scan the remote pane to select the destination folder (your **home\public_html** directory). Drag the local file to the remote pane and drop it onto the destination folder. The *Copy* dialog box appears (Figure 3).

10. Click the **Copy** button to complete the transfer. If the local file has the same name as the remote file the *Confirm* dialog box will appear. Click the **Yes** button to overwrite the remote file.

11. Click the **F10 Quit** button, located in the lower right hand corner of the **Documents** dialog box (Figure 2), to close it. A confirmation dialog box appears (Figure 4). Click the **OK** button to end your session.

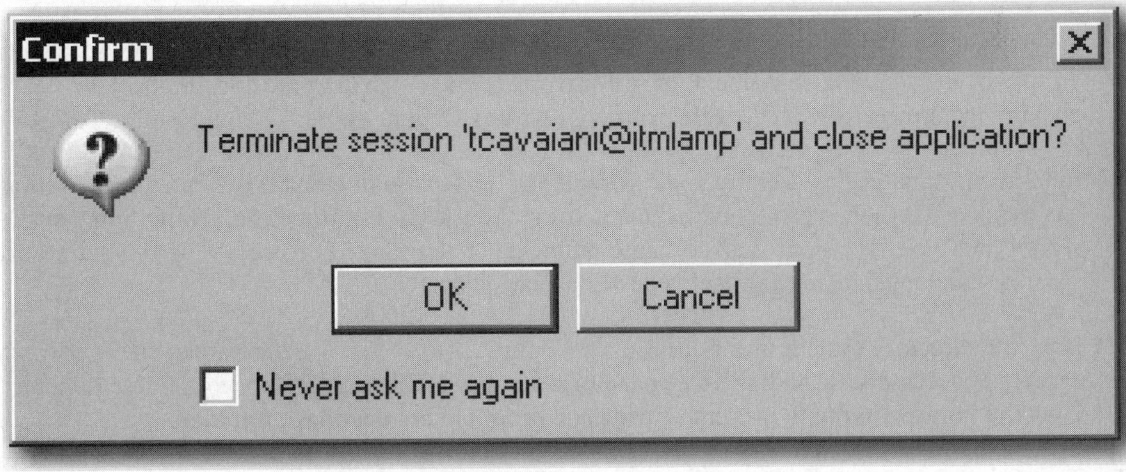

Figure 4: The *WinSCP Copy Confirm* dialog box

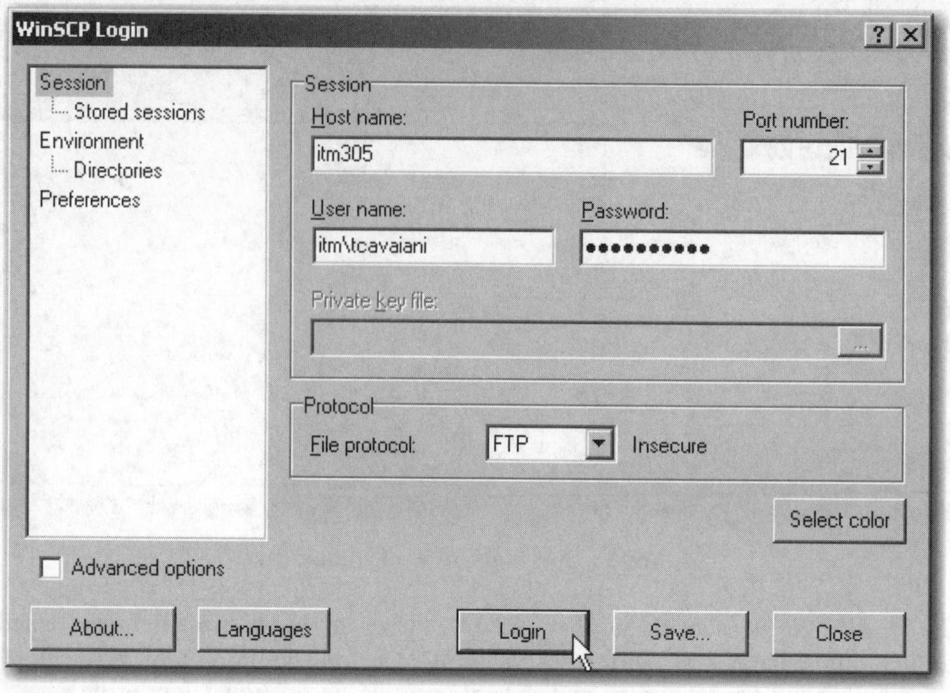

Figure 6: The *WinSCP Login* dialog box configured for a non-secured file transfer

Part Two: Using WinSCP for Non-Secure File Transfers

Some operating systems do not support secure file transfers using SSH. For these systems WinSCP provides an FTP option on port 21 (Figure 6). The next section outline the steps required to transfer files using FTP in WinSCP.

To use WinSCP's FTP file transfer option proceed as follows:

1. Open WinSCP if necessary. Change the port number to 21 by clicking either the up or down arrows of the **"spinner"** in the **Port number text box.** Change the file protocol to FTP by clicking the down arrow on the **File protocol text box** (Figure 6).

2. Enter the host name provided by your instructor in the **Host name** text box. Enter your username and password into the corresponding textboxes and click the **Login** button. **Note**: Some systems require that you type your domain name before your username (Figure 6). If this is the case, separate the domain name and username with a backslash (\).

3. Scan the directory system in the local pane (Figure 2) to locate the **index.htm** file you created earlier. If necessary, scan the remote pane to select the destination folder (your **home** directory). Drag the **index.htm** file to the remote pane and drop it in the **destination folder**.

4. The *Copy* dialog box appears (Figure 3). Click the **Copy** button to complete the transfer. If prompted to overwrite the existing file, click the **Yes** button.

5. When the transfer is complete click the **F10 Quit** button to close the dialog box and then click the **OK** button to terminate your WinSCP session (Figure 4).

6. To verify that you have successfully transferred the file to its remote location, open a browser and enter the destination URL in the browser's **Locator** text box. You instructor will provide the URL.

LAB 3: SELECTED NETWORKING FEATURES IN WINDOWS

OBJECTIVES

After completing this lab you should be able to do the following:

✓ Use basic network utilities such as ping, tracert, ipconfig, and netstat.

✓ Map a network drive

✓ Search for and locate a computer on your network

✓ Change your computer's network name

✓ Join a workgroup or domain

✓ Assign a static IP address to a network adapter

CONTENTS

HARDWARE, SOFTWARE, AND COMMUNICATIONS REQUIREMENTS FOR THIS LAB

➢ A Windows-based computer with Local Area Network access

➢ Access to the Internet

USEFUL LINKS

➢ **http://www.washington.edu/networking/tools/traceroute**

LAB 3

Introduction

This section assumes that you have used Microsoft Windows in the past and are familiar with many of the more common file management procedures used in Windows. It is also assumed that you are currently using Windows XP. Listed below are some of the more commonly used features available in XP that pertain to accessing network files and folders as well as obtaining information about the network and modifying certain network settings. These features include the following:

- Configuring and using the Run option in the Start Menu

- Accessing network computers and resources

- Mapping local and network drives

- Administrative privileges

- Command-line Utilities

- Changing a computer's network name

- Changing a computer's IP address

- Verifying the network adaptor configuration

Start-Run

The *Run* option is a convenient way to open a command window to run some of the more common networking utilities, such as *ping*, *tracert*, *ipconfig*, and *netstat*. In Windows XP the *Run* option appears in the lower right hand corner of the *Start* menu. If you do not see the Run option in this menu you can add it as follows:

1. Right-click the **Start** button to display its shortcut menu (Figure 1).

2. Click the **Properties** choice to display the *Taskbar and Start Menu Properties* dialog box (Figure 2).

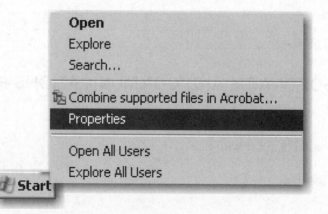

Figure 1: The shortcut menu that appears after right-clicking the *Start* button

Figure 2: The Taskbar and Start Menu Properties dialog box and Customize button

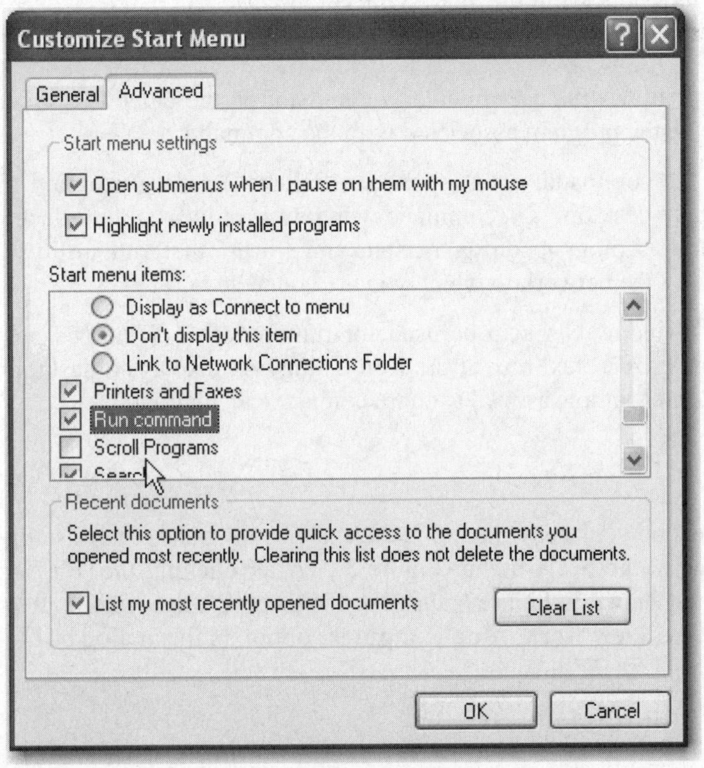

Figure 3: The *Advanced* tab page of the *Customize Start Menu* dialog box showing the *Run* choice

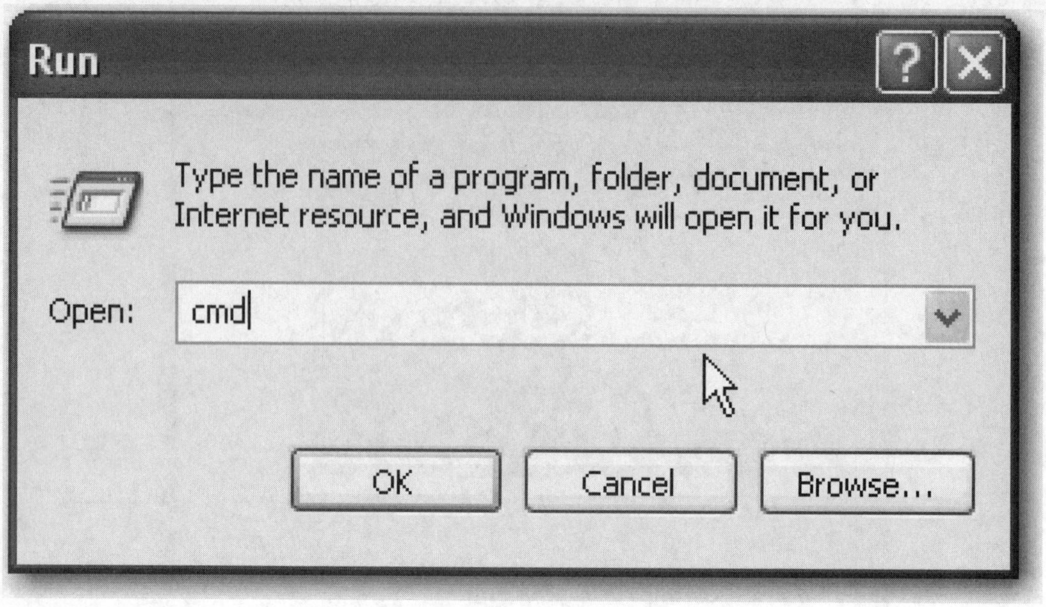

Figure 4: The *Run* dialog box

3. Click the **Customize** button. The *Customize Start Menu* dialog box appears (Figure 3).

4. Click the **Advanced** tab and scroll down until you see the *Run command* choice.

5. Click the **checkbox** next to the Run command choice to place a checkmark in the box.

6. Click the **OK** button to close the *Customize Start Menu* dialog box.

7. Click the **OK** button to close the *Taskbar and Start Menu Properties* dialog box.

8. A *Run* choice now appears in the *Start* menu (Figure 5).

9. Clicking the **Run** choice displays the *Run* dialog box (Figure 4).

10. This dialog box allows the user to enter a command in the *Open* textbox and then click the **OK** button to execute the program associated with the command.

11. For example, the command, *cmd*, (shown in Figure 4) runs a program that opens a command window on your desktop. A command window provides an interface for issuing Windows commands such as ping, ipconfig, netstat, and tracert that run utility programs that provide information about the network to which you are connected.

12. The command window can also be used for running other Windows programs. For example, typing **calc** in the *Open* text box of the Run dialog box displays a desktop calculator that can be used for performing simple as well as more complex calculations.

Networking

You can view computers on your network and make changes to your network settings by clicking the **My Network Places** choice in the **Start** menu (Figure 5). After clicking the *My Network Places* choice a dialog box similar to that shown in Figure 6 appears. To display a list of computers that are connected to your network, click on the **View workgroup computers** option in this dialog box.

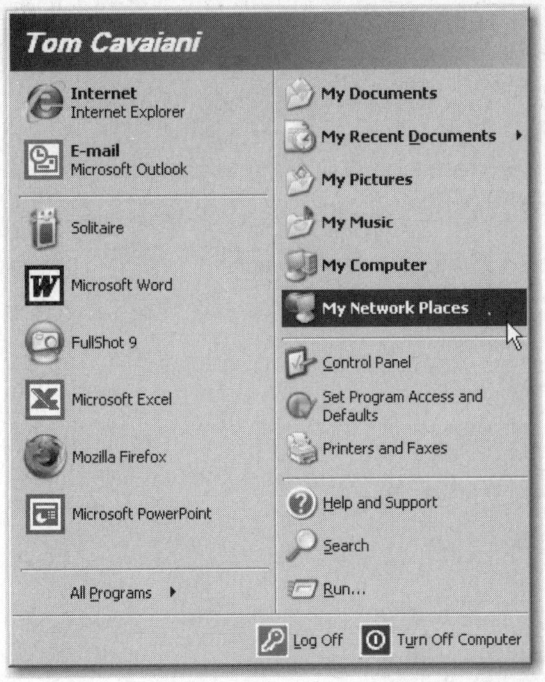

Figure 5: The Windows *Start* menu displayed after clicking the *Start* button on the Windows Task Bar

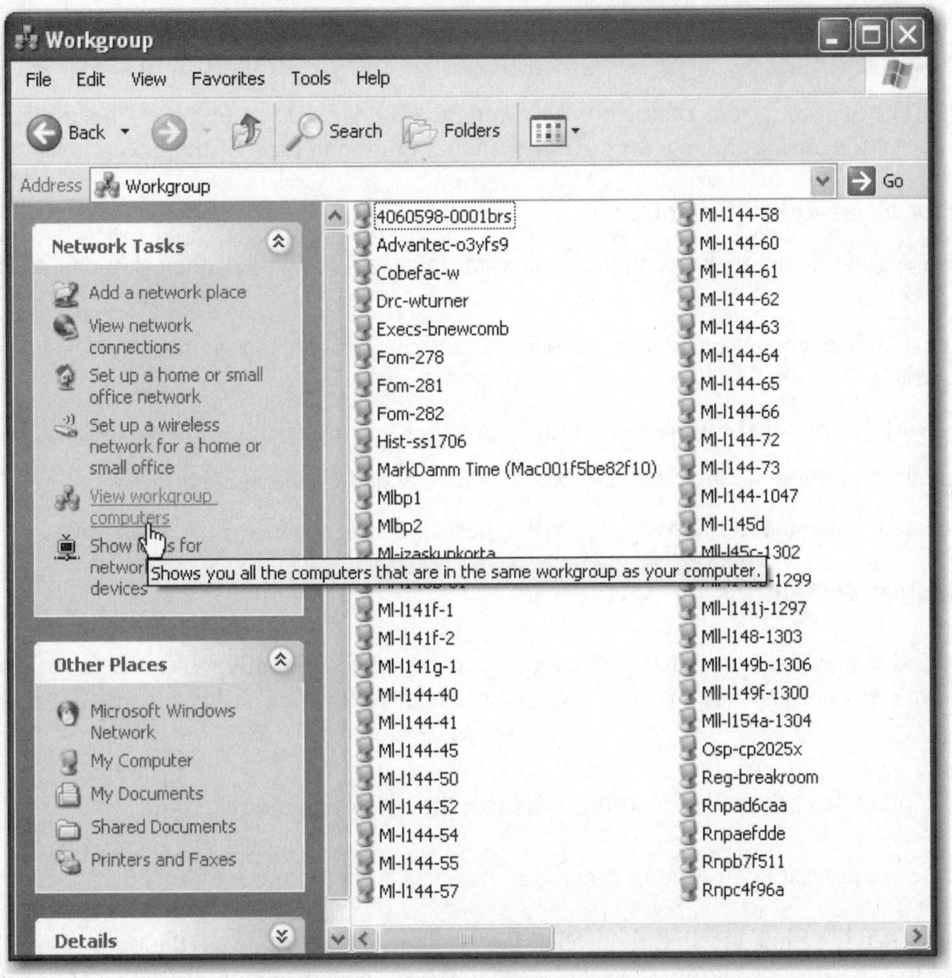

Figure 6: The *Workgroup* dialog box displaying a list of computers attached to a network

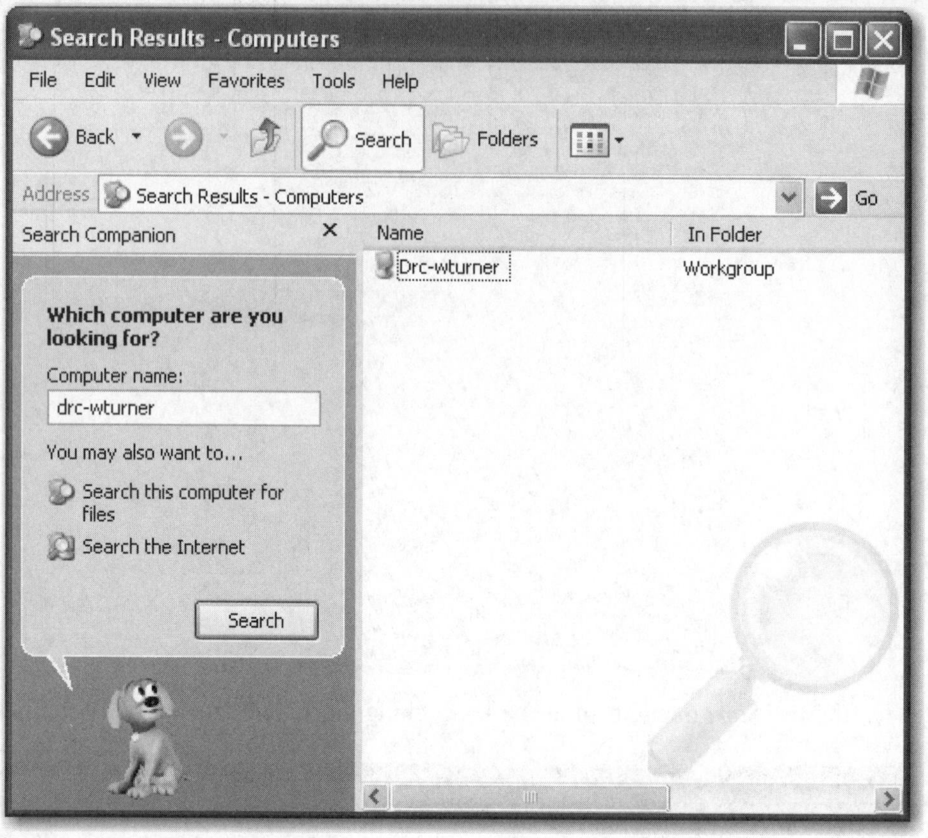

Figure 7: The *Search Results* dialog box showing the *Computer name* text box, the toolbar *Search* button, and search results displayed in the right-hand pane of the dialog box

Searching for a Networked Computer

If you do not see the name of the computer you want to access in the list, then you can search for it as follows:

1. Click the **Search** button in the toolbar shown towards the top of the *Workgroup* dialog box (Figure 6).

2. You will be prompted for the name of the computer you are trying to locate (Figure 7).

3. Type the *Computer name* in the text box provided and click the **Search** button.

4. If located, the name of the computer will appear in the right pane of the dialog box.

Administrative Privileges

It is recommended that you login as an end user so you do not accidentally make unwanted configuration changes to your system and use the *Run As* option when performing tasks that require administrative privileges.

To execute a program as an administrator perform the following steps:

1. Locate the program you want to run.

2. Hold down the **Shift** key and right-click the program icon. A pop-up dialog box appears (Figure 8). Click the **Run as** option. The *Run As* dialog box appears (Figure 9).

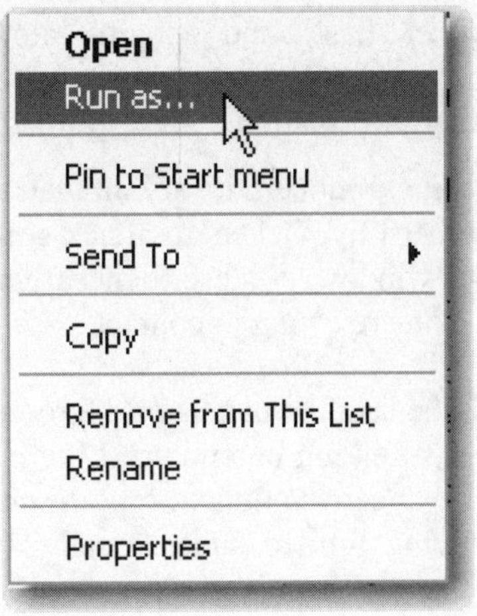

Figure 8: A pop-up menu displaying the *Run as* option

3. Click the option button labeled *The following user*. Enter the administrative password and click the **OK** button to run the application with administrative privileges. When you exit the application your administrative privileges will be canceled.

Command-Line Utilities

The *ipconfig*, *ping*, and *tracert* utilities provide an administrator with convenient methods for obtaining diagnostic and troubleshooting information about a network.

Ipconfig and ***ipconfig/all*** – This utility displays relevant values that pertain to the network configuration of your computer. A command window must be opened before issuing the *ipconfig* command. This can be accomplished by opening a *Run* dialog box and typing *cmd* in its *Open* textbox (See the *Start-Run section* in this lab and Figure 2 for instructions on how to open a *Run* dialog box). Ipconfig shows basic

Figure 9: The *Run As* dialog box displaying the two *user* options

information such as IP address, subnet mask, and default gateway. Ipconfig/all shows additional information including host name, physical address, and IP addresses for DNS and DHCP servers available to your system, as well as other information.

Ping – This utility is useful for checking connectivity to another system. Most network administrators block ping traffic, because it has been used by hackers to attack computer systems and networks. To use the ping command, open a command window as described earlier and type *ping* followed by the *IP address* or *host name* of the computer you are trying to contact.

Tracert (trace route) - This command displays the names of the routers that are involved in transmitting a message from a sending computer to a receiving computer. Like ping, the tracert traffic is also blocked by most organizations. To execute the tracert command type *tracert* followed by the *IP address* of the destination computer. If you are having limited success using tracert, consider using a trace route gateway. The University of Washington supports a *trace route gateway* (**http://www.washington.edu/networking/tools/traceroute**) that can be used to view the addresses of the routers that connect sending and receiving computers.

History

When working with the command-line interface in Windows you can use the *up* and *down* arrows on the keyboard to recall previously entered commands. This can save you considerable typing if you use the same commands repeatedly.

Changing the Computer Name

You can change the name used to identify your computer on the network as follows:

1. Right-click on the **My Computer** option in the **Start** menu (Figure 5), and select the **Properties** choice from the pop-up menu that appears. The *System Properties* dialog box appears (Figure 10).

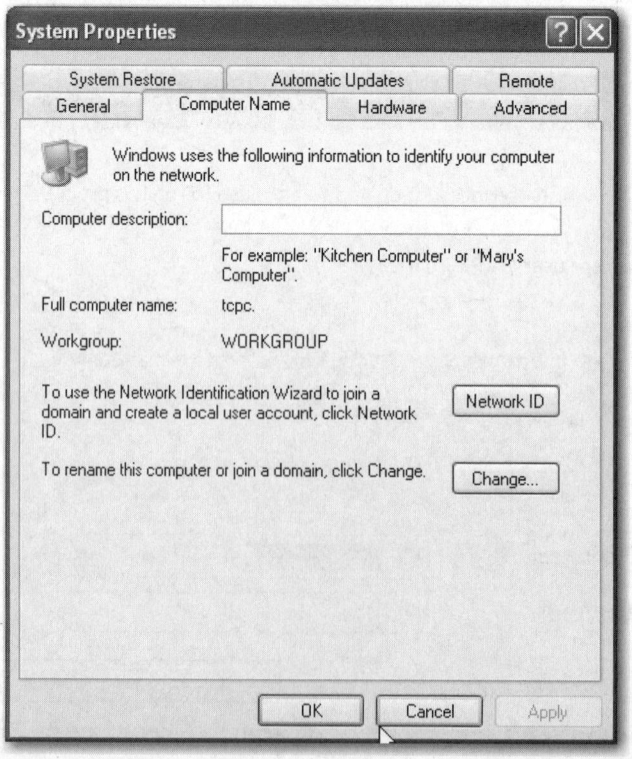

Figure 10: The *System Properties* dialog box showing the options on the *Computer Name* page

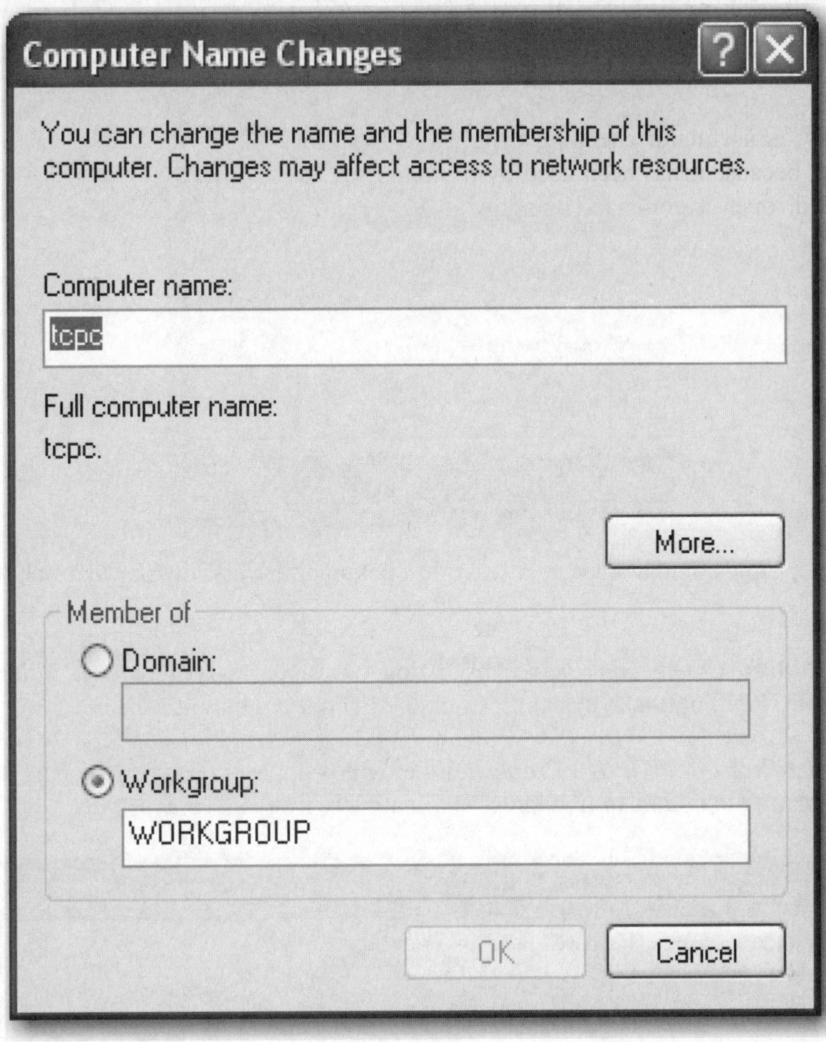

Figure 11: The *Computer Name Changes* dialog box displaying the *Computer name* text box and the option buttons for joining a *Domain* or *Workgroup*

2. Click the **Computer Name** tab (beneath the title bar of the dialog box) to display the choices shown in Figure 10.

3. Click the **Change** button to rename the computer or join a workgroup or new domain (Figure 11). Joining a new domain or workgroup requires administrative privileges. You will be prompted to enter an administrator name and password if you attempt to make these changes.

Changing the System's IP Address

As a network administrator, you will need to know how to configure IP addresses for both desktop computers and network servers. The following steps will show you how to configure a computer to receive an IP address from a DHCP server as well as how to assign a static IP address.

1. Right-click the **My Network Places** option in the **Start** menu (Figure 5). A pop-up menu appears (Figure 12). Click the **Properties** option.

2. A dialog box displaying your network connections appears (Figure 13). Right-click the **Local Area Connection** you want to modify and click the **Properties** option from the pop-up menu that appears.

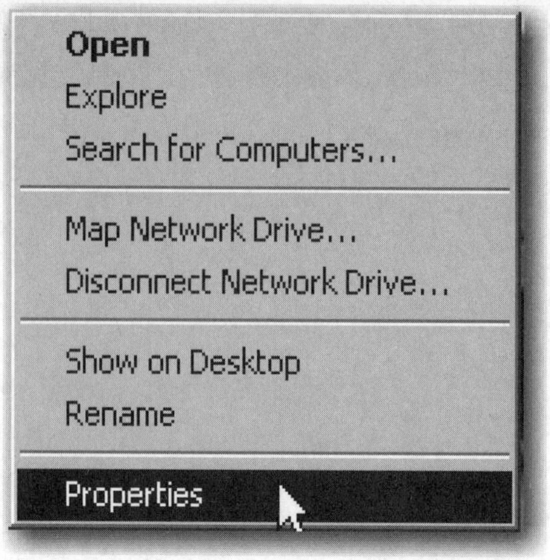

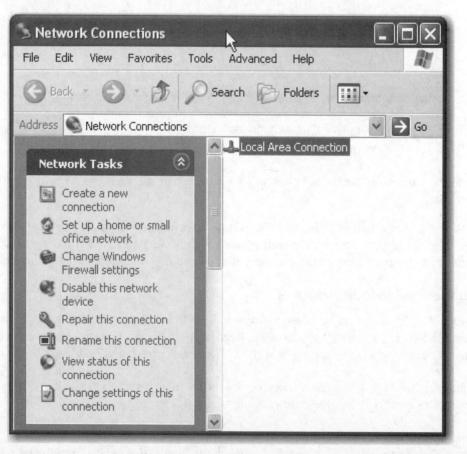

Figure 12: The pop-up menu that appears after right-clicking the *My Network Places* choice in the *Start* menu

3. The *Local Area Connection Properties* dialog box appears (Figure 14). Click the **Internet Protocol (TCP/IP)** option to select it. Click the **Properties** button.

4. The *Internet Protocol (TCP/IP) Properties* dialog box appears (Figure 15). The default setting is for the computer to obtain an IP address automatically from a DHCP server.

Figure 13: The *Network Connection* dialog box showing a *Local Area Connection* icon

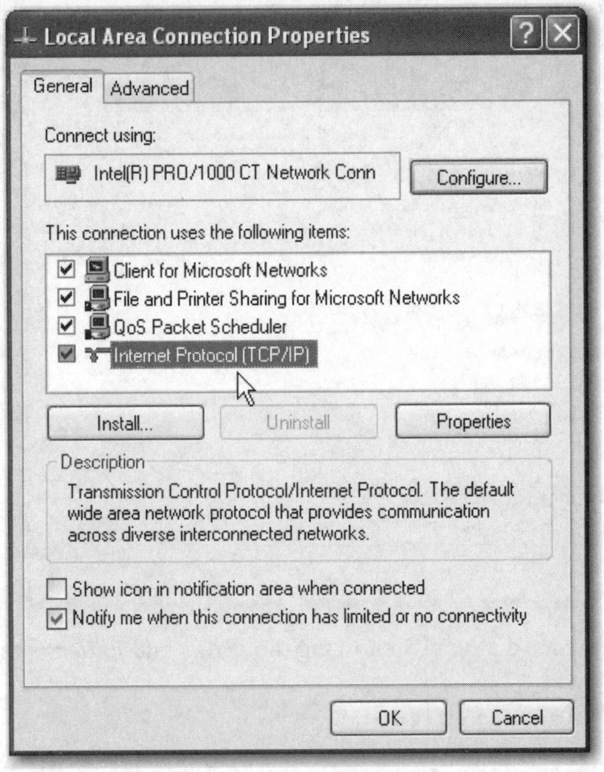

Figure 14: The *Local Area Connection Properties* dialog box showing the *Internet Protocol (TCP/IP)* option selected

5. If you want to configure a static IP address for this computer click the option button labeled **Use the following IP address** and enter the IP address, subnet mask, and default gateway information. You may also assign a static address for DNS.

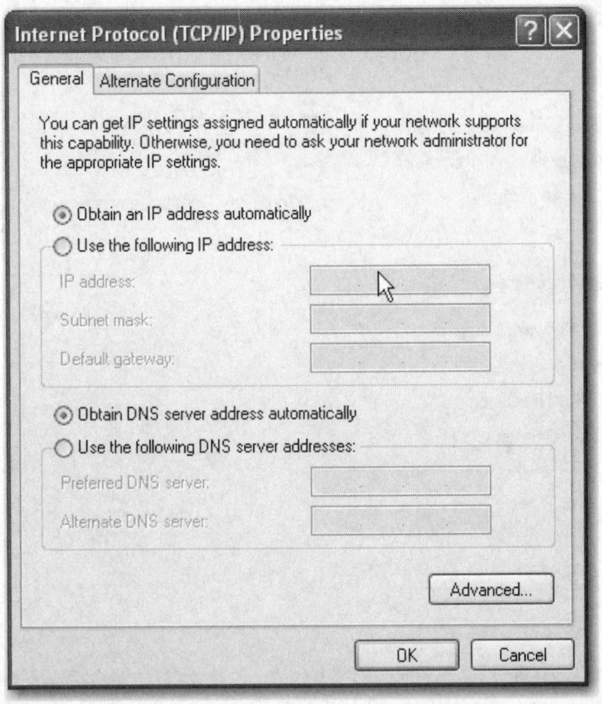

Figure 15: The *Internet Protocol (TCP/IP) Properties* dialog box showing the default settings

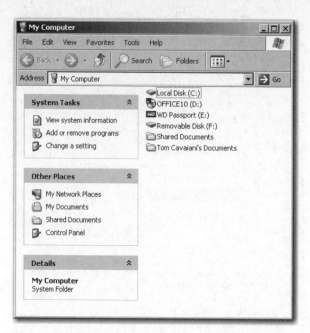

Figure 16: The *My Computer* dialog box showing the *drives* and *folders* available on the computer

Displaying Local and Mapped Drives

Click the **My Computer** choice in the **Start** menu (Figure 5). A listing of all available disk drives and folders similar to that shown in Figure 16 appears.

Figure 17: The *My Computer* dialog box showing the *Tools* menu

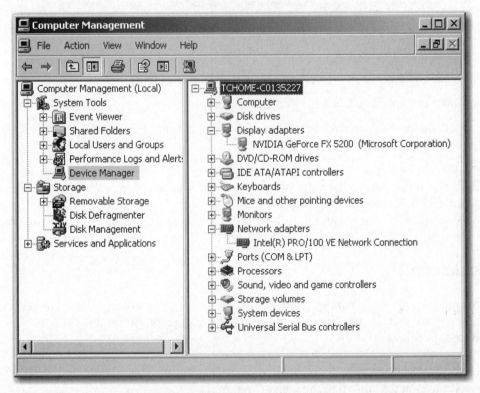

| Open |
| Explore |
| Search... |
| Manage |
| Map Network Drive... |
| Disconnect Network Drive... |
| Show on Desktop |
| Rename |
| Properties |

Figure 18: The pop-up menu that is displayed after right-clicking on the *My Computer Start* menu choice

If you would like to map a network drive, disconnect an existing drive, or change folder *options* click the **Tools** option in the menu bar to display a list with these choices (Figure 17). *Mapping* is a convenient method for associating a network drive with an unused drive letter.

Verifying Network Interface Card Configuration

Settings for your computer's network card are available through the *Device Manager*. To display and modify these settings proceed as follows:

1. Right-click the **My Computer** choice in the **Start** menu (Figure 5). A pop-up menu appears (Figure 18). Click the **Manage** choice.

2. The *Computer Management* dialog box appears (Figure 19). Click the **Device Manager** icon. A list of devices, including one or more network adapters, appears in the right-hand pane of the dialog box.

Figure 19: The *Computer Management* dialog box showing the configurable devices available

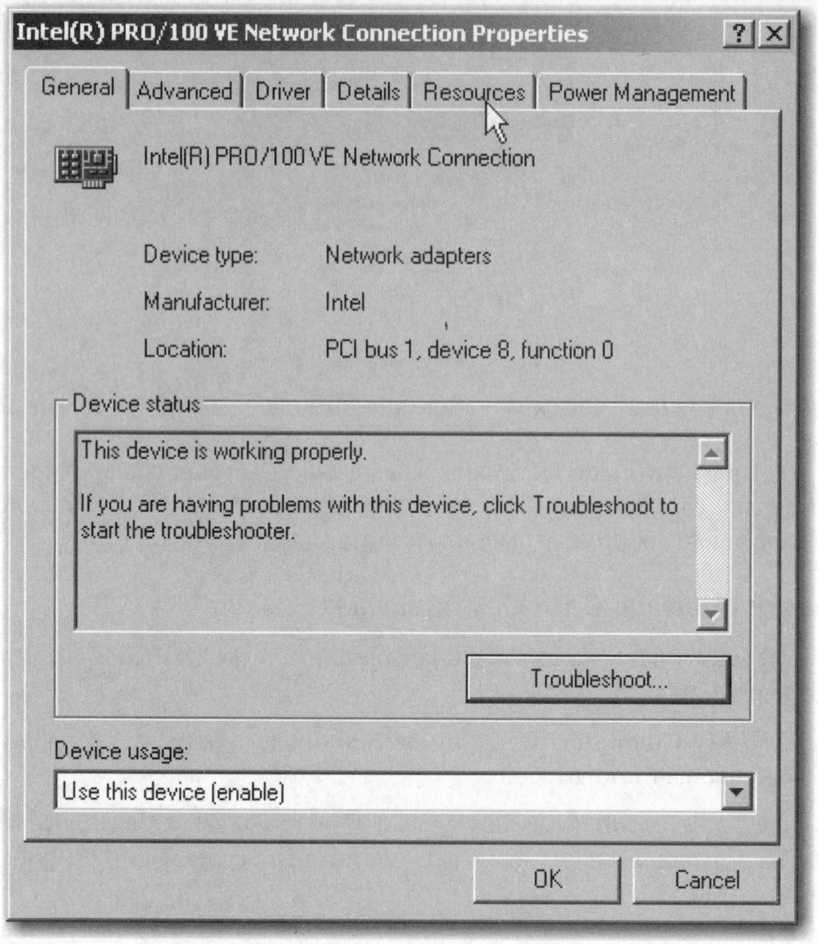

Figure 20: A tabbed network adapter dialog box. Clicking the tabs will display different pages that contain options for the adapter that can be either viewed or modified.

3. Right-click on the name of the network adapter displayed (Figure 19).

4. A pop-up menu appears. Click the **Properties** choice.

5. A tabbed dialog box containing the configurable options for your network adapter appears (Figure 20).

6. **Note**: On a properly configured Windows system, the network adapter options can only be modified by a user with administrator privileges. If you have logged into your network using a standard user account you will not be able to access the *Device Manager*. If you have access to an account that has administrative privileges you can use the *Run as* option to switch to that account so that you can run the Device Manager.

System Shutdown

It is best to either *logout* or *shutdown* your computer when you have completed a session on your computer. Doing so secures the network from access by unauthorized individuals. To logout or shutdown proceed as follows:

1. Click the **Start** button. The *Start* menu appears (Figure 5). The *Log Off* and *Turn Off Computer* options appear at the bottom of the menu (Figure 21).

2. Clicking the **Log Off** option displays the dialog box shown in Figure 22.

Figure 21: The *Log Off* and *Turn Off Computer* options that are shown in the Windows *Start* menu

Figure 22: The *Log Off* dialog box

3. Clicking the **Log Off** button shown in Figure 22 ends your session and leaves the computer running.

4. Clicking the **Turn Off Computer** option shown in Figure 21 displays the dialog box shown in Figure 23. Clicking the **Standby** option puts your computer in a low power state. Clicking the **Turn Off** option ends your session and turns your computer off.

Figure 23: The *Shutdown* or *Turn off computer* dialog box

Questions

1. What information, other than that previously mentioned, is displayed by the ipconfig/all command?

2. What are the IP addresses for the DNS and DHCP servers that are available to your system?

3. What is your system's hostname?

4. What is the physical address associated with your computer?

5. Verify connectivity to one of the DNS Servers available to your system by *pinging* its IP address. Did the DNS server respond?

6. How many bytes long is a DNS server reply?

7. Open a command window and type **tracert www.ibm.com**. Describe the results.

8. What IP address is displayed for **www.ibm.com**?

9. Type CTRL-C to terminate the tracert command.

10. Open a browser and type **http://www.washington.edu/networking/tools/traceroute** in the browser's *locator text box* to display the *University of Washington trace route gateway* homepage. Use this application to obtain information regarding the Internet path the trace takes between the University of Washington's trace route gateway and IBM's server. Use the IP address that you obtained in question 7 above for IBM's server. You may need to scroll the gateway window to see all of the results. Was the entire path between the UW gateway and IBM's server displayed?

11. How many hops were displayed?

12. What is the last IP address or host name displayed? (You may need to click the *Abort* button to terminate the trace)

13. If the host name information being displayed is replaced by one or more lines of asterisks, answer the following question: What do you think the asterisks indicate? (You may need to click the *Abort* button to terminate the trace)

14. Which interrupt (IRQ) has been assigned to this adapter? (**Hint**: Click on the *Resources* tab directly below the title bar in the network adapter dialog box)

15. What other settings can be changed through the Internet Protocol Properties dialog box?

Submitting your Lab Report

Create a new page on your Google site and name it *Lab Three Report*.   Copy the questions and their answers to the Lab Three Report page.

LAB 4: COMPUTER HARDWARE

OBJECTIVES

After completing this lab you should be able to do the following:

- ✓ Describe the basic features of input, output, process, storage, and communications hardware

- ✓ Design a desktop computer system based upon provided requirements

- ✓ Obtain a price quote for a desktop computer system

CONTENTS

HARDWARE, SOFTWARE, AND COMMUNICATIONS REQUIREMENTS FOR THIS LAB

- ➢ A Windows-based computer

- ➢ Access to the Internet

USEFUL LINKS

- ➢ **http://www.wikipedia.com**

- ➢ **http://computer.howstuffworks.com/computer-hardware-pictures4.htm**

- ➢ **http://www.buildyourowncomputer.net/learntobuild.html**

LAB 4

Introduction

In this lab you will perform some basic research to learn more about computer and networking hardware. Based upon the information obtained you will design a computer system for the office staff of an imaginary company.

Part One: Identifying Computer Components

The tangible components of a computer system can be classified into the following five groups: *input, process, output, storage,* and *communications (network)* (Figure 1). This lab is divided into sections based upon these five groups. For each section you will investigate the properties and characteristics of a specific computer component using sources on the World Wide Web. You will then be asked to answer a set of questions regarding your findings. After collecting this background information you will design a computer system for staff members of an imaginary organization. Finally you will create a report based upon your design and post it to your Google site.

Use whatever resources you have available for answering these questions. Include a list of your references at the end of your report. A useful starting point is **http://www.webopedia.com**.

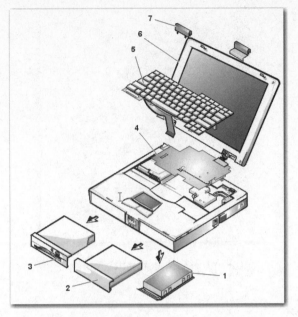

Figure 1: An exploded view of the computer hardware components of a laptop computer

Another is **http://www.wikipedia.com**. Detailed pictures and explanations of motherboard components are available at **http://computer.howstuffworks.com/computer-hardware-pictures4.htm**. Include at least three additional sources in your list of references. Be aware that contributions to Wikipedia are made by volunteers and are not necessarily edited for correctness. Likewise, some information found on either or both of the above mentioned sites may be out-of-date. Include the most accurate and up-to-date information you can find in your report.

Input Hardware

Keyboard

1. How many keys do most modern keyboards have?

2. What keys besides the typical alphabetic and numeric keys are included on a keyboard?

3. What types of connectors are used on modern keyboards?

Figure 2: A computer keyboard

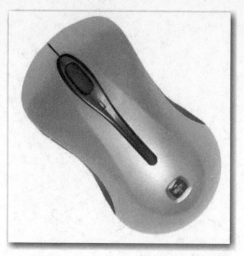

Figure 3: A computer mouse

Mouse

1. What type of mouse has replaced the traditional mechanical mouse?

2. What types of connectors are used on mouses?

3. Name two pointer-type devices that might be used with a computer system.

Scanner

1. What is the purpose of a scanner?

2. List at least two devices that have the capability to scan documents?

3. What type of software is required to convert scanned text into text that can be modified by a word processor?

Process Hardware

Central Processing Unit (CPU) and Motherboard

Figure 4: An external view of a computer processor

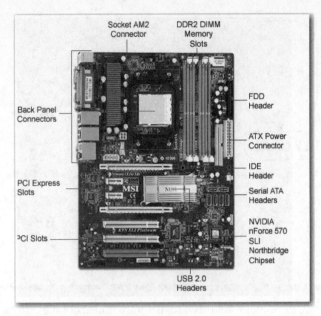

Figure 5: A computer motherboard or system board

1. What speeds (measured in *hertz*) do present-day CPUs attain?

2. Provide definitions for each of the following components of a CPU:

   a. Arithmetic/Logic Unit

   b. Registers/Primary Storage Unit

   c. Control Unit

3. Provide definitions for each of the following components of a motherboard or system board (See **http://computer.howstuffworks.com/computer-hardware-pictures.htm** for a set of pictures that shows detailed pictures of a motherboard and its components)

   a. System bus

   b. Data bus

   c. Address bus

   d. Local bus/Video bus

   e. Expansion bus

4. What is the purpose of the system bus?

5. What is the purpose of the data bus?

Figure 6: A Random Access Memory chip

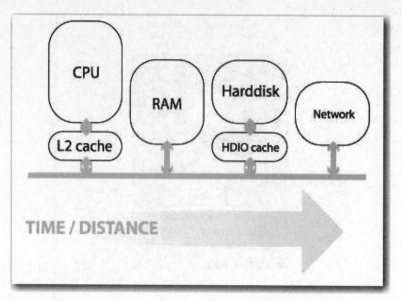

Figure 7: A conceptual view of processor hardware, primary and secondary storage, memory caches, and the network interface. Speeds for these components diminish from left to right.

Memory

1. What is the difference between *Random Access Memory* and *Read Only Memory*?

2. What is the purpose of *cache memory*?

Output Hardware

Monitor

1. What are the two most common types of monitor technologies?

2. Briefly describe how the two technologies differ.

Figure 8: A flat-screen computer monitor

Figure 9: A computer video adapter

Video Cards

1. What is the purpose of a video card?

2. Why would you want lots of memory on your video card?

Printers

1. Early computer printers were based upon typewriter technology. Newer printer technologies discarded the older approach were the print head contacted the paper to create a character image. List three advantages that non-impact printers have over the older typewriter-style printers.

2. Search for information on dot-matrix and daisy-wheel printers. Briefly describe the differences between these older typewriter-based technologies.

3. The two most common types of printer used today are laser jets and ink jets. Briefly explain the difference in these technologies. List 3 advantages of each type of printer.

Figure 10: A modern desktop printer

Figure 11: A dedicated FAX machine

Fax

1. Is it reasonable to consider a fax machine as a type of computer? Explain.

2. Describe two different approaches to sending a fax (*Hint*: one approach uses dedicated hardware and the other does not).

Storage Hardware

Hard Disk Drives

1. List three different hard disk drive interface technologies.

2. What is meant by a *track* on a hard disk drive?

3. What is a sector?

4. Describe how data are physically stored on hard disk drives.

5. What does the acronym RAID refer to?

6. List and describe three different classes of RAID

7. What does the expression "hot swappable" mean with regard to drives in a RAID array?

Figure 12: A hard disk platter and read-write head and mechanism

Figure 13: A floppy disk and drive

Floppy Disk Drives

1. List three ways in which a floppy disk drive differs from a hard disk drive.

2. Why are floppy disk drives no longer available on most computers?

3. What is a zip drive?

4. What is a thumb drive?

Other Types of Storage

1. Provide a description for each of the following types of storage hardware:

   a. CD-ROM

   b. Blu-Ray

   c. DVD

   d. Thumb drives

   e. Network disk drives and arrays

Figure 14: A CD-ROM/DVD drive

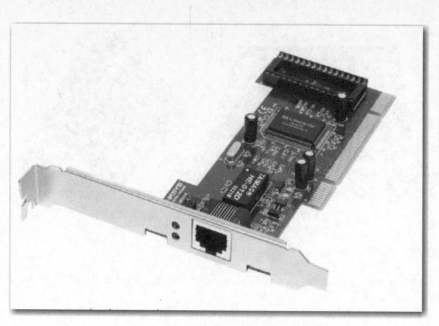

Figure 15: A Network Adapter Card

Communications Hardware

Network Interface Cards (network adapters)

1. What is the purpose of a network adapter?

2. What two different types of network adapters are typically included in laptop computers?

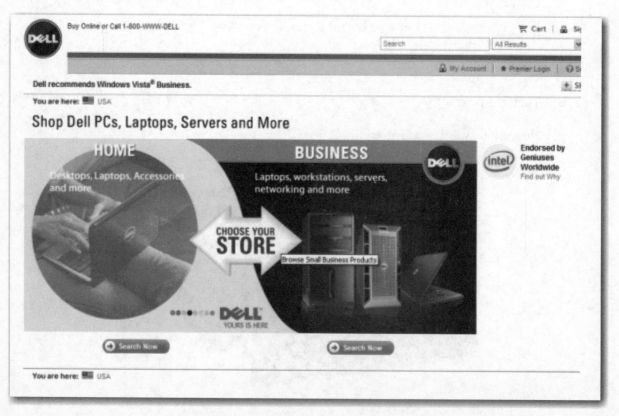

Figure 16: Dell Computer's home page

Part Two: Designing a Computer System

In this part of the lab you will use the knowledge gained in Part One to help you design a computer system for the office staff of a fictional organization. You will not be given specific budget information, but must attempt to design the most cost-effective system you can, based upon the resources available. The system should be capable of accomplishing the tasks performed by the office workers, but should not contain unnecessary features.

Scenario

Assume that you work in the IT department of a large corporation name Acme Productions and that it is your job to periodically provide management with price quotes for new office computers. You are required to obtain quotes from two different vendors. The quotes must include an itemized list of components and a justification for why each component is appropriate and necessary. Both quotes must be for a computer that includes a set of components that meet the needs of the office staff, but do not exceed these needs. Specifically your quotes must be for computers that have sufficient computing power and storage capacities, but are reasonably priced.

In general, the office staff uses computers for email and word processing purposes. They also need access to the company intranet to download purchase forms. The staff also needs to access the Internet to exchange orders with Acme's business partners. Office workers store documents that include large graphics files on their PCs. They also need to access network storage drives for archiving older documents.

Designing a Computer System

Design a computer system for the office staff. If you have never designed a computer system before consult **http://www.buildyourowncomputer.net/learntobuild.html** for a set of guidelines describing how to build your own computer including short explanations of each type of component. Obtain price quotes from two different vendors. Use on-line resources and include the names of the vendors in your quotes. Sources for information used in your quotes must be well-known reputable companies such as Dell, Gateway, Hewlett-Packard, etc. Write a short summary indicating the differences and similarities between the computer systems you have designed. Also include a short justification for any price differences that are encountered.

Submitting your Lab Report

Create a new page on your Google site. Name this page *Lab Four Report*. Copy the questions on computer hardware and their answers by category to the Lab Four Report page. Clearly label the categories. Create a separate section for your price quote summaries. Attach the actual itemized price quotes to your report using the *Google Attachments* feature (refer to the lower right hand corner of Figure 16).

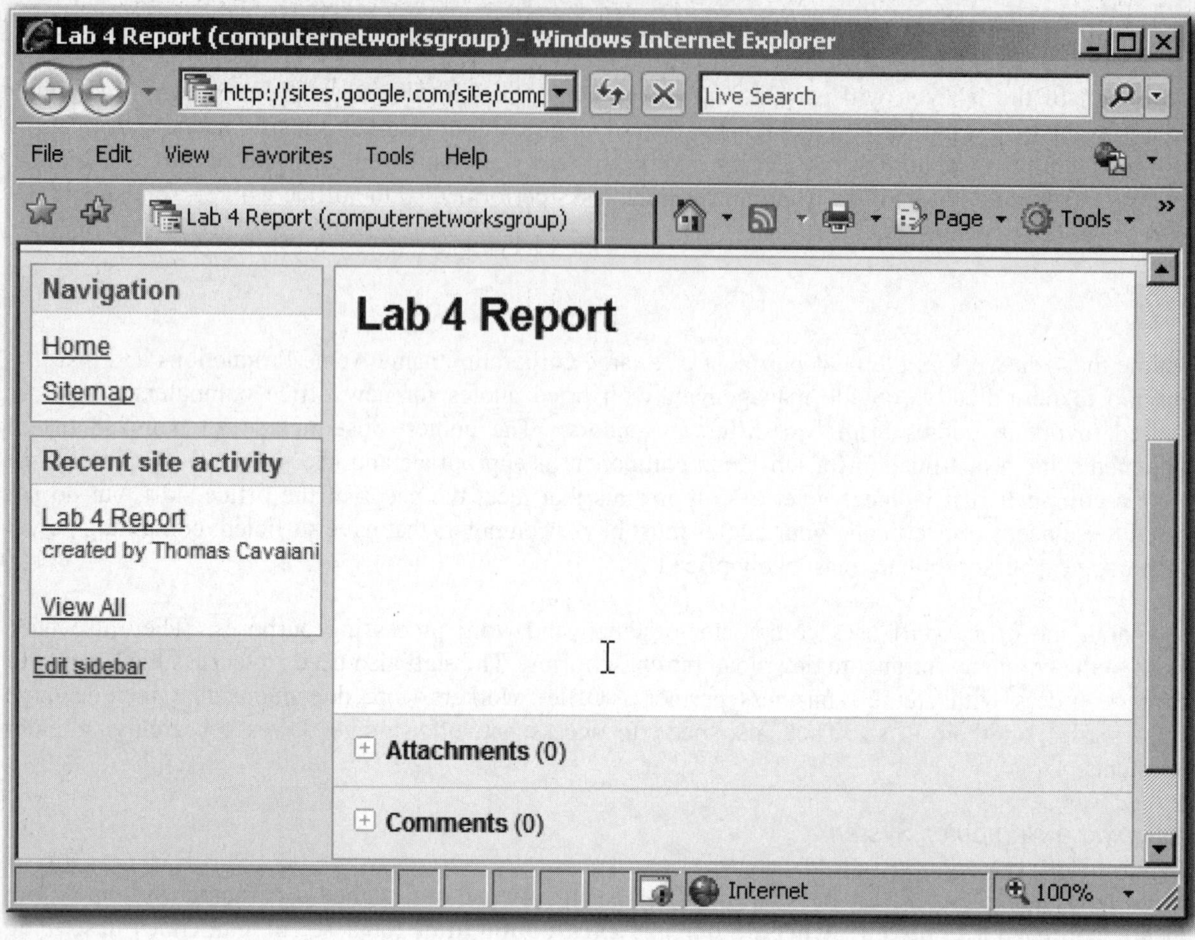

Figure 17: A sample Google site report page showing the *Attachments* feature

LAB 5: THE HYPERTEXT MARKUP LANGUAGE

OBJECTIVES

After completing this lab you should be able to do the following:

- ✓ Use basic HTML tags to format web pages

- ✓ Create tables and forms using HTML

CONTENTS

HARDWARE, SOFTWARE, AND COMMUNICATIONS REQUIREMENTS FOR THIS LAB

- ➤ A Windows-based computer

- ➤ Access to the Internet

USEFUL LINKS

- ➤ **http://www.w3schools.com/html/**

LAB 5

Introduction

This lab is designed to introduce you to HTML, the HyperText Markup Language used to create pages that can be displayed in a browser on the World Wide Web. HTML allows you to create files that use different *tags* for labeling information in the file so that it appears in the appropriate format when displayed in a browser.

Part One: Learning HTML Basics

This is an on-line lab. You will work on tutorials found on the *W3 Schools* home page to learn about the basics of HTML. The following steps will get you started:

1. Open a browser and copy the URL, **http://www.w3schools.com/html/**, into the **Locator** text box (Figure 1). Click the **Go to** arrow to the right of the **Locator** text box or press the **Enter** key to display the *W3 Schools HTML Tutorial* page (Figure 2).

Figure 1: The *Windows Internet Explorer* browser showing the URL for the *W3Schools* home page in the *Locator* text box. The *Go to* arrow is located to the right of the Locator text box.

50

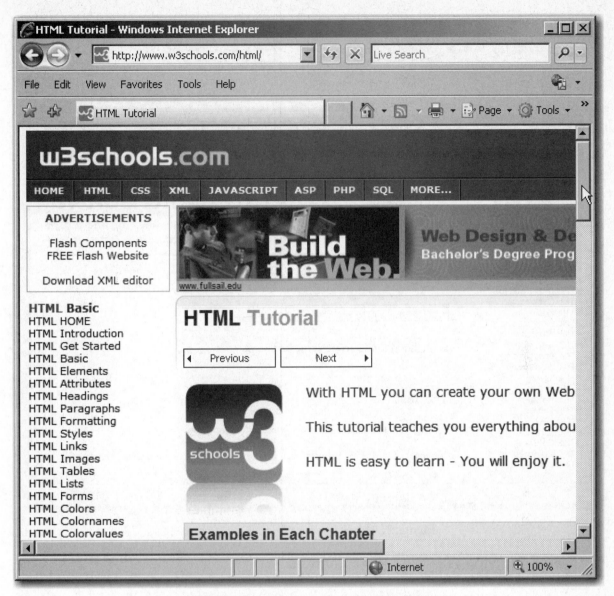

Figure 2: The *W3 Schools HTML Tutorial* page

2. Complete *HTML Basic* section (Figure 2). Instructions for completing the lessons are included on the lesson pages. The *Previous* and *Next* buttons can be used to move from one lesson to another. Scroll the screens to see more information. This section has 17 lessons beginning with an *Introduction to HTML* and ending with a lesson on *Colorvalues*.

3. After completing the 17 lessons in the HTML *Basic* tutorial take the on-line HTML *Quiz* to test your knowledge (Figure 3). The link to the HTML tutorial is located on the W3School page homepage and is provide here: **http://www.w3schools.com/html/html_quiz.asp**. The test has 20 questions and can be re-taken.

4. After completing the quiz, check your score and then review the topics associated with the questions you answered incorrectly.

5. Retake the quiz after you have reviewed the topics. Although the test is not official you may wish to record your scores to determine if they improve based upon any extra studying and review that you may perform.

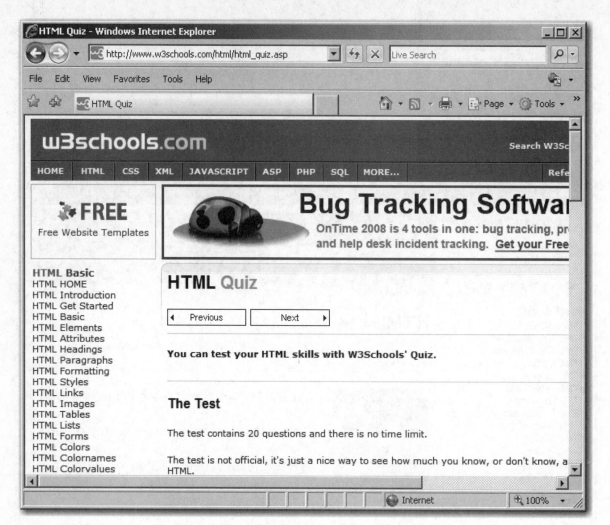

Figure 3: The *W3 Schools HTML Quiz* page

Part Two: Applying What you Have Learned

To apply the information learned in Part One, proceed as follows (**Note**: the *W3Schools Quick List* is available at **http://www.w3schools.com/html/html_quick.asp**. This list includes a summary of all the commands discussed in the HTML Basic tutorial. A portion of the list is shown in Figure 4).

1. Open a word processor that supports the HTML file format (Microsoft Word supports this file format).

2. Create a new file. Name the file *index.htm* and be sure to save it as an HTML file type.

3. Add your name, course name, section number, instructor's name, and session name (for example, Fall Semester 2009). Format this information by changing the fonts and colors, centering the names, adding bolding and italics, etc.

4. Add a table. List your weekly schedule in this table. Add the days of the week to the top row of the table and bold these labels.

5. Create a survey form. Include three questions in your survey.

6. Add option buttons to the survey form so that users can conveniently indicate there survey choices.

Submitting your Lab Report

Create a new page on your Google site and name it *Lab Five Report*. Copy the *index.htm* file that you created in Part 2 to the Lab Five Report page. Include a subheading in your report to label the index.htm file.

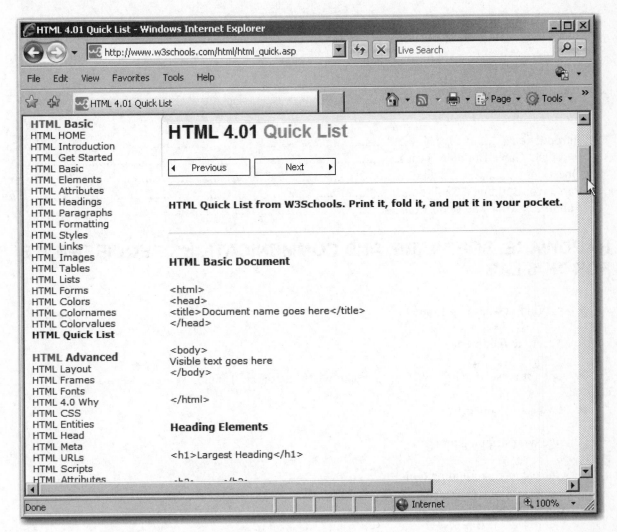

Figure 4: The *W3 Schools Quick List* summary of basic HTML commands

LAB 6: CONSTRUCTING A NETWORK CABLE

OBJECTIVES

After completing this lab you should be able to do the following:

- ✓ Describe TIA/EIA-568-B cabling and termination standards

- ✓ Build a Category 5 UTP patch cable

CONTENTS

HARDWARE, SOFTWARE, AND COMMUNICATIONS REQUIREMENTS FOR THIS LAB

- ➤ A Windows-based computer

- ➤ Access to the Internet

- ➤ One 6 foot section of CAT 5 unshielded twisted pair (UTP) cable

- ➤ Two RJ 45 connectors

- ➤ One wire stripping tool

- ➤ One cable-end crimping tool

- ➤ One cable tester

USEFUL LINKS

- ➤ **http://en.wikipedia.org/wiki/T568B**

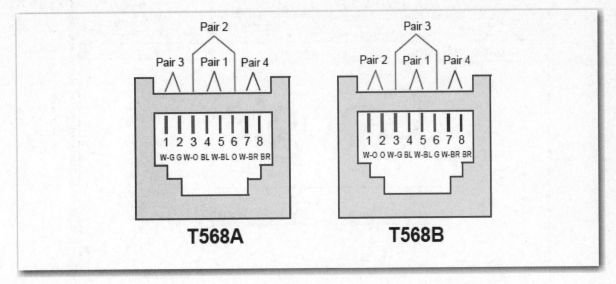

Figure 1: 8-Position modular jack wire pair assignments for UTP

Introduction

Most organizations hire wiring contractors to design and install the cabling systems required for their internal networks. For new construction special unshielded twisted pair cabling is typically used for this purpose. This cabling is composed of four wire pairs (8 separate insulated wires) wrapped in plastic sheathing to create a wire bundle. The cabling can be purchased in bulk, cut to the desired lengths, and then *terminated* by installing special connectors to the ends of the cable. This process involves inserting individual wires in the bundle into slots in specially designed connectors. Wiring patterns defined by the *Telecommunications Industry Association* specify the alignment of the wires in the connectors (Figure 1). In this lab you will build and test your own network cable to gain a better understanding of the procedures required and problems encountered during this process.

Part One: Cable Building Basics

Cable Standards

This section provides you with information regarding wiring standards. Standards are essential so that cables transmit data in a consistent manner regardless of the manufacturer of the cable. Besides learning about wiring patterns you will also learn about the history and origins of the standards organizations.

Proceed as follows to learn more about the TIA/EIA cable standards:

1. Double-click the **Internet Explorer** icon on the Windows Desktop. An Internet Explorer browser window appears (Figure 2).

2. Enter the URL, **http://en.wikipedia.org/wiki/T568B**, into IE's *Locator* text box and click the **Go to** button (Figure 2).

3. A Wikipedia page displaying historical and technical information about the TIA/EIA-568-B wiring standards appears.

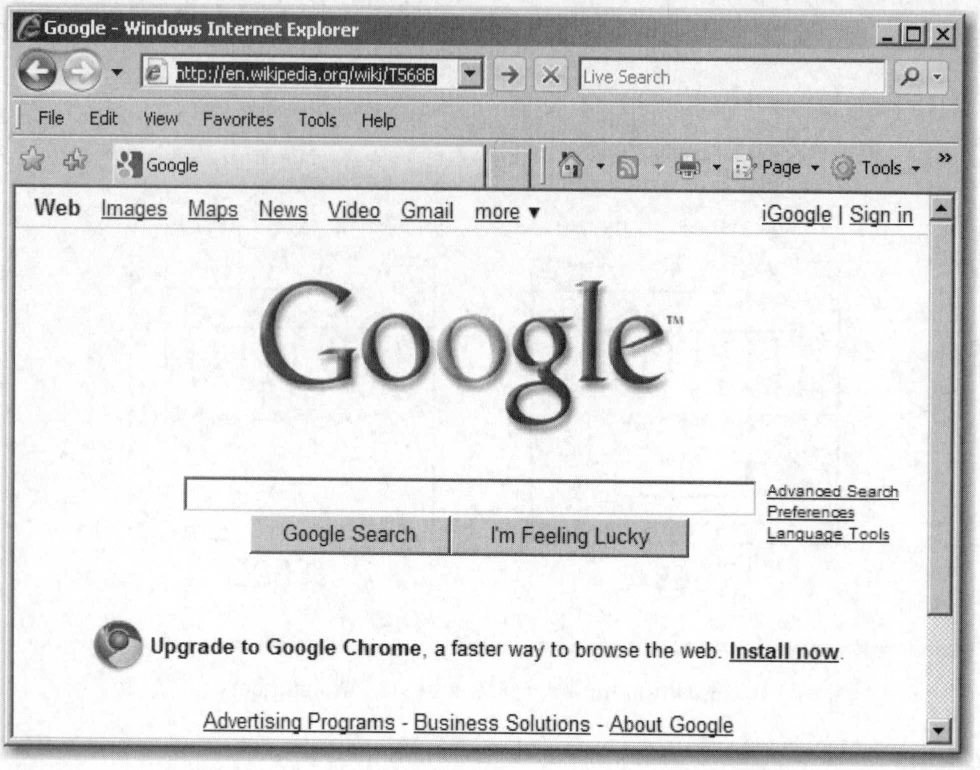

Figure 2: The Windows Internet Explorer showing the *URL* to the Wikipedia page on cable wiring standards in the *Locator* text box and the *Go to* button to the right of the text box

4. Review the information on the Wikipedia page and answer the questions that follow:

Questions

1. In which year were the TIA/EIA-568-B standards were first published?

2. What types of organizations were involved in developing the TIA/EIA-568-B standard?

3. The development and popularization of what type of cabling drove significant changes in the standards?

4. Under TIA/EIA-568-B standard, what is the range of allowable horizontal cable distances for twisted-pair cable types?

5. What is the widest known and most discussed feature of TIA/EIA-568-B.1-2001 standard?

6. What is the correct specification for RJ 45 connectors?

7. What is the correct sequence of wire color assignments to connector pins 1-8 using the T568B standard?

8. What type of cable standard would need to be used to support 10GBase-T connections?

9. What is a crossover cable?

10. You decide to convert a TIA/EIA 568-B straight-through cable into a crossover cable. What changes do you have to make?

Part Two: Building a Cable

Tools and Materials Required

The following is a list of tools and materials that are needed to build a short *Category 5e* (CAT 5e) network cable.

- One 6 foot section of CAT 5 unshielded twisted pair (UTP) cable (Figure 3)

- Two RJ 45 connectors (Figure 4)

- One wire stripping tool (Figure 5)

- One cable-end crimping tool (Figure 6)

- One cable tester (Figure 7)

A Category 5e cable meets the requirements for transmitting data on an IEEE 802.3 computer network at speeds of 100 Mbps or less. According to specifications published by the *Telecommunications Industry Association* (TIA) these cables may vary in length from a minimum of about 3 feet to a maximum of 100 meters (about 328 feet).

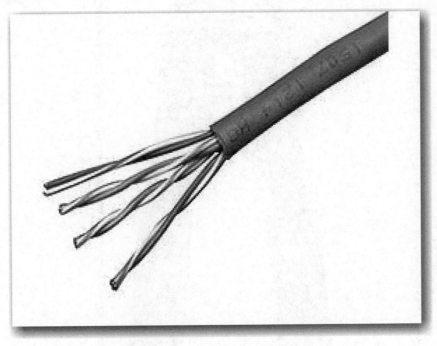

Figure 3: A short section of CAT 5 cable

Figure 4: An RJ-45 connector

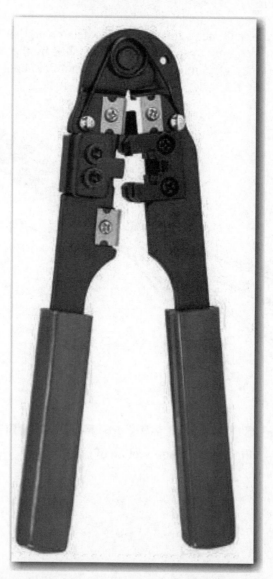

Figure 5: A combination wire stripping/crimping tool

Figure 6: Cable testers

The tools and materials needed to build a CAT 5 patch cable will be available during your regularly scheduled lab session. Follow the steps shown below to build and test your cable. Your instructor will assist you in testing the cable, and will assign credit for completing this part of the lab when your cable passes the tests described below.

1. Strip about 1 inch of cable housing off of each end of a section of CAT 5 cable.

2. Align the individual wires in the correct pattern according to the T568B standard.

3. Trim the individual cable straight across until only about ½" of each cable remains

4. Insert the cable ends into the connector.

5. Check the alignment of the individual cables to determine if the color pattern is in accordance with the standard.

6. Crimp the connector ends using the cable-end crimping tool.

7. Pull on the cable to determine that the connectors are firmly crimped. Crimp loose ends again if necessary.

8. Test your cable for continuity using the cable tester provided.

9. Have your instructor verify that your cable functions properly.

10. Congratulations! You have successfully built a functioning CAT 5 patch cable.

Submitting your Lab Report

Create a new page on your Google site. Name it *Lab Six Report.* Copy the *Cable Standards* questions and their answers to the Lab Six Report page.

LAB 7: LOCAL AREA NETWORKS FUNDAMENTALS

OBJECTIVES

After completing this lab you should be able to do the following:

✓ Describe basic LAN topologies and media access methods

✓ Describe LAN types and security models

✓ Describe the basic characteristics of Virtual LANs

CONTENTS

HARDWARE, SOFTWARE, AND COMMUNICATIONS REQUIREMENTS FOR THIS LAB

➢ A Windows-based computer

➢ Access to the Internet

USEFUL LINKS

➢ http://www.google.com

➢ http://telecomm.boisestate.edu/itm305l.fall.2008/slides/vlans.pdf

LAB 7

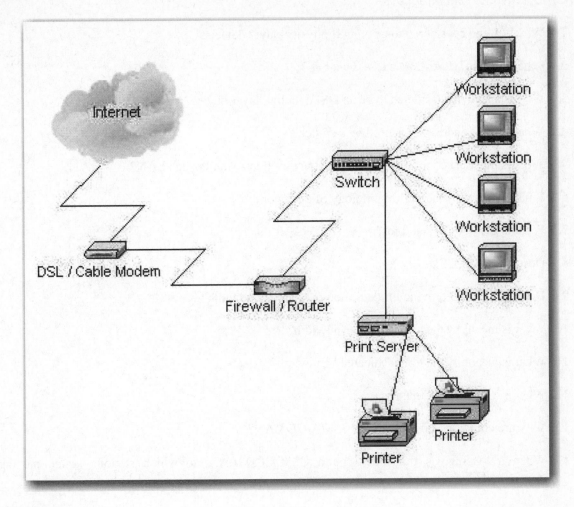

Introduction

Local Area Networks provide a convenient and secure means for office workers to share data and system resources. Once management personnel become aware of these LAN benefits, they probably will make the design and implementation of a LAN a top priority. Many organizations have already done so.

LANs can be implemented by using either hubs, devices that simply retransmits signals, or switches, more "intelligent" devices that use addressing to minimize network traffic and increase throughput. Since a hub transmits information to all of the computers connected to it, bandwidth is shared. A switch, on the other hand, creates temporary circuits between message senders and receivers so that all available bandwidth is dedicated to each message transmitted.

Researching the Concepts

To help you become aware of some of the issues affecting the design of a LAN, review and answer the following questions. Sources for answers to these questions include your textbook, those resources you used in previous labs, and any other additional resources you find while searching for answers for these questions. Make note of these sources because you will be required to include a list of them in your lab report.

Questions

LAN Topology and Media Access

1. Why is a hub considered to be an OSI physical layer device?

2. What types of addressing is used by a hub?

3. Why is a switch considered to be an OSI data link layer device?

4. What type of addressing is used by a switch?

5. What is the most common physical topology used in a small office LAN?

6. What is meant by the logical topology of a network?

7. What is CSMA/CD stand for?

8. Describe CSMA/CD.

9. Does CSMA/CD provide for dedicated or shared bandwidth?

10. What is meant by the term shared bandwidth?

11. What is meant by the term dedicated bandwidth?

12. What is a collision domain?

13. Why are collisions a problem on a CSMA/CD LAN?

14. When a message is transmitted on a CSMA/CD LAN, to which stations is the message transmitted?

15. When a message is transmitted on a switched LAN, which stations are involved in the data transmission?

LAN Types and Security Models

To help you better understand some of the issues affecting the security of a LAN, perform some basic research on *peer-to-peer* and *client/server* networks and answer the following questions.

1. What is a peer-to-peer network?

2. What is a client/server network?

3. Which network model uses a centralized security model?

4. Who controls access to files and shared printers in a peer-to-peer model?

5. Who controls access to systems, files, and shared printers in a client/server model?

6. Which security model provides better management and protection for systems and their resources?

VLANS

Virtual Local Area Networks (*VLANs*) overcome many of the physical and security issues that are inherent in a Local Area Network. Double-click the Internet Explorer icon on your Windows Desktop and enter the URL, **http://telecomm.boisestate.edu/itm305l.fall.2008/slides/vlans.pdf**, into IE's locator text box and click the **Go to** button to view a slide show on VLANs. Review the information presented in the slide show to gain a basic understanding of the characteristics of VLANs. Based upon the information provided in these slides and any additional research you may wish to conduct, answer the following questions:

VLANs

1. What is a VLAN?

2. What types of collision domains do VLANs break up?

3. List three features of a VLAN.

4. List three ways in which a VLAN can be organized.

5. Explain how VLANs can be used to overcome the physical limitations of a departmental office.

Submitting your Lab Report

Create a new page on your Google site and name it *Lab Seven Report*. Copy the question headings, the questions, and their answers to the Lab Seven Report page. Also include the list of the sources that you consulted while answering the questions. Use a standard reference format for each resource.

LAB 8: DESIGNING A LOCAL AREA NETWORK

OBJECTIVES

After completing this lab you should be able to do the following:

- ✓ Design a Local Area Network based upon a given scenario

- ✓ Create a spreadsheet that outlines the cost of implementing a LAN that you designed

CONTENTS

HARDWARE, SOFTWARE, AND COMMUNICATIONS REQUIREMENTS FOR THIS LAB

- ➤ A Windows-based computer

- ➤ Access to the Internet

USEFUL LINKS

- ➤ **http://elena.aut.ac.nz/homepages/weblandesigner/index.php?fuseaction=home.main**

LAB 8

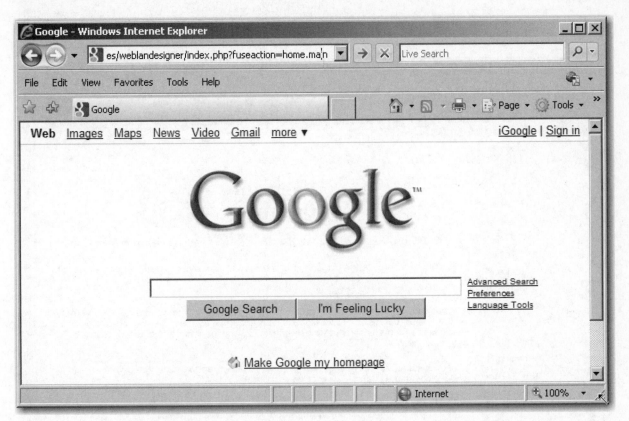

Figure 1: The Windows Internet Explorer showing the URL for the *AUT WebLan-Designer* home page in the *Locator* text box and the *Go to* arrow to the right of the text box

Introduction

In the previous lab you learned about computer and communications hardware, cable standards, LAN fundamentals and media access. In this lab you will extend your knowledge of computer technology and local area networks by designing a LAN for a fictional organization. You will create the LAN by first reviewing design concepts. You will then use on-line tools to design a pictorial representation of the LAN. Tutorials available at the *AUT's WebLan-Designer's* home page will provide you with the conceptual knowledge and tools you will need to learn how to design a LAN.

Part One: Accessing the Design Tools

The following steps outline the procedures required to design your local area network.

1. Double-click the **Internet Explorer** icon on the Windows Desktop. The Internet Explorer browser window appears (Figure 1).

2. Enter the URL, **http://elena.aut.ac.nz/homepages/weblandesigner/index.php?fuseaction=home.main**, into the **Locator** text box.

3. Click the **Go to** button to the right of the **Locator** text box or press the **Enter** key.

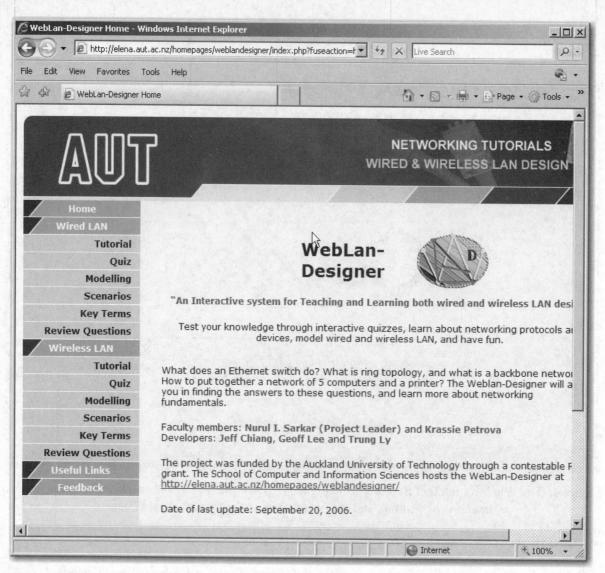

Figure 2: The *AUT WebLan-Designer* home page showing the *Wired* and *Wireless* LAN links in the left column of the page

4. The *AUT's WebLan-Designer's* home page appears (Figure 2).

Part Two: Weblan-Designer Links

1. Notice the links in the left column of the AUT WebLan-Designer home page.

2. Click the **Tutorial** link to display a pre-test that you can take to review your existing knowledge of LANs and LAN terminology, and learn how to use the *Modeling* tools that can be used to create LAN diagrams.

3. Click the **Quiz** link to display a quiz that you can take to test your knowledge of LAN components, topology, and concepts.

4. Click the **Key Terms** link to display a Glossary of LAN-related terms.

5. Click the **Review Questions** link to display a list of questions with answers that can be used for reviewing or confirming your knowledge of LANs and the OSI model.

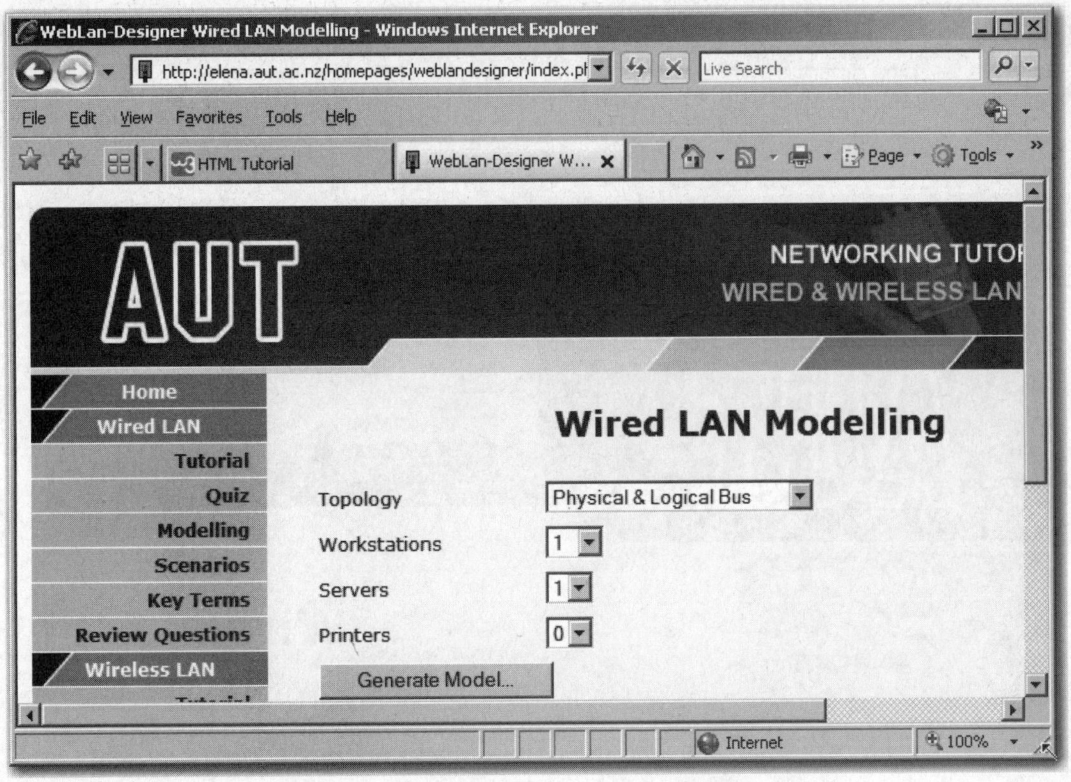

Figure 3: The AUT *Wired LAN Modeling* page

Part Three: Modeling

1. Click the **Modeling** link in the *Wired LAN* section.

2. The *Wired LAN Modeling* page appears (Figure 3). This page is quite intuitive and easy to use. First select the **Topology** for your LAN by clicking the **down-arrow** in the *Topology* text box to display a list of choices.

3. Next select the number of workstations, servers, and printers required you want to add to the LAN by clicking the **down-arrow** and selecting a value from the list that appears. You can also type the value from the keyboard.

4. Click the **Generate Model** button. The *Information Bar* dialog box appears (Figure 4).

Figure 4: The *Information Bar* dialog box

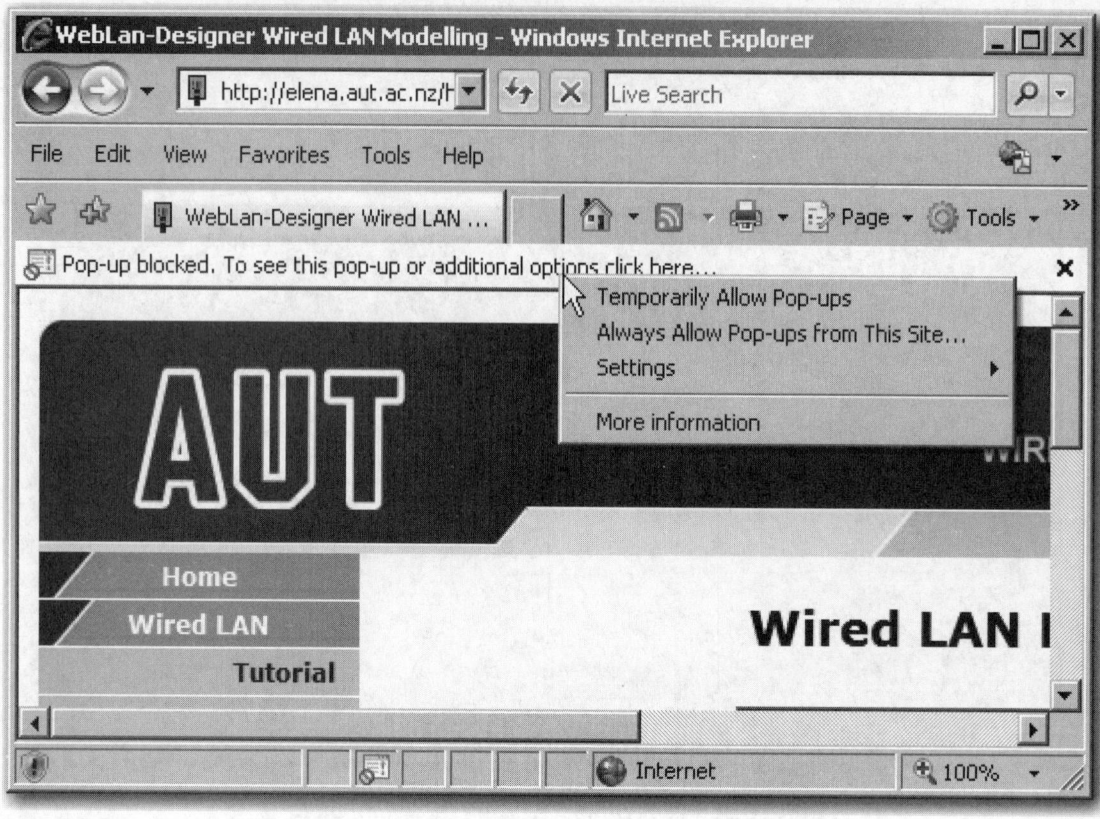

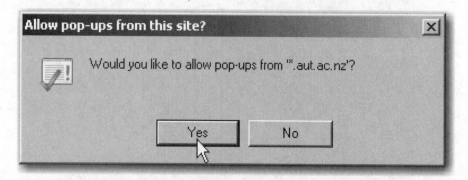

Figure 5: The *Information Bar pop-up* menu that is displayed after right-clicking the Information Bar

5. The *Modeling tool* needs to use a JavaScript pop-up. Click the **Close** button in the *Information Bar* dialog box (Figure 4).

6. Right-click the **Information Bar** on the *Wired LAN Modeling* page to display a pop-up menu with 4 choices (Figure 5).

7. Click the **Always Allow Pop-ups for this Site** choice.

8. Click the **Yes** button in the dialog box that appears to allow pop-ups from this site (Figure 6). Click the **Retry** button in the dialog box that appears next (not shown).

9. A diagram of the LAN appears (Figure 7). From this point on the diagrams that you create with the modeling tool will appear without displaying the *Information Bar* or any warning messages.

Figure 6: The *Allow pop-ups from this site*? dialog box

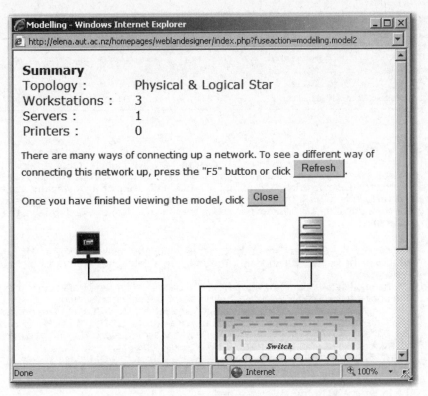

Figure 7: A sample LAN model diagram

Part Four: Scenarios

Click the **Scenarios** link in the *Wired LAN* section. The *Wired LAN Scenarios* page appears (Figure 8). Review the four example scenarios. Create solutions for the two exercise scenarios. Your solutions must include both a written design description and diagrams generated with the *WebLan Modeling* tool.

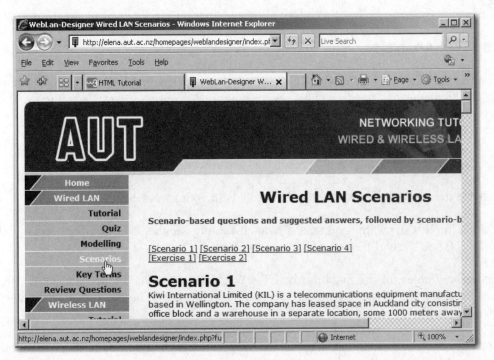

Figure 8: The *Wire LAN Scenarios* page

Exercise 2

KIWI BUSINESS LIMITED (KBL), an International company (with a head office in Auckland), has recently established three regional branches located in Wellington, Christchurch, and Singapore. Based on the following description, **draw up a detailed diagram of the company's networking Infrastructure.** Include the whole internal network (all LANs) with the connecting devices, the Internet connections, and all telecommunication links in your diagram. Clearly label the elements of the diagram.

- The company's eBusiness site (B-to-C) is hosted by the company itself and is physically located in the head office Auckland. The company's databases are physically located in Wellington.
- The head office (Auckland) has one Novell NetWare server, one Web server, eight PCs and one printer networked together in a LAN using STAR physical topology.
- The Singapore branch has one Novell NetWare server, eight PCs and one printer networked together in a LAN using BUS physical topology.
- The Christchurch branch has one Novell NetWare server, eight PCs and one printer networked together in a LAN using RING physical topology.
- The Wellington branch has one Novell NetWare server, one Database server, eight PCs and one printer networked together in a LAN using STAR physical topology.
- The Auckland and Singapore branches use a high-speed digital link (1.54 Mbps) to access the Internet and to contact each other.
- Both the Auckland and Christchurch branches have an ADSL (740 Kbps) for fast Internet access and linking with other branches.
- Each branch has a dedicated router for linking to the outside world over the Internet. The branches and the head office are connected through the Internet.

Figure 9: *Exercise Scenario 2.* Use this information and your design for creating your costs spreadsheet.

Part Five: Cost Analysis

1. After completing the designs for your LANs create a spreadsheet that includes the costs that would be incurred by implementing the design that you created for *Exercise Scenario Two* (Figure 9).

2. Use the following guidelines for designing and completing your spreadsheet.

   a. List each of the items that must be purchased separately.

   b. Indicate the cost per unit and the number of units in your spreadsheet.

   c. Include the cost of cabling and assume that all cabling is either UTP or fiber. Assume that a pre-built UTP patch cable, 10 feet in length costs $50.

   d. Include estimates for the monthly costs for WAN services (the T1 line and DSL connections). Assume that the company has agreed to a two-year contract for both services from either the same or different service providers.

   e. You may assume that all workstations are similar in design and costs to those that you obtained price quotes for in lab 4.

f. Include a cost estimate for all servers, switches, and hubs (if included in your design). Indicate the number of ports per switch or hub since this affects the cost.

g. Include the installation expense. Assume that installation rates are $100 per person hour. Use the following time estimates in your calculations:

    i. 45 minutes to install and configure each switch or hub.

    ii. 30 minutes to install each UTP connection

    iii. 60 minutes to install each fiber optic connection

    iv. 30 minutes to install and configure each workstation

    v. 20 minutes to install and configure each printer

Submitting your Lab Report

Create a new page on your Google site and name it *Lab Eight Report*. Copy your Modeling Exercise solutions to the Lab Eight Report page. Attach your cost estimates spreadsheet to this page.

LAB 9: CONFIGURING A WIRELESS ACCESS POINT

OBJECTIVES

After completing this lab you should be able to do the following:

✓ Describe the basic functionality of a wireless access point

✓ Describe how to determine the default settings for a Cisco wireless access point

✓ Describe how to configure the access point's IP address, hostname, radio settings, and assign an SSID via the Cisco command line interface

✓ Know the Cisco IOS commands for changing configuration modes and how to use the IOS command help feature

CONTENTS

HARDWARE, SOFTWARE, AND COMMUNICATIONS REQUIREMENTS FOR THIS LAB

➤ A Windows-based computer

➤ Access to the Internet

➤ A Cisco Aironet 1240AG Series wireless access point (optional)

USEFUL LINKS

➤ **http://en.wikipedia.org/wiki/Wireless_access_point**

➤ **http://www.cisco.com/en/US/docs/wireless/access_point/12.2_13_JA/configuration/guide/i12
213sc.html**

LAB 9

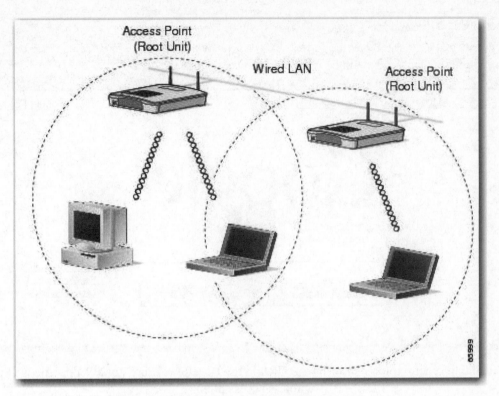

Figure 1: Wireless Access Point topology (source:
http://www.cisco.com/en/US/docs/wireless/access_point/12.2_13_JA/configuration/guide/s13ovrv.ht
ml#wp1034639*)*

Introduction

In this lab you will review different sections of the Cisco Aironet 1240AG Series on-line manual
(available at
http://www.cisco.com/en/US/docs/wireless/access_point/12.2_13_JA/configuration/guide/i12213sc.ht
ml*)* to learn how to configure a Cisco wireless access point (WAP). The topics discussed will include
using Cisco operating system (IOS) commands to configure the access point via a command line interface
(CLI). You will be required to answer questions and list configuration settings as you review different
pages of the manual. Create a word processor document or use paper and a pencil to record your answers
as you read through the manual pages.

Cisco provides both command-line and graphical interfaces for configuring their wireless access points
(WAPs). The graphical interface is much more convenient to use than the command-line interface
because it is menu driven and does not force administrators to learn a set of commands for configuring
purposes. The graphical interface is accessed via a browser. The IP address of the WAP is used instead
of an URL. Brand new Cisco WAPs are configured to obtain an IP address from a DHCP server. Since
the IP address of the access point must be known to connect to it, users must be able to answer one or
both of the following questions:

1) How does one obtain the IP address value assigned to the AP by a DHCP server?

2) How does one change the AP's default setting for obtaining an IP address?

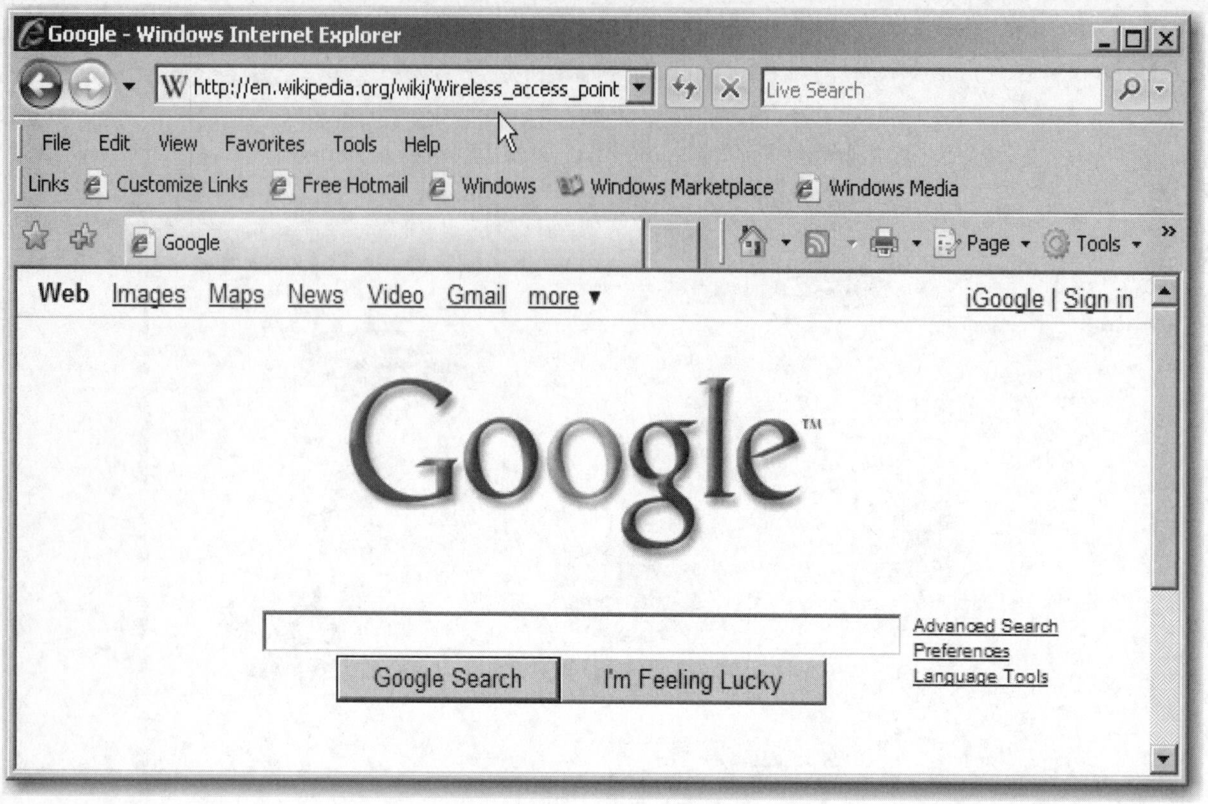

Figure 2: The Internet Explorer showing the URL in the Locator text box for a Wikipedia web page on wireless access points

The answer to both of the above questions is "by issuing IOS commands at the command prompt". Once the IP address of the WAP has been either obtained or set, then the graphical interface can be accessed and used to complete the configuration. Knowledge of at least a minimal set of Cisco IOS commands is essential for configuring a WAP.

Therefore, the discussion in this lab will be limited to commands that are used to set the AP's IP address and enable its radio. Securing the AP will be discussed briefly, but it is recommended that this job be done using the GUI since the command line process is somewhat complex.

Part One: Wireless Access Point Basics

To learn more about the general characteristics of wireless access points open Internet Explorer on your Windows desktop and enter the URL, **http://en.wikipedia.org/wiki/Wireless_access_point**, into IE's Locator text box (Figure 2). Click the **Go to** button or press the **Enter** key to display a Wikipedia page discussing the basics of *Wireless access points*.

After reviewing the characteristics and limitations of WAPs answer the following questions. You may need to consult other sources to answer all of the questions

Questions

1. What are the most common applications of wireless access points?

2. How does an ad-hoc network differ from one that uses wireless access points?

3. What is needed to allow wireless users to "roam" from one location to another?

4. List three factors that limit the range of communications for wireless access points.

5. Why is interference such an issue with 802.11 devices operating in the 2.4 GHz range?

6. Why does EAP provide the highest level of security for a wireless network?

Basic Features of a Cisco Wireless Access Point

Next we will investigate some of basic features of a Cisco WAP. Open a browser on your desktop and enter the URL, **http://www.cisco.com/en/US/docs/wireless/access_point/12.2_13_JA/configuration/guide/s13ovrv.html** in the locator text box in your browser. Click the **Go to** button or press the **Enter** key to display the *Cisco IOS Configuration Guide for the AP* page (Figure 3).

Review the **Features and Management Options** on this page and answer the following questions.

Questions - Features and Management Options

1. List and explain the different modes available with this access point.

2. What three different types of interfaces can be used to manage this access point?

3. What are the three different roles that this access point can play in a wireless network configuration?

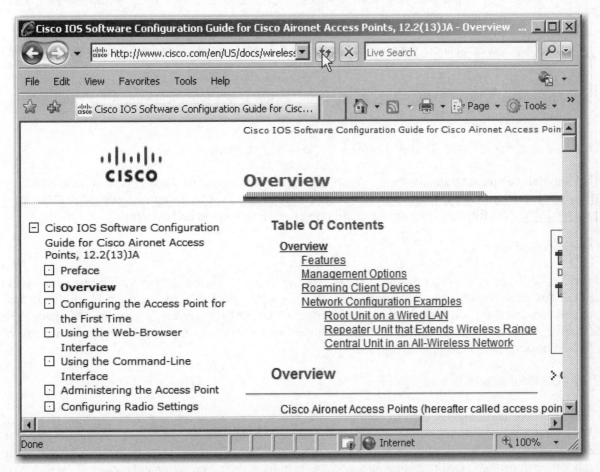

Figure 3: The *Cisco Aironet Access Point Configuration Guide* page

Default Settings for a Cisco Aironet 1240AG Series Access Point

Knowledge about the factory default settings is essential for configuring the access point. Use the following URL,
http://www.cisco.com/en/US/docs/wireless/access_point/12.2_13_JA/configuration/guide/s13frst.html#wp1034814) to determine and record the default setting for each of the following:

1. Login userID

2. Password

3. SSID and guest SSID

LED Display Settings

The Aironet access point has light emitting diodes (LEDs) that display different colors depending upon the state of the access point. Use the following URL,
http://www.cisco.com/en/US/docs/wireless/access_point/12.2_13_JA/configuration/guide/s13trb.html#wpmkr1043622), to determine what condition is indicated when the LED displays a certain color, then answer the following questions:

Questions – LED Display Settings

1. What is indicated about the operating status of the access point when the Radio Indicator LED color is blinking green?

2. What is indicated about the operating status of the access point when the Ethernet Indicator LED color is green?

3. In general what is indicated about the status of the access point when the LED color is either amber or red?

Requirements for a Cisco Aironet 1240AG Series Access Point

Click the **Before you start** link in the *Configuring the Access Point for the First Time* section available at **http://www.cisco.com/en/US/docs/wireless/access_point/12.2_13_JA/configuration/guide/s13frst.html#wp1002608.** List five requirements for configuring the Cisco Aironet access point.

The Cisco IOS

Cisco has developed the IOS to provide a command-line interface for configuring their routers and access points. An administrator who knows how to use the IOS commands can effectively configure and manage these devices. A basic working knowledge of the IOS is essential if you need to change the default settings (as discussed earlier in this lab) of a Cisco wireless access point. A short summary of Cisco commands and access modes follows.

Cisco IOS Command Modes

There are four access modes used to configure a Cisco router. They are *user EXEC mode, privileged EXEC mode, global configuration mode,* and *interface configuration mode.* Each mode provides different levels of access to the device. Passwords are used to provide security for the device. It is important to understand the different modes because they have their own command set.

1. *User EXEC mode* is the initial startup mode. A router configuration session can be initiated using terminal emulation programs such as Kermit, HyperTerminal, or telnet, or puTTY.

2. *Privileged EXEC mode* is the system administrator mode. In this mode configuration files can be read, the router can be rebooted, and operating parameters can be changed.

3. *Global configuration mode* is used to modify system-wide configuration parameters, such as routing tables and routing algorithms.

4. *Interface configuration mode* is used to modify the Ethernet and serial port configurations.

Changing Modes

1. *User Exec mode* is the startup mode. When you connect to the command line interface of the device from a workstation running a terminal emulation program, such as puTTY, or start a telnet session from the workstation, the Cisco device will display an *Exec mode* command prompt. Your workstation must physically be connected to the console port on the device by either a rollover cable or to an Ethernet port by a standard patch cable. Typically a password must be entered to establish the connection. The *user Exec mode* prompt displays the device name followed by a *greater than sign*. For example, *RouterName>*.

2. *Privileged Exec mode* is entered from user Exec mode by typing **enable** at the Exec mode prompt. A password must be supplied to enter Privileged Exec mode. The *privileged Exec mode* prompt displays the device name followed by a pound sign. For example, *RouterName#*.

3. *Global configuration mode* is entered from privileged Exec mode by typing **configure terminal** or **config t**. No password is required. The g*lobal configuration mode* prompt displays the device name, the word *config* in parentheses and a pound sign. For example, *RouterName (config)#*.

4. *Interface configuration mode* is entered from global configuration mode by typing **interface** *InterfaceName*, where the *InterfaceName* is the name of the interface you want to configure. Examples of interface names are *F0/0 and F0/1* (Fast Ethernet) and *S0/0 and S0/1* (Serial). The *interface configuration mode* prompt displays the device name, the word *config-if* in parentheses and a pound sign. For example, *RouterName(config-if)#*.

Exit Modes

1. To exit *interface configuration mode* type **exit**. This will return the system to *global configuration mode*.

2. To exit *global configuration mode* type **exit**. This will return the system to *privileged Exec mode*.

3. To exit *global configuration mode* type **disable**. This will return the system to *user Exec mode*.

4. To exit *user Exec mode* type **logout**. This will end the session.

Exit Mode Alternatives

1. To return to *privileged Exec mode* directly from any configuration mode type **end**.

2. Typing **logout** or **exit** from *privileged Exec mode* will also end the session.

Getting Help

Typing a question mark (?) at any prompt will display a list of commands that apply to that mode. It is helpful to remember the following points:

- *User EXEC mode* is the initial startup mode.
- In *Privileged EXEC mode* configuration files can be read, the router can be restarted, and operating parameters can be changed.
- *Global configuration mode* allows modification of routing tables and routing algorithms.
- *Interface configuration mode* allows modification of logical router interfaces.

Selected Commands – Privileged Exec Mode

- *show running-config* – displays current router configuration for the router
- *show startup-config* – displays the startup configuration for the router
- *reload* – restarts the router. Discards running configuration and reloads startup configuration.
- *copy running-config starting-config* – saves the current configuration to NVRAM. The new configuration takes effect after the router is rebooted.
- *show interfaces* – displays information about the configuration of network interfaces

Selected Commands – Global Configuration

- *hostname* – resets the logical device name

Selected Commands – Interface Configuration Mode

- *no shutdown* – enables a network interface
- *shutdown* – disables a network interface
- *ip address IPaddress netmask* – Sets the IP address and subnet mask for an interface

Questions – Cisco IOS

1. Which computer programs may be used to allow an administrator to enter user Exec mode?

2. Which mode is used for configuring an access point?

3. Which mode must be entered before global configuration mode?

4. Which password must be known to enter privileged exec mode?

5. Which command is used to show the settings for an Ethernet interface?

Accessing the Cisco Command Line Interface

Accessing the Cisco Command Line Interface (CLI) requires a physical connection from a workstation to the AP. Review the **Connecting to the 1200 Series Access Point Locally** link on the *Configuring the Access Point for the First Time* page (available at

http://www.cisco.com/en/US/docs/wireless/access_point/12.2_13_JA/configuration/guide/s13frst.htm l#wp1002608) to determine how to connect to the WAP and access the command line interface.

Exercises

1. List the two general steps required to allow communication to a wireless access point.

2. List the IOS commands required for configuring a static IP Address to an access point interface.

3. List the IOS commands required for setting an access point hostname. Assume you are starting in Privileged Exec mode.

4. The access point radios on the 1242 APs are *disabled* by default. Beginning in Privileged Exec mode, list the steps to *enable* the access point radio.

5. Review the **Configuring Authentication Types** section on-line in the manual available at **http://www.cisco.com/en/US/docs/wireless/access_point/12.2_13_JA/configuration/guide/s13aut h.html#wpxref31911**. Provide descriptions for the following:

    a. Static WEP key

    b. EAP authentication – RADIUS server (hostname or IP address required)

    c. WPA

Part Two: Configuring a Cisco Aironet 1240AG Series Access Point (Optional)

In this part of the lab you will work with your classmates in a team to configure an actual Cisco Aironet AP. Use the information you collected in Part One to configure the IP address and enable the WAP radio on the Cisco 1200 Series wireless access point. All of the equipment and materials needed for this part of the lab will be available during your regularly scheduled classroom lab session. The WAPs will be set to their default values before you begin configuring them.

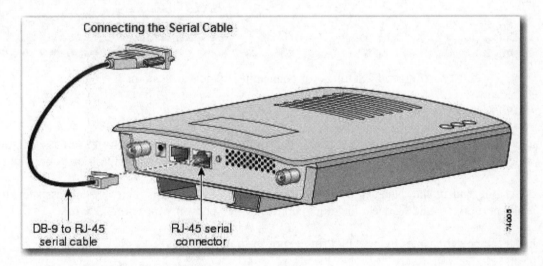

Figure 4: Physical interfaces on a Cisco Wireless Access Point (Source:
http://www.cisco.com/en/US/docs/wireless/access_point/12.2_13_JA/configuration/guide/s13frst.htm l#wp1034762)

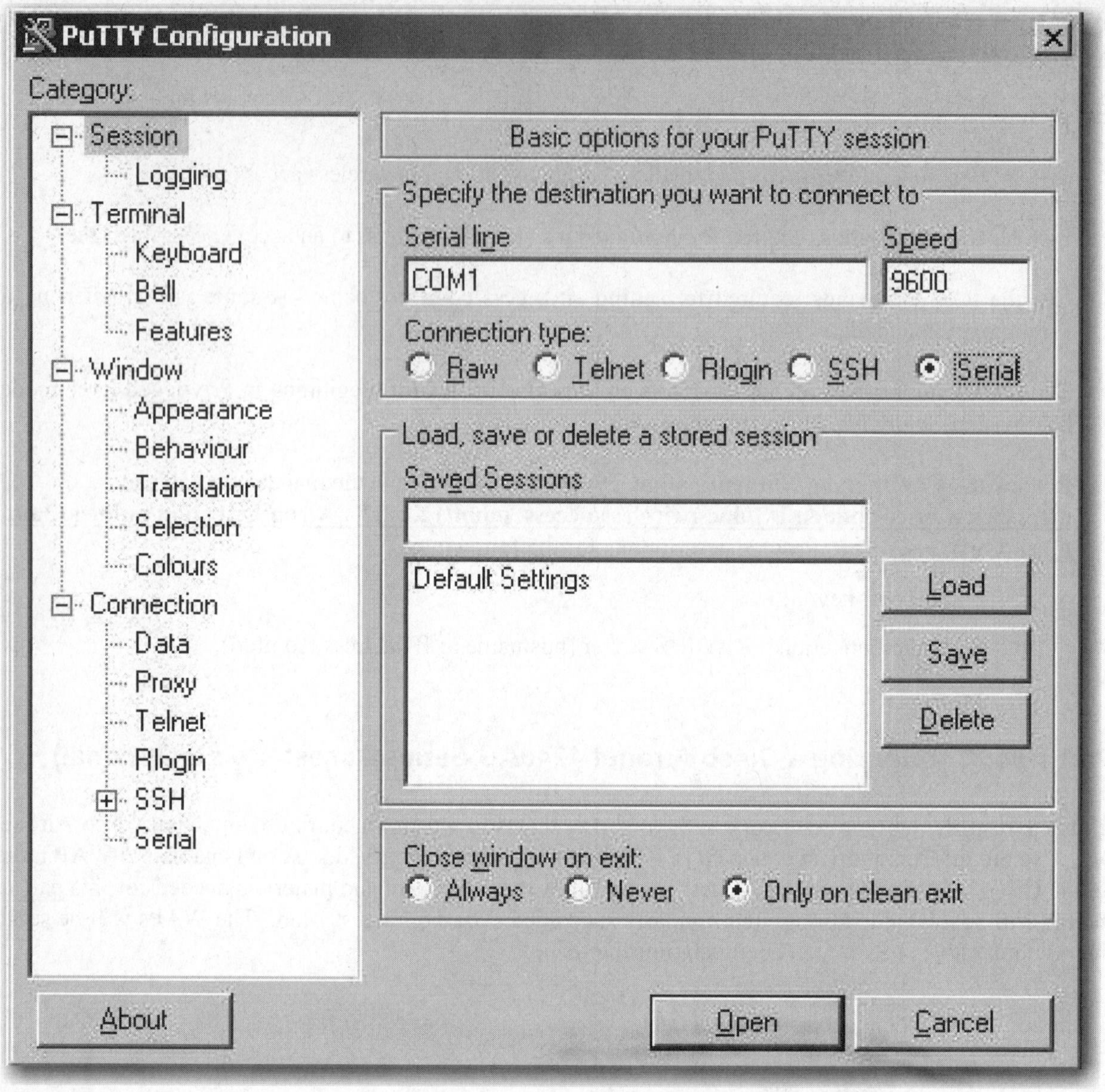

Figure 5: Settings for connecting to the access point

Configuration Procedures

1. Connect one end of the blue rollover (serial) cable provided by your instructor or lab assistant to the console port on the WAP. Connect the other end of the cable to serial port COM1 on your computer.

2. Connect one end of the category 5 UTP cable provided by your instructor or lab assistant to the Ethernet port on the AP. Connect the other end to a switch port on your wired network.

3. Connect the power adapter to the AP. Provide power to the adapter.

4. Double-click the **putty.exe** icon on your Windows Desktop to display the puTTY Configuration dialog box (Figure 5). Change the *Connection type* to serial. Click the **Open** button.

5. A command window appears (Figure 6) displaying "ap #" prompt. If no prompt appears, press the **Enter** key.

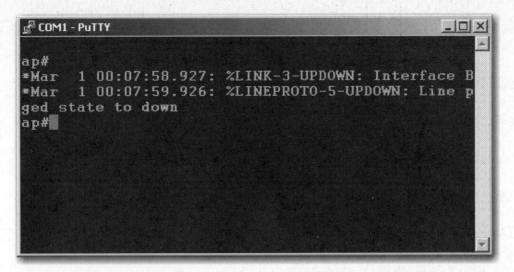

Figure 6: Command-line interface window and startup prompt

6. Type **enable** at the command prompt and press the **Enter** key. Type the **password** provided by your instructor and press **Enter**.

7. Type **show interfaces** and press the **Enter** key. A listing of the current settings for the interfaces on the WAP is displayed one screen at a time (Figure 7). Press the **space bar** to see the next screen. Record the default value for the **IP address**. Also record the default values for the **radio interfaces**.

8. Change the IP address to 10.10.0.2 with subnet mask 255.0.0.0 using the commands you learned in Part One of this lab.

9. Enable the radio interfaces using the commands you learned in Part One of this lab. **Note:** To fully configure the WAP the antenna must be connected and an authentication type needs to be configured to secure it.

Submitting your Lab Report

Create a new page on your Google site. Name it *Lab Nine Report*. Copy the questions headings, questions, and their answers to the Lab Nine Report page.

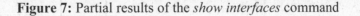

Figure 7: Partial results of the *show interfaces* command

LAB 10: THE LINUX COMMAND LINE INTERFACE

OBJECTIVES

After completing this lab you should be able to do the following:

- ✓ Access a remote Linux computer using terminal emulation software

- ✓ Open a terminal window

- ✓ Understand how to use basic file management commands in Linux

- ✓ Modify file permissions

- ✓ Use the grep command to extract data from a text file

CONTENTS

HARDWARE, SOFTWARE, AND COMMUNICATIONS REQUIREMENTS FOR THIS LAB

- ➢ A Windows or Linux-based computer or remote access to a Linux computer

- ➢ The bootable version of the Knoppix operating system on a CD-ROM

- ➢ Access to the Internet

USEFUL LINKS

- ➢ http://www.knopper.net/knoppix-mirrors/index-en.html

- ➢ http://linux.softpedia.com/get/System/Operating-Systems/Linux-Distributions/KNOPPIX-Live-DVD-2621.shtml

LAB 10

Introduction

This lab provides an introduction to the Linux command line interface and some of the more common file management commands available in Linux. You will learn how to create files and directories, copy and delete files, navigate the Linux directory hierarchy, and search for specific information contained in a file.

You will need to have access to a Linux operating system to complete this lab. Numerous options are available. The first and perhaps simplest option is to use a computer that already has a version of Linux installed on it. If this option is available to you, skip the remainder of this section and begin working on the section entitled *Opening a Terminal Window*.

A second option is to run Linux from a bootable CD or DVD. A bootable CD contains all the files required to run Linux on any Windows computer. The operating system runs from the CD. No actual Linux files are installed on your computer and your Windows operating system will not be affected in any way. When you end your session, simply remove the CD from its drive and reboot your computer to again work with Windows.

A third option is to use terminal emulation software, such as puTTY, to connect to a remote Linux computer that is connected to your organization's network. Appendix B describes how to download and use puTTY. If you have chosen this option skip the next section and begin working on the section entitled *Opening a Terminal Window*.

Lastly, if you plan to access your organization's network from off-campus and your network administrator has configured a *Virtual Private Network (VPN)* for this purpose, then you can still connect to the remote Linux computer, but must first run VPN client software before starting puTTY. Appendix A describes how to install and configure the Cisco VPN client software on your computer. If you have chosen this option skip the next section and begin working on the section entitled *Opening a Terminal Window*.

Running Knoppix

A bootable version of Linux is readily available from the Knoppix site on the World Wide Web. Consult Appendix C to learn more about obtaining a copy of a bootable Knoppix CD. To transform your computer into a Linux computer, simply insert the Knoppix CD into the CD player and restart the computer. If you have problems loading Knoppix from the CD, consult Appendix D.

Startup Screens

The Knoppix *Boot* window is the first screen to appear as files are loaded from the CD-ROM into computer memory. This window displays the Knoppix version number across the top of the screen and a message indicating that you must press the Enter key to start Linux from the CD. The message also indicates that you can terminate your session by removing the CD from its drive and restarting your computer to resume running the operating system installed on it.

Towards the bottom of the screen is another block message comprised of three lines of text. The first line indicates that you can press the F2 or F3 keys for help and boot options. The next displays the Linux Live CD version number, the URL to the Knoppix home page, and the product release date. A *boot* prompt is shown as the last line on this screen. Any special parameters that are required for loading Linux onto your system will appear after this prompt as you type them at the keyboard. An example of a boot parameter is "knoppix nodma". This boot parameter is required to suppress the error message "cannot find file system on CD". You will not know in advance which parameters are needed to make Linux run from the CD on your particular computer. Some trial and error may be required to determine the correct parameters. It is best to simply press the Enter key when initially loading Linux from the Knoppix Live CD and then record any error messages that are displayed. With the aid of the error message and a little searching on the web you should be able to find the appropriate parameter or parameters that are required to boot Knoppix from the CD. You may also consult Appendix D for more information regarding some of the more common error messages that are displayed and the boot parameters that are required to suppress these errors.

After you have determined which, if any parameters are required to get Knoppix to boot from the CD and have pressed the **Enter** key. a screen containing the familiar Linux penguin logo and a "Welcome to the KNOPPIX live GNU/Linux on CD!" message appears if the upper portion of your computer display screen. This graphic is followed by a line-by-line display of configuration messages that appear on the screen as information is loaded from the CD into memory on your computer. These messages will indicate which features are being installed and if the feature was successfully installed or not. For example, the network interface card on your computer will be configured with an IP address during this part of the installation process. If an IP address can be located and assigned to your computer's NIC, then a message indicating that this task was accomplished will be displayed. The configuration process will take a few minutes depending upon the amount of memory installed on your computer and the speed of your CPU.

When all devices have been configured this screen disappears and a dialog box displaying the progress of peripheral initialization appears. This dialog box displays the Knoppix version number towards the top of the window and a row of seven icons towards the bottom. The icons include a disk drive, wrench, a globe, a desk lamp, a monitor, a file folder, and the KDE logo, and represent different peripheral devices that require installation of device drivers to make them function correctly. Don't worry, none of these drivers will be installed on your computer's hard disk drive. Instead they are being installed on a "RAM disk" in computer memory that can emulate your computer's hard disk drive. This dialog box will disappear automatically after all peripheral devices have been initialized.

Preliminary Messages

You may see one or more preliminary dialog boxes during the boot process and that overlay the KDE desktop. One such dialog box is a language selection dialog box. Knoppix is available in German, Danish, Dutch, English, Spanish, French, Italian, Japanese, and Russian. The two-character country code abbreviations are shown on the language selection screen. Select your language choice from the available options by clicking on the appropriate country code. For example, you would click the *EN* abbreviation to run the English language version of Knoppix. After you have selected a language choice, the dialog box containing the language codes disappears.

The *What is Knoppix* dialog box appears after the language selection dialog box disappears. This page is a short presentation written by Klaus Knopper that describes the Live Knoppix CD and its features. Review the information in this dialog box to learn more about Knoppix and the features it supports. When you have finished reading this material, click the **Close** button on the right-hand end of the dialog box's title bar to close the dialog box.

Once these dialog boxes have been closed the KDE desktop will be fully visible. **Note**: Depending upon the resolution of your monitor you may need to scroll the screen to see the KDE task bar and desktop icons. If scroll bars are not displayed, moving the display is accomplished by positioning the mouse pointer on the appropriate window boundary and moving the mouse pointer in the direction you want to scroll the window.

A *terminal window* provides an interface for issuing Linux commands. Commands are issued at a command-line prompt displayed in the terminal window. You can open a terminal window from the KDE menu system or from the shortcut menu that is displayed when you right-click anywhere on the KDE desktop. The most convenient way to open a terminal window is to simply click the **Terminal** icon on the KDE task bar. A terminal window looks at lot like the command window you use when issuing commands like ping, tracert, ipconfig, etc., in MS Windows (Figure 1).

Figure 1: A command window and prompt

UNIX Overview

UNIX was developed in 1969 by Dennis Ritchie and Kevin Thompson at Bell Laboratories. UNIX was designed to be easily portable to different hardware platforms. One factor that contributes to the portability of UNIX is that most of the UNIX operating system is written in the high-level programming language C, which was specifically developed for the purpose of implementing UNIX. A UNIX operating system consists of a kernel and a set of common utility programs. The kernel is the core of the operating system. It manages the computer hardware, provides essential facilities, such as the control of program execution, memory management, a file system, and mechanisms for exchanging data with attached devices, programs, or over a network. The utility programs provide user-level commands, such as those needed to create and edit files.

Since its inception, many different versions of UNIX operating systems have emerged. Most computer companies have developed their own version of UNIX. Examples include AIX (IBM), HP-UX (Hewlett Packard), SunOS and Solaris (Sun Microsystems), Ultrix (DEC), and Xenix (Microsoft Systems). By the early 1990s, when PCs had become powerful enough to run UNIX-like operating systems, UNIX versions for PCs, such as FreeBSD, NetBSD, OpenBSD, and Linux began to emerge. The BSD systems are based upon the very significant version of UNIX developed at the University of California at Berkeley. Linux was created by Finnish computer science student Linus Torvalds and has become quite popular in a very short period of time.

The source code for most of UNIX versions for PCs is distributed freely. The Linux operating system, which is sometimes packaged with proprietary software, is distributed by different vendors. Popular Linux distributions include Red Hat (Fedora), Caldera, and Suse Linux.

For the most part, the different distributions of Linux are quite similar. There are some obvious differences in the ways in which the graphical user interfaces are implemented and some of the tools available for configuring system settings. Although these differences exist among the different versions of Linux, the file system characteristics and commands described in this lab apply to essentially all UNIX systems.

The Linux File System

Like other modern operating systems, Linux organizes files in a hierarchical tree of directories. Figure 2 provides an example of the directory hierarchy in Linux. The directory at the top of the tree is called the *root directory*. The directories shown directly beneath the root are typically a part of the hierarchy on all Linux file systems. User directories typically have names that identify actual users.

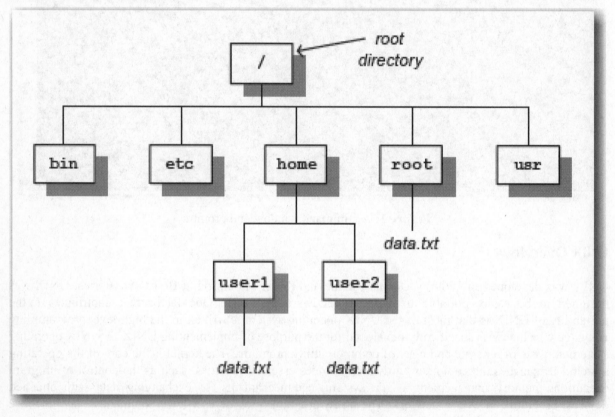

Figure 2: The Linux directory hierarchy

Each file and directory in a Linux file system can be uniquely identified by a *pathname*. Pathnames can be absolute or relative. Absolute pathnames start at the root directory. The absolute pathname for the root directory is a slash (/) character. In the file hierarchy in Figure 2, the absolute pathname of directory *home* in the root directory is */home*. That of the directory *user1* is */home/user1*, and the absolute pathname of file *data.txt* under */home/user1* is */home/user1/data.txt*.

Pathnames that do not begin with a slash are relative pathnames and are interpreted relative to a *current (working) directory*. For example, if the current directory is */home*, then *user1/data.txt* is equivalent to the absolute pathname */home/user1/data.txt*.

When using relative pathnames, a single dot (.) denotes the current directory and two dots (..) denote the *parent directory*, which is the directory immediately above the current directory in the hierarchy. For example, if the current directory is */home/user1*, the relative pathname **..** refers to directory */home,* while the relative pathname **.** refers to *user1* directory (Figure 9).

Linux file systems contain a *home directory*. For regular user accounts (accounts other than root) the home directories are located under */home*. Thus */home/user1* is the home directory for the *user1* account. The home directory of the root account is */root*. The currently logged-in user's home directory is used as the *current directory prompt* whenever a new terminal window is opened. If you log in as the *root* user, then the current directory prompt displayed in a new terminal window is */root*.

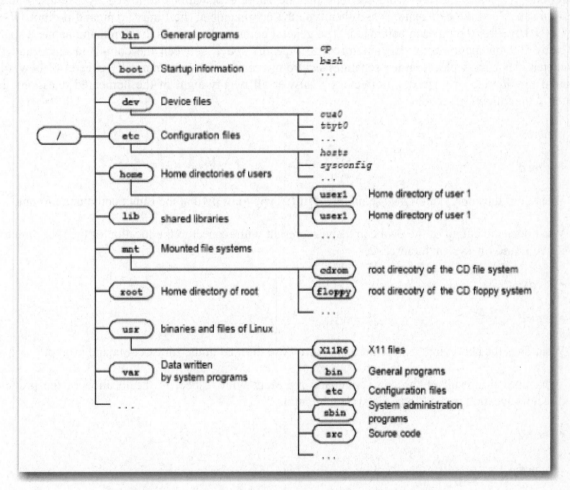

Figure 3: The Linux directory hierarchy in greater detail

A more complete list of the top level directories in a Linux file system is shown in Figure 3. Most of these directories and files can only be modified by the root user. Linux configuration files are located in directories /etc, /usr/etc, /var and their subdirectories. Whenever you modify the configuration of a Linux system, you are working on the files in these directories.

Each file and each directory has an owner. Regular users own there home directory (/home/user1 for example) and all files that they create. *Root* is the owner of all other files on the system.

Linux Command Structure

The commands used in Linux have the following general syntax: *commandname option*(s) *argument*(s), although the options and arguments may be omitted. For example, in the *command* **ls –l data.txt**, **ls** is the command, **l** is an *option*, and **data.txt** is the *argument*. Options are generally preceded by a – (dash). Multiple options can be specified for a single command.

On-line help for commands is provided by the Linux *man pages*. These pages offer detailed information on a command, are quite technical and assume that you are familiar with the command and need only to lookup certain details. Desktop environments, such as *Gnome* and *KDE*, may provide additional documentation. Type the keyword, **man,** followed by the name of a command, to display the on-line documentation provided by the manual pages. For example, typing **man** *ls* displays the manual pages for the command **ls**.

Directions: This and the following sections include short explanations followed by exercises and a question set. Read the explanations and then type the commands at the Linux command prompt. Press the **Enter** key after typing each command. The general command syntax is the command name, a space, and zero or more parameters. Do not forget to type the *space* between the command name and the parameters. For example, a **space** separates *cd* from **..** in the **cd ..** command. Create all new files required for this lab in your *home* directory. Answer all twenty-eight of the numbered questions that appear in the following sections.

Begin here:

- *pwd*

1. What does the abbreviation *pwd* stand for? **Hint:** Type **man pwd** at the Linux command prompt.

2. What does the output of the pwd command represent with respect to the location of the root directory in the Linux file system hierarchy?

- *cd ..*

- *pwd*

3. What does the abbreviation *cd* stand for? **Hint:** Type **man cd** at the Linux command prompt.

4. What does the result of the cd .. command represent with respect to the location of the previous directory location in the Linux file system hierarchy?

- *cd /*

- *pwd*

5. Which directory in the Linux file system does the **cd /** command take you to?

- *cd*

- *pwd*

6. Which directory in the Linux file system does the **cd** command take you to?

Creating Files

- *touch file1*

- *touch file2*

- *touch file3*

- *touch Ab.txt*

- *touch A1.txt*

- *touch Ab*

- *touch A1*

- *touch Albert.txt*

- *touch Annette.txt*

7. Is it obvious what the touch command is designed to do?

8. Type **man touch** and press the **Enter** key. What does the MAN page for touch say about the purpose of this command?

File Access Permissions

In Linux, each file has a set of access permissions. The permissions are *read ("r"), write ("w"),* and *execute ("x"),* and give, respectively, permission to read the contents of a file, modify the file, or execute the file as a program. Permissions are set by the owner of a file. Linux specifies access permissions for three different groups: the *owner* of the file, a user *group* which is associated with the file, and the set of *all* users. The owner of a file has exclusive rights to the file, and can modify the permissions so that others can access the file. For example, the owner of a file can set the permissions so that all users can read the file, but not modify it. There is one exceptional account that you need to know about. The *root* account or administrative user account often, called the *super user* account, overrides all end-user access permissions and can even change the ownership of files.

- *ls -l file1*

9. What are the permissions assigned to users and groups for file1?

- *chmod 777 file1*

- *ls –l file1*

10. What are the new *file1* permissions for users and groups?

11. Are these permissions reasonable for file1? Answer the question in terms of who can modify these files and what you currently do or do not know about file1.

Shells

A *shell* is a program that interprets and executes Linux commands. Whenever you create a new terminal window, a shell is started. The shell displays a prompt to indicate where to type commands. The prompt provides useful information to the user. For example, the prompt **root@PC1 root#** displays the *username*, the *computer name*, and the *current directory*. The *username* is separated from the *computer name* by an @ symbol.

When you type a command at the prompt, and press the enter key, the shell interprets the command, and if it is valid, the command is executed. A shell can be closed by typing **exit** at the command prompt. If the shell is running in a window, the window also closes.

Linux offers a variety of shell programs with names such as *sh, csh, ksh, tcsh*, or *bash*. Different shells provide different features for different purposes. To learn more about these features, double-click the **Internet Explorer** icon on your Windows Desktop and enter the URL, **http://telecomm.boisestate.edu/Linux/ShellDetails.htm**, into IE's *Locator* text box. Click IE's **Go to** button to open a web page that discusses the features of the different shells. The *bash shell* is one of the more popular shells and is the one used in these exercises.

- *csh*

- *bash*

12. Which shell should be activated after typing *csh*?

13. Which shell should be activated after typing *bash*?

14. What changes, if any, occurred to the command prompt after typing *csh*?

15. If you did not notice any change, can you speculate why the command prompt remained the same?

Directory Commands

You will need to become familiar with navigating the directory tree so that you can locate the files you want to modify. Descriptions of some of the more frequently used directory commands are provided below:

pwd prints the current directory.

cd *dirpath* changes the current directory to the relative or absolute pathname of the directory *dirpath*. If no directory name is provided, the command changes the current directory to the user's home directory.

mkdir *dirname* creates a new directory in the current directory with name *dirname*.

rmdir *dirname* deletes the directory *dirname* from the current directory. A directory must be empty before it can be deleted; otherwise an error message is displayed.

- *cd /usr/bin*

- *mkdir xyz*

16. Why is it not possible for you to create the xyz directory in the /usr/bin directory?

- *cd*

- *mkdir xyz*

- *mkdir files*

- *ls –l*

17. Which character in the listing displayed after typing ls -l indicates that xyz is a *directory*?

- *cd files*

- *mkdir subfiles*

- *cd subfiles*

- *touch file1*

- *cd ..*

- *rmdir subfiles*

18. Why was it not possible to delete the subfiles directory?

Listing Files

ls *dirname* lists information about files and directories. If a directory name is typed, then the command lists the files in that directory. The **ls** command has several options. The most descriptive is **ls –l**, which includes extensive information on each file, including, the access permissions, owner, file size, and the time when the file was last modified.

- *ls*

- *ls –l*

- *ls /*

19. How does the output of the ls command differ from that of the ls –l command?

20. A file listing for which directory is displayed after typing ls / ?

Wildcards

The wildcard character * matches any sequence of zero or more characters, and the ? is used to match any single character. Wildcard characters are useful for describing multiple files with similar characters in their names in a concise manner.

- *cd*

- *ls A*.txt*

- *ls A?*

21. Which files in your home directory are listed after typing ls A*.txt?

22. What do these files have in common?

Moving Files

mv *fname newfile,* **mv** *fname dirname* renames or moves a file. The file or directory *fname* is renamed as *newfile*. If the destination file (*newfile*) exists, then the content of the file is overwritten, and the old content of *newfile* is lost. If the first argument is a file name and the second argument is a directory name (*dirname*), the file is moved to the specified directory.

- *cd*

- *touch data.txt*

- *mv data.txt text.txt*

- *ls –l data.txt*

- *mv * */root* (**Note**: spacing in critical for this command. There is a space after the m and also after the asterisk)

23. Explain the error messages that are displayed after typing the *ls* and *mv* commands.

24. Which account could perform the *mv* command without getting the error message (**Hint**: Which account can override all user permissions)?

Copying Files

cp *fname newfile,* **cp** *fname dirname* copies the content of file *fname* to *newfile*. If a file with name *newfile* exists the content of that file is overwritten. If the second argument is a directory, then a copy of *fname* is created in directory *dirname*.

- *mkdir tmp*

- **cp *.txt tmp**

- *cd tmp*

- *ls -l*

25. Procedurally, how does copying a file differ from moving a file?

Deleting Files

rm *fname* removes a file. Once removed, the file cannot be recovered. **Note:** No warning is issued when a file is overwritten or when a file is removed. When you use the option –i, you are asked for confirmation before deleting the file. It is strongly recommend that you use the –i option for copying, moving, and removing files (**cp –i** instead of **cp**, **mv – i** instead of **mv**, and **rm –i** instead of **rm)**. Many shells are configured to always use the **-i** option. It is important to remember that an *undo* shell command that reverses the effects of a previously issued command is not supported.

- *touch newFile*

- *rm –i newFile*

- *y*

- *ls –l newFile*

- *touch oldfile*

- *rm oldfile*

- *ls –l oldfile*

26. What additional feature does the rm –i command offer over the rm command ?

Viewing Files

more *fname* displays the contents of file *fname*, one page at a time. The display can be scrolled with the '↑' and '↓' keys, and the 'Page Up' and 'Page Down' keys. Keyboard controls are the space bar or *'f'* for the next page (forward), *'b'* for the previous page (back), and *'q'* to close the display (quit).

cat *fname* is similar to the *more* command, but the contents of the file is displayed without stopping at the end of each page.

- *cd /etc*

- *cat auto.net*

- *more auto.net*

- *cd*

File Redirection

cmd > fname — The output of the command *cmd* is written to file *fname*. The file is created if it doesn't already exist, and the contents are overwritten if the file already exists.

cmd >> fname — The >> operator appends the output of command *cmd* to the end of existing file *fname*.

- *touch mlist*

- *echo "This is the first line of the file" > mlist*

- *cat mlist*

- *clear*

- *ls > mlist*

- *more mlist*

- *echo "This is the last line of the file" >> mlist*

- *more mlist*

27. What output is produced for the command *cat mlist* ?

Grep

Grep is a utility program that facilitates searching for information embedded in a data file. Grep filters data in the file by performing a key word search. The output of a grep command is a new file composed of each line of the original file that contains the key word. Grep has a very simple syntax that can be learned quickly. An excellent tutorial on Grep is available at **http://www.panix.com/~elflord/unix/grep.html**.

For example, the command *grep "ACK" ftpSummaryLarge.rtf* displays only those lines in the *ftpSummaryLarge.rtf* file that contain the key word *ACK*. Grep can also be used to determine how many lines in a given file contain a specific keyword. For example, one may wish to know the number of packets exchanged during a data transfer between two computers that meets a specific condition, such as the number of packets that contain application data. Issuing a command such as *grep –c "Data" tftpSummaryLarge.rtf,* would instantly reduce a potentially large file into a single value that represents the number of data packets transferred.

28. Assume the previous paragraph is stored in a file called *textfile3.rtf*. What would be the output for the following grep command? *grep –c "Data" textfile3.rtf*

Terminating a Remote Session

Read this section only if you are accessing the Linux server via telnet or a terminal emulation program like puTTY.

After completing a remote session with a Linux server you must terminate your connection to the server. When using telnet, the *quit* command is typically used to disconnect from the server. If you are using other terminal emulation software, the termination command may be different or depend upon settings of the software. Putty.exe allows you to click the **Close** button on the terminal window to end a session. Putty.exe may also be configured so that you can type **exit** at the command prompt to close the session.

Terminating a Knoppix session

Select the *Logout* option from the *KDE Start Menu*. Click the appropriate **choice** to end your Knoppix session.

Submitting your Lab Report

Create a new page on your Google site. Name the page *Lab Ten Report*. Copy questions 1 through 28 and their answers the Lab Ten Report page.

LAB 11: THE LINUX DESKTOP

OBJECTIVES

After completing this lab you should be able to do the following:

- ✓ Access the Linux desktop on a remote Linux computer using terminal emulation software

- ✓ Use graphical tools to create files and folders

- ✓ Use graphical tools to modify file permissions

- ✓ Browse the Internet from the Linux desktop

- ✓ Terminate a remote desktop session

CONTENTS

HARDWARE, SOFTWARE, AND COMMUNICATIONS REQUIREMENTS FOR THIS LAB

- ➢ A Windows-based computer

- ➢ Remote access to a Linux computer preferably running Suse Linux

- ➢ The TightVNC viewer

- ➢ The bootable version of the Knoppix operating system software on a CD-ROM (optional)

- ➢ Access to the Internet

USEFUL LINKS

- ➢ **http://www.tightvnc.com/**

LAB 11

Introduction

The two most common desktop environments used on Linux computers are *KDE* and *Gnome*. These desktops are similar enough that the skills you develop while working with one of the desktops will provide you with a good background for developing skills on the other desktop.

This lab will provide you with an opportunity to learn more about the *KDE Desktop* available with most Linux distributions. This desktop environment is somewhat similar to Windows, but has some differences worth noting, the most significant being the organization of the *Start* menu. Using the KDE desktop environment simplifies common file management activities that are regularly performed by most users and administrators. Creating new files and folders, copying and pasting files from one folder to another, and saving and retrieving existing files from the file system are just a few of examples of the file management activities that will be covered in this lab.

You will need to have access to a Linux computer to complete this lab. Numerous options are available. The first and perhaps simplest option is to use a computer that already has a version of Linux installed on it. If this option is available to you, skip the remainder of this section and begin working on the section entitled *Accessing the Linux KDE Desktop*.

A second option is to run Linux from a bootable CD. A bootable CD contains all the files required to run Linux on any Windows computer. The operating system runs from the CD. No actual Linux files are installed on your computer and your Windows operating system will not be affected in any way. When you end your session, simply remove the CD from its drive and reboot your computer to again work with Windows. A bootable version of Linux is readily available from the Knoppix site on the World Wide Web. Consult Appendix C to learn more about obtaining a copy of a bootable Knoppix CD.

A third option is to use a viewer, such as *TightVNC*, to access the desktop of a remote Linux computer that is connected to your organization's network. TightVNC provides a view of the desktop that is identical to what you would see if you were working locally on the Linux computer. Consult Part Two of Appendix F for instructions regarding the installation and configuration of the Tight VNC viewer software.

Lastly, if you plan to access your organization's network from off-campus and your network administrator has configured a *Virtual Private Network (VPN) for this purpose*, then you can still connect to the remote Linux computer, but must first run VPN client software before starting the viewer. Appendix A describes how to install and configure the Cisco VPN client software on your computer.

The procedures required for accessing the KDE desktop are outlined below.

Accessing the Linux KDE Desktop

1. Begin by logging into a Windows lab computer. Click the **Start** button on the Windows Task Bar to display the *Start Menu*. Click the **All Programs** option in the Start menu (Figure 1) to display a menu that displays a TightVNC choice.

Figure 1: The Windows *Start* menu with the All Programs option selected

2. A *TightVNC* choice will be displayed in the menu. Locate and click the **TightVNC** choice to display a sub-menu that contains additional *TightVNC* options (Figure 2). Click the **TightVNC Viewer** option to launch the application.

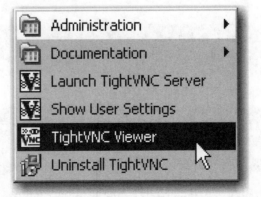

Figure 2: The TightVNC sub-menu options

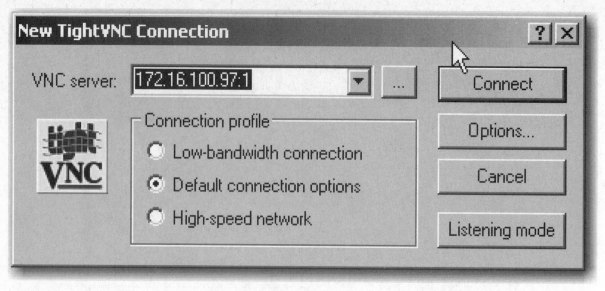

Figure 3: The *New TightVNC Connection* dialog box

3. The *New TightVNC Connection* dialog box appears. Type the **IP address** of the Linux server (provided by your instructor) in the *VNC server* textbox (Figure 3). Click the **Connect** button to access the Linux computer. The *KDE authentication* window appears after a short delay (Figure 4).

4. Enter your **user name** and **password** in the respective textboxes. Press the **Enter** key or click the ***bent arrow*** icon to the right of the *Password* textbox to authenticate to the Linux computer. If you have entered this information incorrectly, the message "Login failed" will appear briefly in the window. The textboxes will be reset and you will need to re-enter your username and password. When you have correctly entered this information the KDE desktop appears (Figure 5). For this lab we will be investigating the *Suse* Linux version of the KDE desktop.

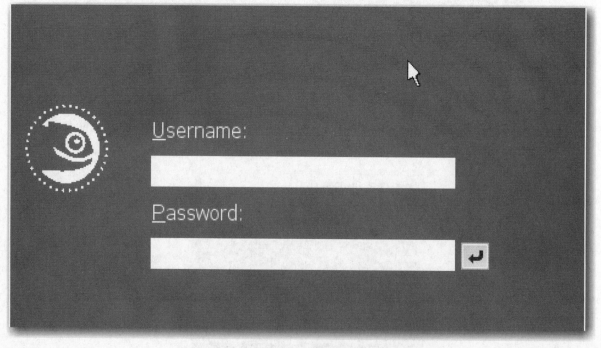

Figure 4: The KDE authentication window

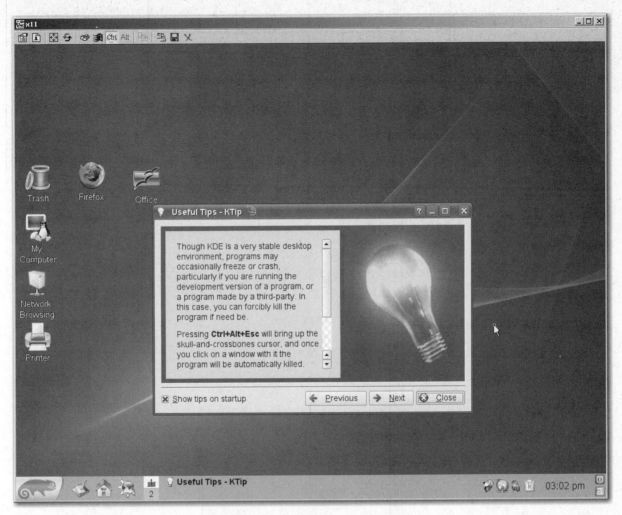

Figure 5: The Suse KDE desktop

The KDE Desktop

The KDE Desktop includes the desktop icons, the taskbar, and menu system. You may need to scroll the window to see all of the components of the KDE desktop. Scroll bars will be displayed on the right and bottom borders of the window if the window is too small to display its entire contents. A *Useful Tips* dialog box appears initially. Numerous useful tips are displayed by clicking the **Previous** and **Next** buttons. Click the **Close** button in the dialog box's title bar to close the dialog box and obtain an unobstructed view of the KDE desk top.

The desktop icons provide shortcuts for connecting to the Internet using the *Firefox* browser, running applications from the *OpenOffice* suite, accessing your printers, and for browsing the network.

The KDE taskbar appears across the bottom of the desktop. The taskbar contains the *Start Button* (on the left end of the taskbar), a shortcut to your *Home* directory, the *Konqueror* browser icon, a search tool, some status indicators, and the current time.

The **Start Button** displays a menu system when clicked. This menu is quite extensive and provides access to utility programs that can be used for configuring your desktop, as well as change system settings. On the Suse KDE desktop the menu system is tabbed to separate and organize the available options. There are five tabbed pages in the menu – *Favorites, History, Computer, Applications*, and *Leave*.

Figure 6: The Suse *KDE desk top* with the *Favorites* menu selected

The *Favorites* tab (Figure 6) allows access to your desktop settings, a terminal window for running directory and configuration commands, your home directory for managing your files, and a word processor, as well as other options.

The *History* tab provides convenient access to the documents you have worked on most recently by providing a list of those documents.

The *Computer* tab (Figure 7) provides access to *YaST*, a system configuration utility available in the Suse distribution of Linux. This utility allows an administrator to make changes to the files used for maintaining and configuring the Suse Linux operating system. As an example, network settings, such as IP address settings can be configured using YaST. When you click on the **YaST** icon you will see the *Run as root* dialog box (Figure 8).

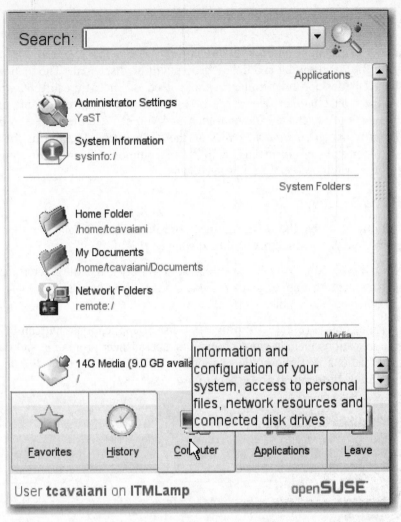

Figure 7: The KDE desktop with the *Computer* menu tab selected

Making changes to the system configuration requires *root user* (administrative) privileges. The root password must be entered into the *Password* textbox before one can continue to use YaST. Changing system configuration settings is beyond the scope of this lab.

The *Applications* tab provides access to both end user applications and system utilities that are designed to edit common end-user file types (both text and graphics files) and modify system configuration files.

The *Leave* tab allows the user to end a session by logging out, locking a session, or shutting down the computer altogether.

Figure 8: The Suse KDE desktop displaying the *Run as root* dialog box

File Management

This section focuses on managing files and directories. The steps required for creating files and directories, modifying files, and saving and deleting files will be discussed. The techniques used for file management on the KDE desktop are similar to those used on the Microsoft *Windows* desktop. For example, you move the mouse pointer over a file or folder to **select** it, you double-click the mouse to **open** (display the contents of) a selected file or folder, and you can use the mouse to **drag and drop** or **move** a selected file or folder. *Directional arrows* on the toolbar provide a means for moving from one directory level to another and *pop-up* menus, with many common file property options, appear if the pointer is held over a file or folder icon for a few seconds.

Accessing your Home Directory

1. Click the **Home** icon on the KDE toolbar. A dialog box displaying the files and folders (directories) in your *Home* directory will be displayed (Figure 9).

2. To modify a file located in your home directory, right-click the file's **icon** and select an option from the pop-up menu that appears. *Cut, copy, delete (Move to trash), rename,* and *Open with...* options (and others) are available.

3. The *Open with ...* option (Figure 10) provides a list of applications that can be used to modify a file. These applications include word processors, spreadsheet programs, and database programs, and other applications that allow you to modify different file types. For text files *KWrite* is probably the easiest of the word processors to use.

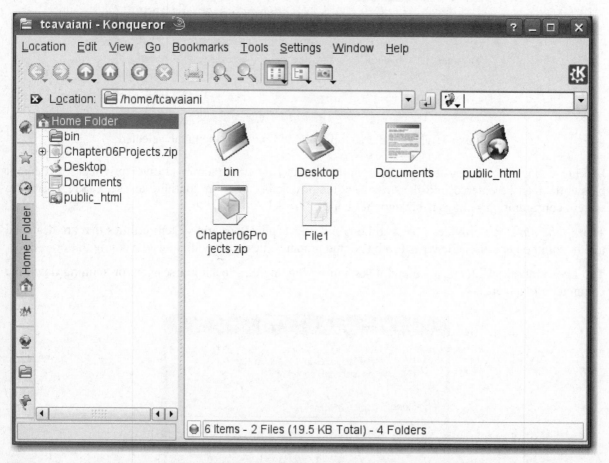

Figure 9: A KDE *Home* directory showing the folder list in the left pane and the file and folder *icons* in the right pane

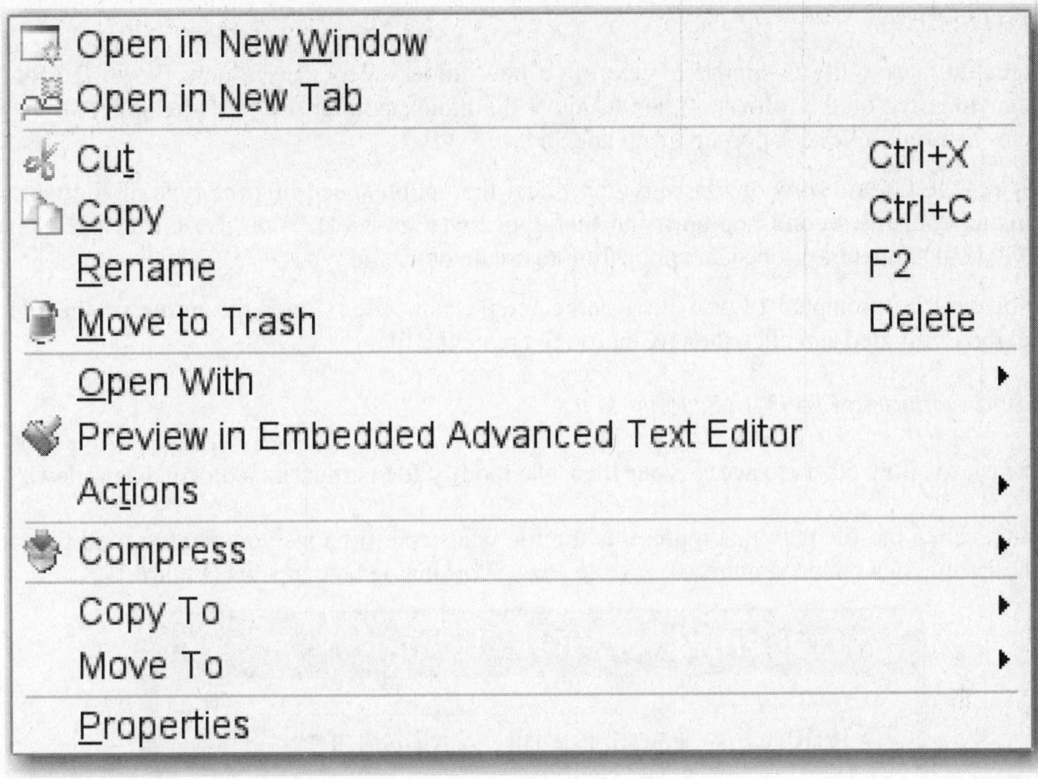

⬚ Open in New **W**indow		
⬚ Open in **N**ew Tab		
✂ Cu**t**		Ctrl+X
📋 **C**opy		Ctrl+C
Rename		F2
🗑 **M**ove to Trash		Delete
Open With		▶
🖐 Preview in Embedded Advanced Text Editor		
Ac**t**ions		▶
🐚 Compress		▶
Copy To		▶
Move To		▶
Properties		

Figure 10: The pop-up dialog box that appears when right-clicking a file icon in the Home directory

Creating a New Folder

1. To create a new folder, move the mouse pointer to the white space in the file pane and **right-click** your mouse. A pop-up menu appears.

2. Select the **Create New** option, and then select the **Folder** option from the second pop-up menu that appears (Figure 11).

3. You will be prompted to provide a name for the new folder. Enter the **name** and click the **OK** button to create the folder.

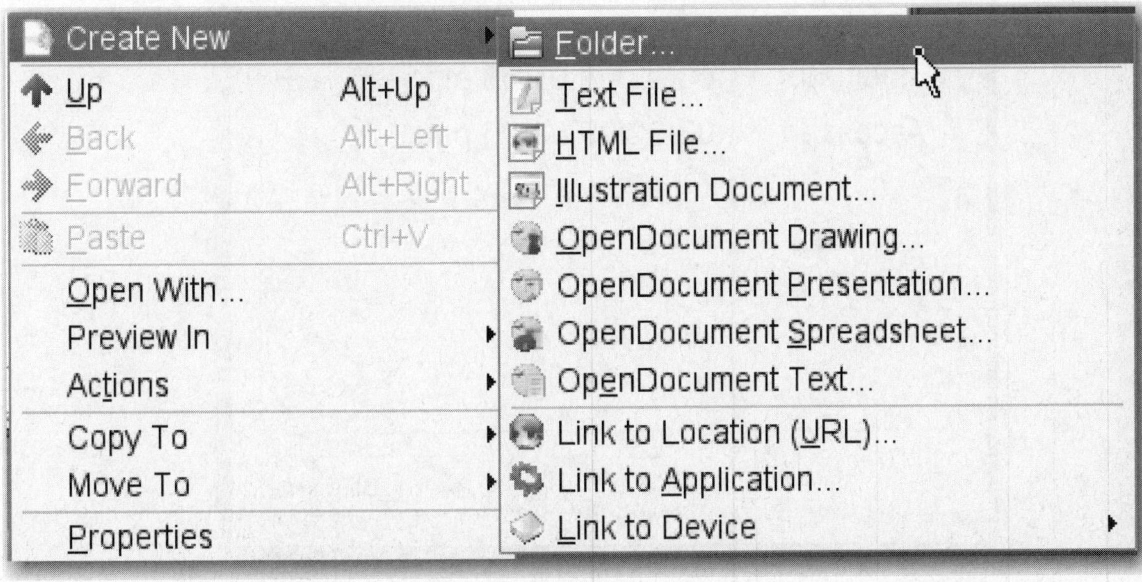

📄 Create New		▶	📁 **F**older...	
⬆ **U**p	Alt+Up		📄 **T**ext File...	
⬅ **B**ack	Alt+Left		🖼 **H**TML File...	
➡ **F**orward	Alt+Right		🖼 **I**llustration Document...	
📋 **P**aste	Ctrl+V		🐚 OpenDocument **D**rawing...	
Open With...			🟠 OpenDocument **P**resentation...	
Preview In		▶	🟢 OpenDocument **S**preadsheet...	
Ac**t**ions		▶	📄 OpenDocument **T**ext...	
Copy To		▶	🌐 Link to Location (**U**RL)...	
Move To		▶	🔌 Link to **A**pplication...	
Properties			💿 Link to Device	▶

Figure 11: Pop-up menus for creating a new folder or files of different types

Creating a New File

1. Creating a new file is similar to creating a new folder. To create a new file in the folder just created, click on the **folder** to open it, move the mouse pointer to the **white space** in the folder, and then right-click. A pop-up menu appears.

2. Select the **Create New** option, and then select the option specifying the type of file you wish to create from the second pop-up menu that appears (Figure 11). You can create plain text files, HTML documents, or open an application to create other file types.

3. You will be prompted to provide a name for the new file. Enter the **name** of the file in the textbox provided and click the **OK** button to create the file.

Viewing and Changing File Permissions

You may wish to allow others to access your files. To modify file permissions proceed as follows:

1. Right-click the **file icon** that represents the file whose permissions you want to modify, and click the **Properties** option (Figure 10). A file *Properties* dialog box appears (Figure 12).

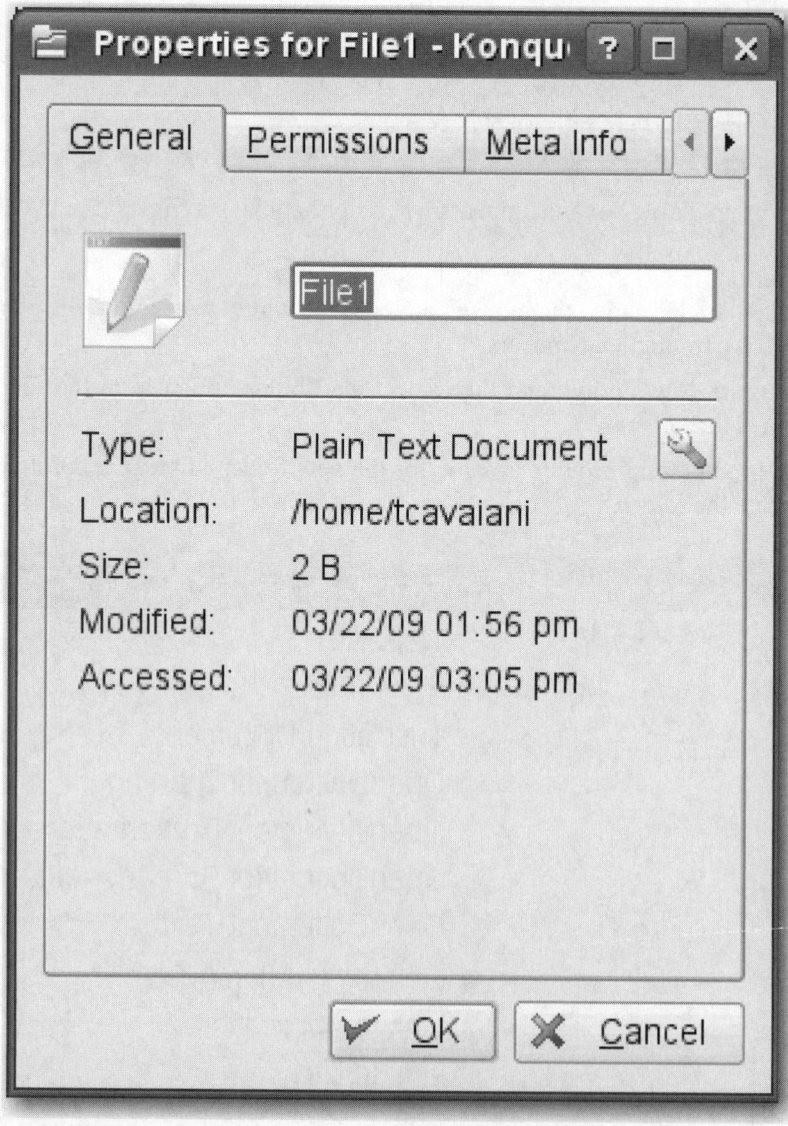

Figure 12: A *Properties* dialog box for a selected file

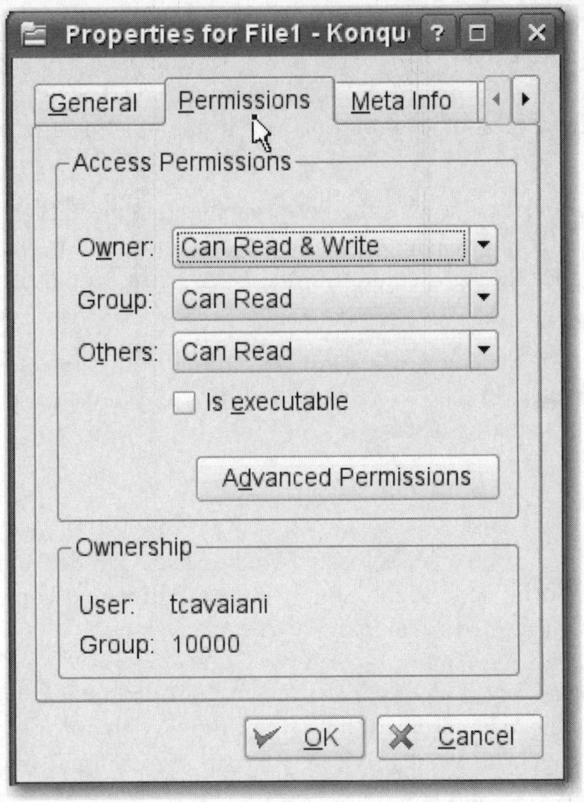

Figure 13: The *Permissions* page of the *Properties* dialog box

2. Click the **Permissions** tab in this dialog box to view existing permissions for the file. This dialog box allows you to make changes to file permissions by clicking the **down arrows** next to the current permission setting (Figure 13).

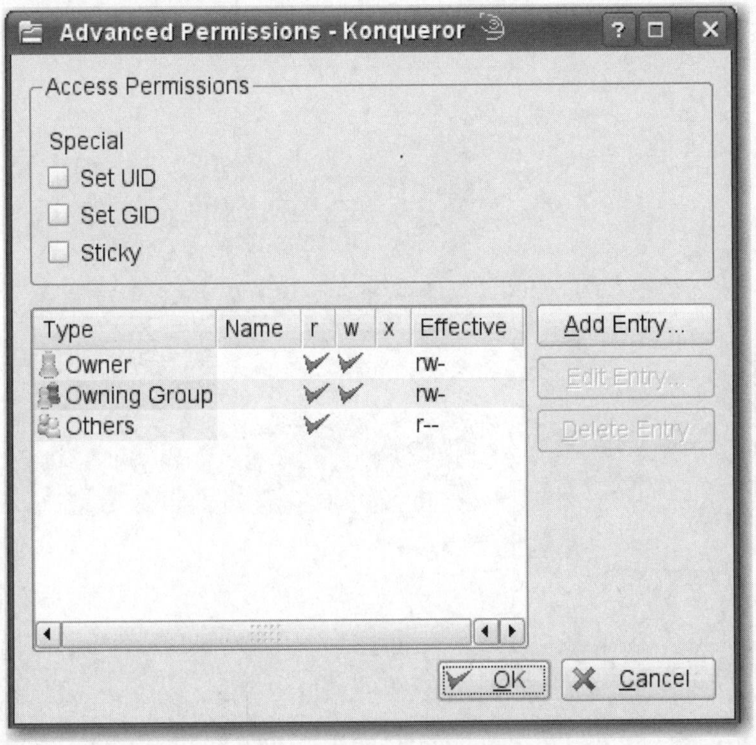

Figure 14: The *Advanced Permissions* dialog box

3. Clicking the **Advanced Permissions** button on the Permission page displays the *Advanced Permissions* dialog box (Figure 14). This dialog box displays the same permission settings that were shown on the *Permissions* page plus it lets you add *Special* permissions by marking the appropriate **check box** or another group or user to the existing file permissions by clicking the **Add Entry** button.

4. Clicking on a **green arrow** removes the permission and denies access to the group shown in the *Type* column. For example, in Figure 14 the *read (r)* attribute is checked for *Others*. Clicking the **green arrow** under the *read* column of the *Others* row would deny Others from reading the file.

5. To save any permissions changes, click the **OK** button in the *Advanced Permissions* dialog box, then click the **OK** button in the *Permissions* dialog box. To cancel any changes made, click the **Cancel** buttons in these dialog boxes.

Browsing the Web

An icon for activating the *FireFox* browser is located on the Suse KDE desktop (Figure 5). Firefox allows you to access pages on the World Wide Web. Simply click the **FireFox** icon to access the web and view a preset default homepage for this browser (Figure 16).

To access a site on the *World Wide Web*, **type** its **URL** in the **Locator** text box at the top of the Firefox browser window and click the *green arrow* to the right of the text box or press the **Enter** key. If you do not know the URL of the page you want to view, you can search for it by typing a **key word** in the Google text box located to the right of the Firefox Locator (Figure 15).

Figure 15: A preset *default* home page displayed by the *Firefox* browser

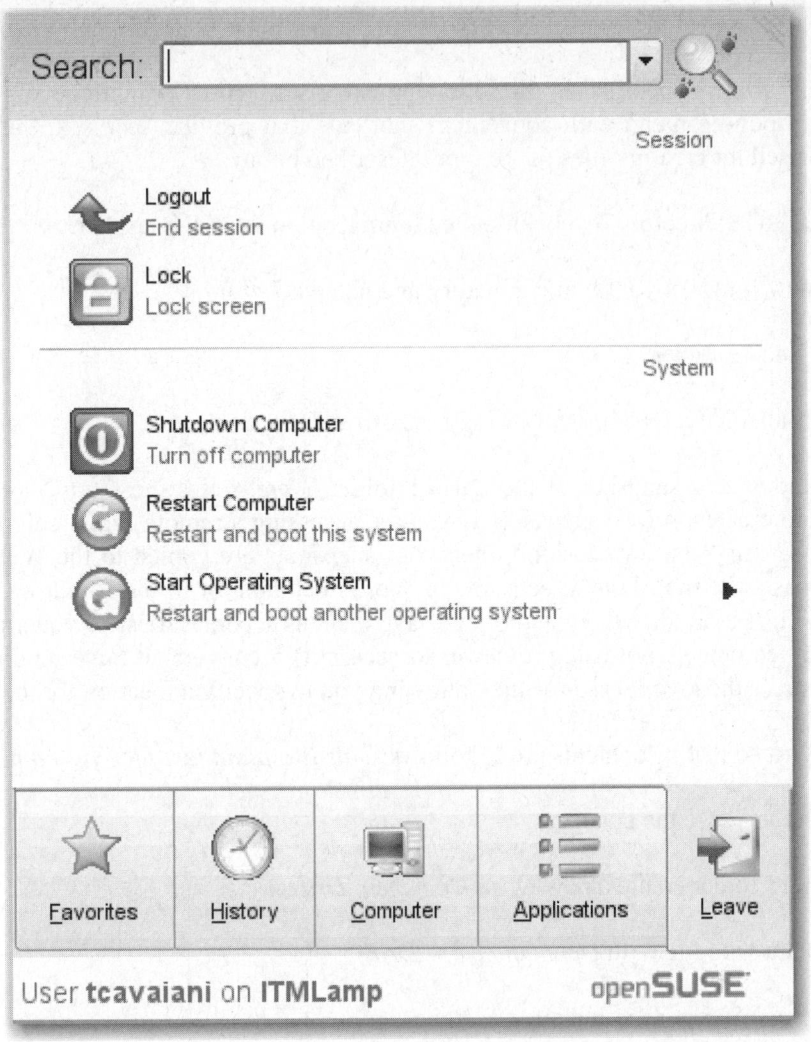

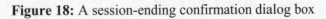

Figure 17: The Suse Linux *Start* menu with the *Leave* tab selected

Ending a Session

1. Click the Suse **Start** button. The *Start Menu* appears (Figure 17).

2. Select the **Leave** tab. Options to *logoff, switch user, switch off, reset, or suspend* your computer are provided. Click on the **Logoff** option to end your session.

3. A confirmation dialog box appears (Figure 18). Click the **Confirm** button to end your session.

> **Would you like to end your current session?**
>
> This session will end after 30 seconds automatically.
>
> [Confirm]   [Cancel]

Figure 18: A session-ending confirmation dialog box

Exercises

Create the files and folders specified in the following exercises. **Hint**: Right-clicking in the **directory** window displays a pop-up menu with convenient shortcuts that provide access to the most commonly used applications used for creating files of the types described below.

1. Open your home directory by clicking the **Home** icon on the KDE taskbar.

2. Create a new folder in your home directory and name it *Lab 11*.

3. Open the Lab 11 folder.

4. In the Lab 11 folder create the following files: *A.txt, B.txt, and C.txt*.

5. Capture and save a snapshot of the Lab 11 folder. *Note*: Press the *Print Screen* button on the keyboard to create a screen snapshot. If you are accessing a remote Linux computer via a viewer running on your Windows desktop, then your snapshots are copied to the Windows clipboard. You can paste the snapshots directly into a Word document or to the Windows *Paint* program if you would like to modify them and/or and save them as separate files. If you are working locally on a Linux computer (not using a viewer to access it) a convenient *Save As* dialog box appears after you press the *Print Screen* button, allowing you to specify a location for the file.

6. Modify A.txt so that its contents are as follows: *This is a plain text file. It's name is A.txt*.

7. Close A.txt and save the changes.

8. In the Lab 11 folder create a new *Open Document Drawing*.

9. Open this drawing file with *OpenOffice.org Draw*.

10. Create a *green Smiley face* and a *red rectangle*.

11. Capture and save a snapshot of this file.

12. Save the changes and close the file.

13. Rename the drawing *Smile*.

14. Change the *Permissions* (Use the *Advanced Permissions* option) for B.txt to *rwx* for all groups.

15. Create a new child folder under the Lab 11 folder and call it *Special files*.

16. Move *C.txt* to the *Special files* folder.

17. Rename *B.txt* to *List.txt*.

18. Open a terminal window and send a listing of the files in the *Lab 11 folder* to *List.txt*. **Hint**: Open a terminal window from the *Favorites* menu. Use Linux commands to change your directory to Lab 11 if necessary. Use the *redirection* option (discussed in Lab 10) to send a listing of the files in the Lab 11 folder to the List.txt file. File or directory names that include spaces must be enclosed in double quotes (" ").

19. Capture and save a snapshot of the Lab 11 folder.

20. Create a report that includes the above questions statements and their answers. Include any requested screen snapshots in your report.

21. Close all dialog boxes and terminate your session.

Submitting your Lab Report

Create a new page on your Google site. Name the page *Lab Eleven Report*. Copy the report created in this lab to the Lab Eleven Report page. *Note*: If you need to copy images to your Google page use the *Insert* option available in *Edit* mode.

LAB 12: PACKET CAPTURE AND ANALYSIS

OBJECTIVES

After completing this lab you should be able to do the following:

- ✓ Start a packet capture session using Wireshark

- ✓ Capture packets and save packet capture files

- ✓ Create display filters

- ✓ Use the Wireshark Expression Builder

- ✓ Analyze captured packet data

CONTENTS

HARDWARE, SOFTWARE, AND COMMUNICATIONS REQUIREMENTS FOR THIS LAB

- ➢ A Windows-based computer

- ➢ Wireshark

- ➢ Access to the Internet

USEFUL LINKS

- ➢ **http://www.wireshark.org/**

LAB 12

Introduction

In this lab you will use the *Wireshark* packet analyzer to capture and display the control information and data stored in packets transmitted over a network. Wireshark collects network traffic data and creates files that display packet header information in a layered format like that used by the Internet model. These layers can be expanded to view details that may prove helpful in determining the source of problems that your network might be experiencing. Creating filters that hide unwanted data and facilitate data analysis will also be discussed in this lab.

Starting Wireshark

To begin click the **Start** button on the Windows *Task Bar*. Click the **All Programs** option in the *System* menu to show all menu choices (Figure 1). Click the **Wireshark** choice to start the application. **Note**: If you do not see the Wireshark choices in the menu then you will need to install Wireshark on your computer. Consult Appendix E for detailed instructions on how to download, install, and configure Wireshark.

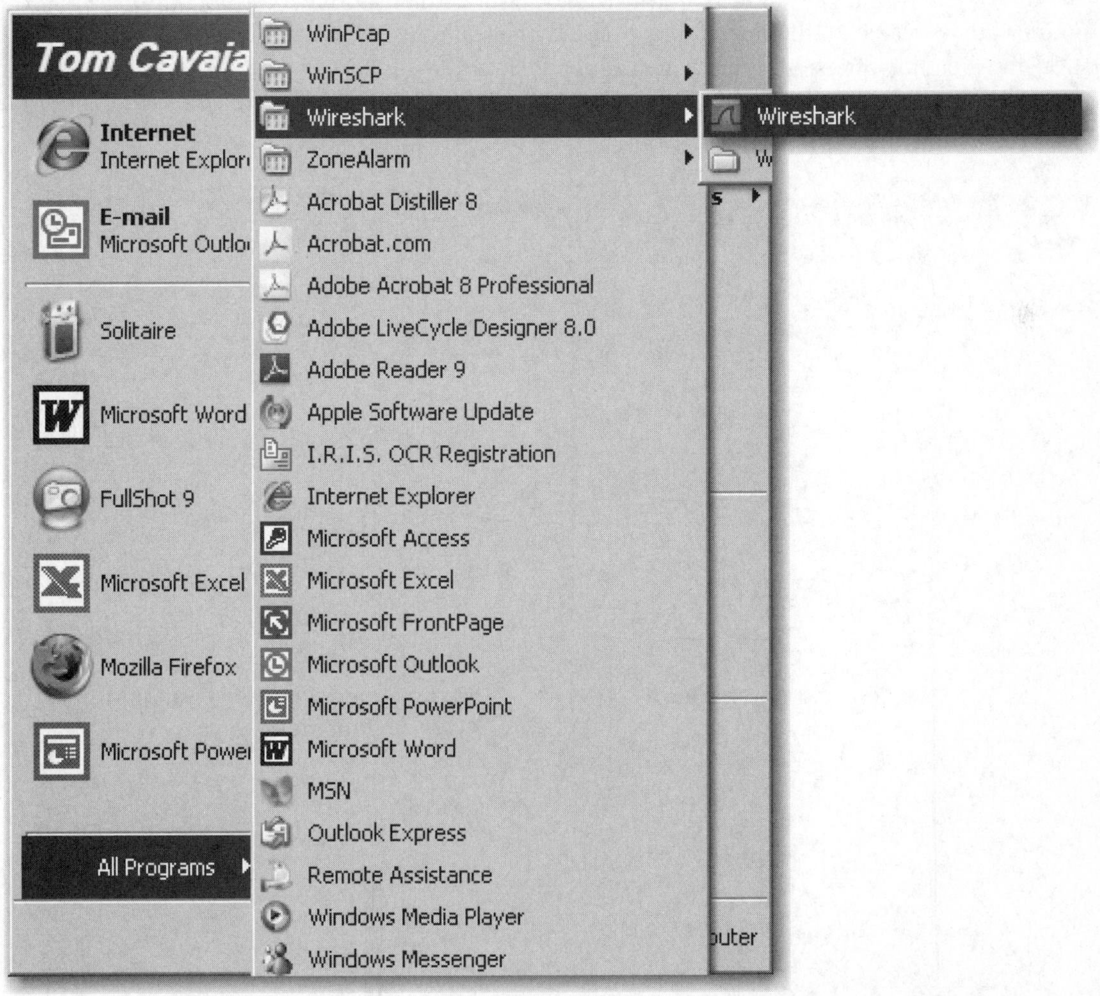

Figure 1: The *All Programs* menu showing the *Wireshark* choices

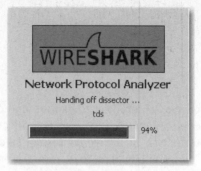

Figure 2: The Wireshark *splash* screen

After launching Wireshark, the Wireshark splash screen (Figure 2) appears while the application is loading program components into computer memory. After all components are loaded the splash screen disappears and the Wireshark application window appears (Figure 3).

The Wireshark application window includes a *menu bar*, the *main toolbar*, and a *filter toolbar*. In Figure 3 the *Capture* menu has been expanded to show its menu choices. The *Interfaces* choice lets you assign a network adapter for capturing packet data transmitted over the network. Clicking the **Stop** choice terminates a capture session. The *Capture Filters* choice provides an interface for specifying conditions that hide unwanted information in the capture display. Notice that shortcuts for the *Interfaces*, *Start*, and *Stop* options are available on the main toolbar directly beneath the menu bar. The *Filter* toolbar provides an option for creating filters by typing them directly into the *Filter text box*. The *Expression* button provides a list of pre-defined expressions and operators that can be used to minimize the amount of typing needed to create a display filter.

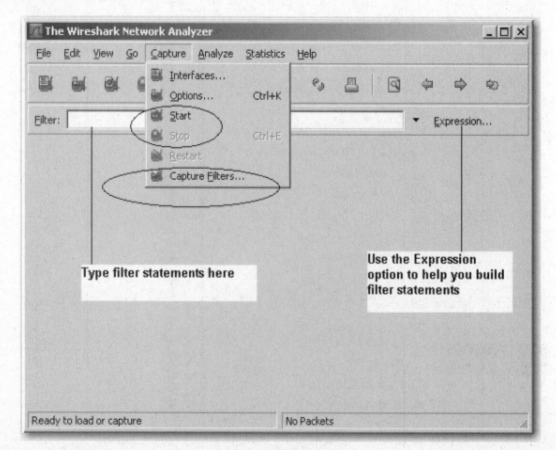

Figure 3: The Wireshark application window with the *Capture* menu displayed

Figure 4: The Wireshark *Capture Interfaces* dialog box

Capture Session Basics

When you start a Wireshark capture session all packets transmitted over the network to your computer are collected, stored in a temporary file, and then displayed in the main Wireshark application window. To start the capture process you first identify which network interface on your computer will be used for collecting packet data. When you are satisfied that your computer has collected the desired information, you then terminate the capture session by clicking the **Stop** button. If the data file created is too complex, you can create a filter to hide unwanted packets from view. The filtered packet information can then be used to analyze network-related problems or to gain insight into the protocols used during a message transfer.

Starting a Capture Session

This section outlines the steps required to run a capture session. Begin by clicking on the **Interfaces** option in the Capture menu (Figure 3). The *Wireshark Capture Interfaces* dialog box appears (Figure 4). Select a network interface that can be used for data collection purposes from those listed in the *Description* column. Such an interface will have an IP address corresponding to the network segment where the traffic you are interested in originates. Click the **Start** button corresponding to the interface you have chosen (Figure 4) to start a capture session. The dialog box will close and Wireshark will begin capturing packets immediately.

Packet capture will continue until you stop the capture session. During the capture, collected data will be displayed in the Wireshark Application Window (Figure 5). When it is displaying captured packets, the application window is divided into three panes. The top pane displays one row of information for each packet captured. The information displayed in this row includes a *sequence number* for the packet, the *time* the packet was captured relative to a starting time of zero seconds, the packet's *source* and *destination* addresses, the *protocol* used by the packet, and an *information* column describing the packet's purpose. Source and destination addresses may be IP addresses, MAC addresses, or port numbers depending upon the protocol associated with the packet. The values under a given heading can be sorted in either descending or ascending order by pointing and clicking on the **heading**.

The center pane displays the protocols associated by the selected packet. Protocols are organized in layers as outlined by the Internet Model (physical, data-link, network, transport, and application). A layer can be expanded so it displays field information by clicking the + sign to the left of the layer name. To hide the field information you can click the − sign to the left of the field or protocol name.

The bottom pane displays the hexadecimal representation of data contained in the selected packet on the left and a character-based version of the same information on the right. Beneath the bottom pane is a status bar that displays the total number of packets captured and the total number of packets marked. The value for marked packets is zero unless a filter has been applied to the raw data.

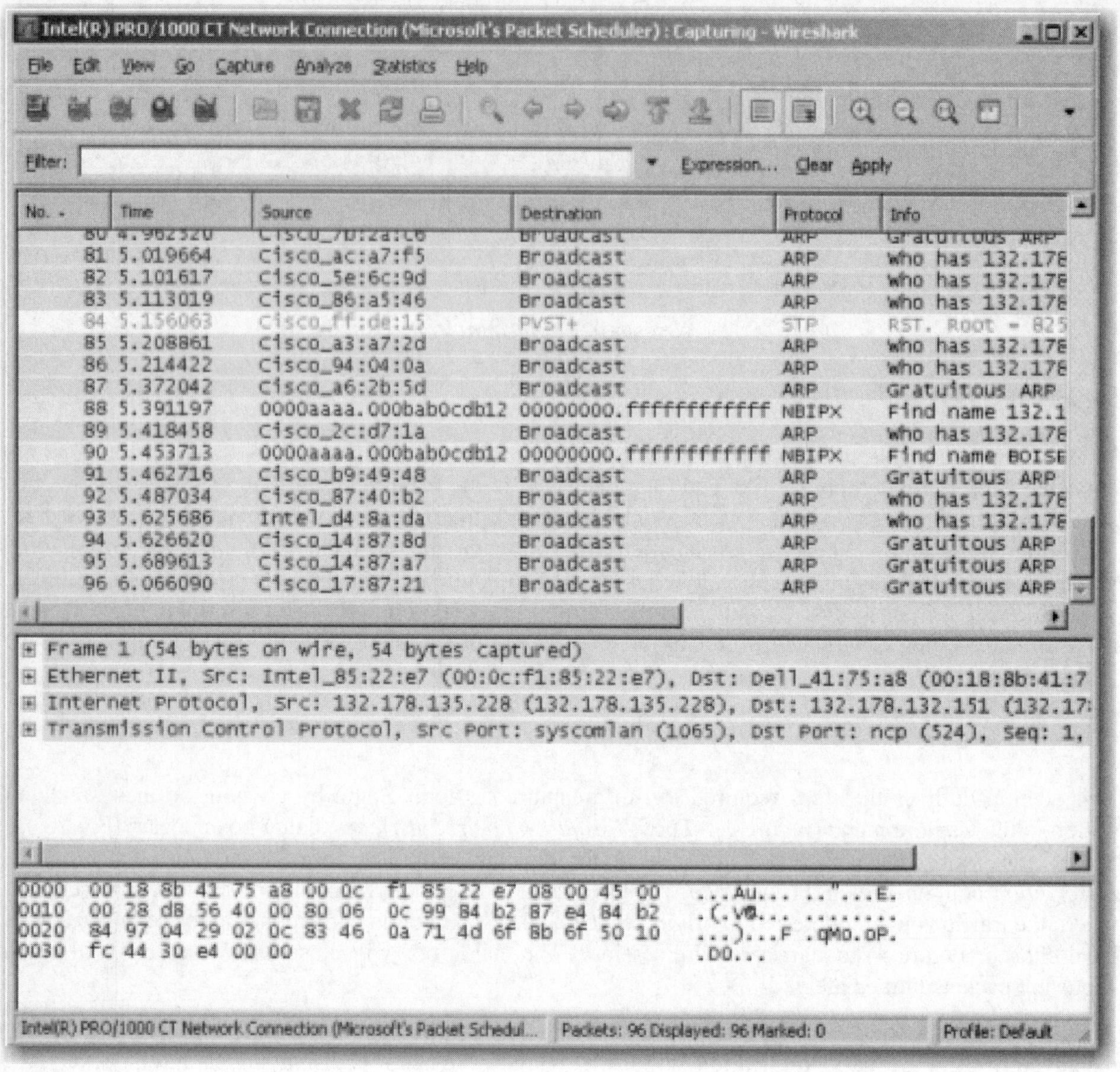

Figure 5: Wireshark *application* window and *capture* panes

Capturing Packets

1. Start a capture session and observe the Wireshark display for a few minutes. Observe the center pane of the application window.

2. While Wireshark is capturing packets open a browser and enter **http://www.ibm.com** into the Locator text box. Press the **Enter** key or click the **Go to** button to the right of the Locator text box (Figure 6) to display the IBM homepage.

3. Once this page is displayed click the **Close** button on the browser's title bar. Stop the Wireshark capture by clicking the **Stop** button. Minimize the Wireshark window.

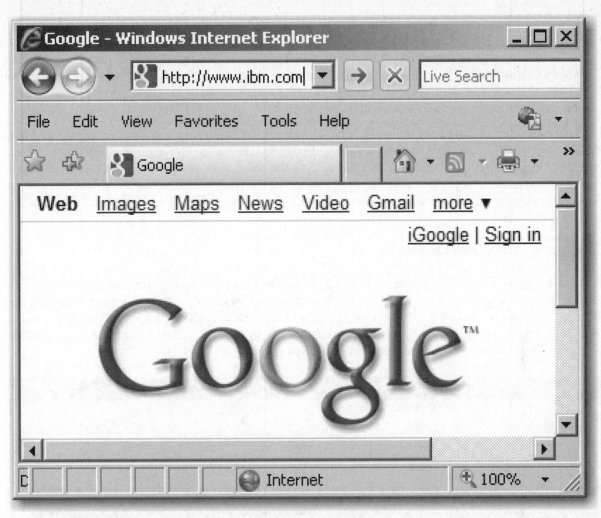

Figure 6: A browser window showing the *URL* for IBM in the *Locator* text box

Packet Filter Basics

Wireshark was designed to provide network administrators with a tool for troubleshooting their networks. By capturing packets that are being transmitted to and from a network segment that is experiencing communication problems, a network administrator could obtain information that might prove helpful in determining the source of the problem.

The data captured could amount to thousands of packets. Analysis of the data would be very tedious and time-consuming if an administrator had to review it line-by-line. Fortunately Wireshark has built-in filtering utilities that can be used to hide extraneous information and allow administrators to focus on just those packets that are relevant to the problem at hand. The next section describes the steps required to create a display filter in Wireshark.

Creating a Wireshark Display Filter

Creating a display filter in Wireshark can be quite simple if you have a good working knowledge of the protocols used in message transfers over a network. The Internet model defines a layered approach that describes the different functions involved in sending a message. Protocols have been created for each of these layers. Knowledge of the Internet layers and their associated protocols and fields provides you with a basis for selecting key words that you would use to create a display filter (for example, if you want to determine how many of the packets you just captured use the TCP protocol). To obtain the answer, you

115

can create a display filter by simply typing the keyword "TCP" into the *Filter text box* on the Wireshark Filter toolbar (Figure 7). No other key words are required. When you type TCP in the Filter textbox, Wireshark assumes that you want to display only those packets that contain the TCP protocol. Clicking the **Apply button** on the Filter toolbar causes the existing set of packets to be scanned. All packets that do not meet the selection criteria are then hidden from view and the status bar then displays the number of packets that meet the criteria as *Marked* packets.

Thus, in general, you can create a display filter for any packet capture by simply entering the common acronym for that protocol into the *Filter* text box. Doing so reduces the number of packets displayed and provides a count of the number of packets that display the protocol of interest. It should be noted that if you enter the name of a protocol that is not contained in the packet capture, then zero packets will be displayed. To remove such a filter and return to a full view of all packets simply click the **Clear** button on the Filter toolbar.

Logical and Comparison Operators

Wireshark display filters also include logical and comparison operators so that you can specify a specific value or range of values for a given keyword. These operators include *equals (eq)*, *greater than (ge), less than (le),* and *and*, *or*, and *not*. For example, if you want to view only those packets that contain a source IP address equal to 172.16.216.60, then you would type *ip.src eq 172.16.216.60* into the Filter text box (Figure 8). Variations on the above filter text also exist.

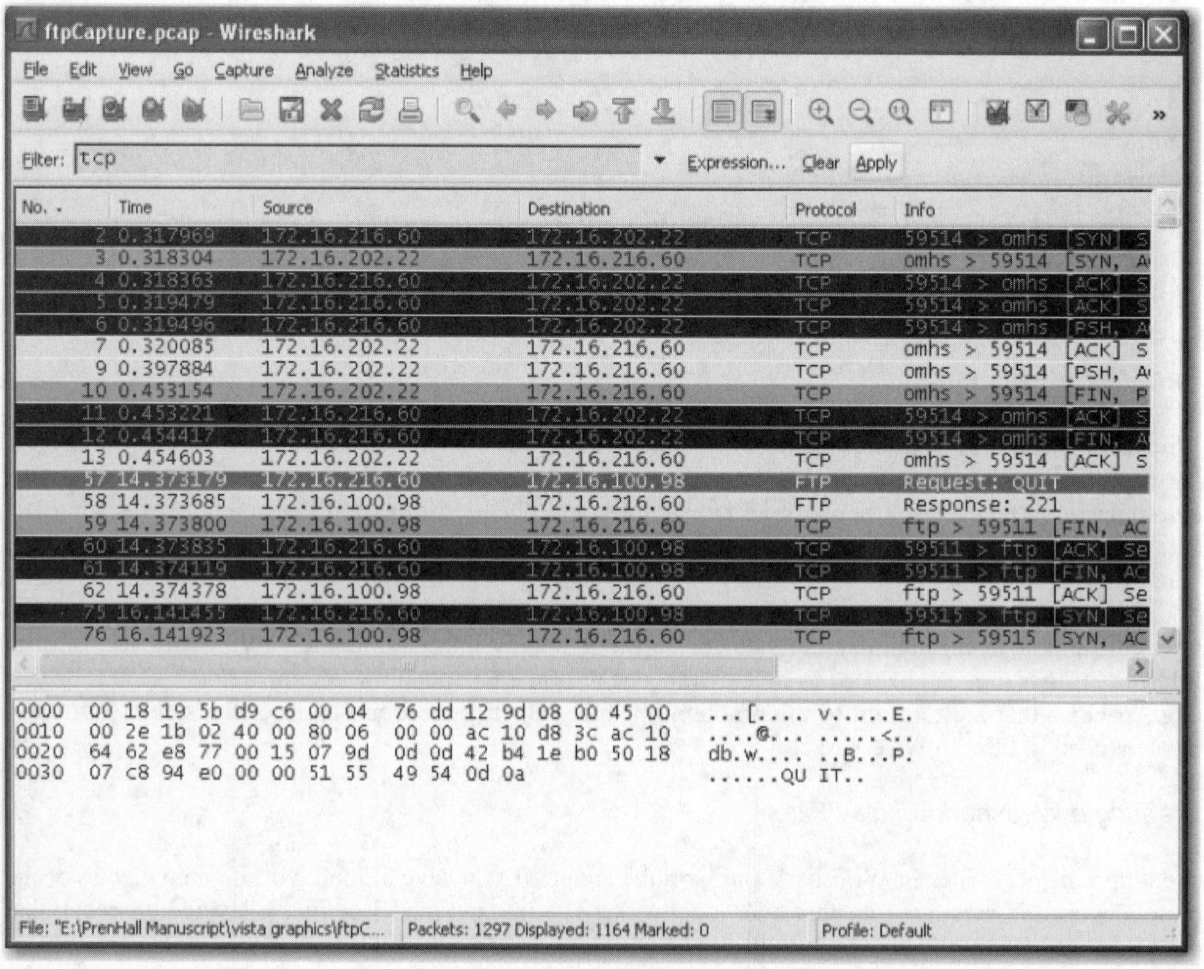

Figure 7: The *Filter* text box, a simple key word filter, and the status bar count

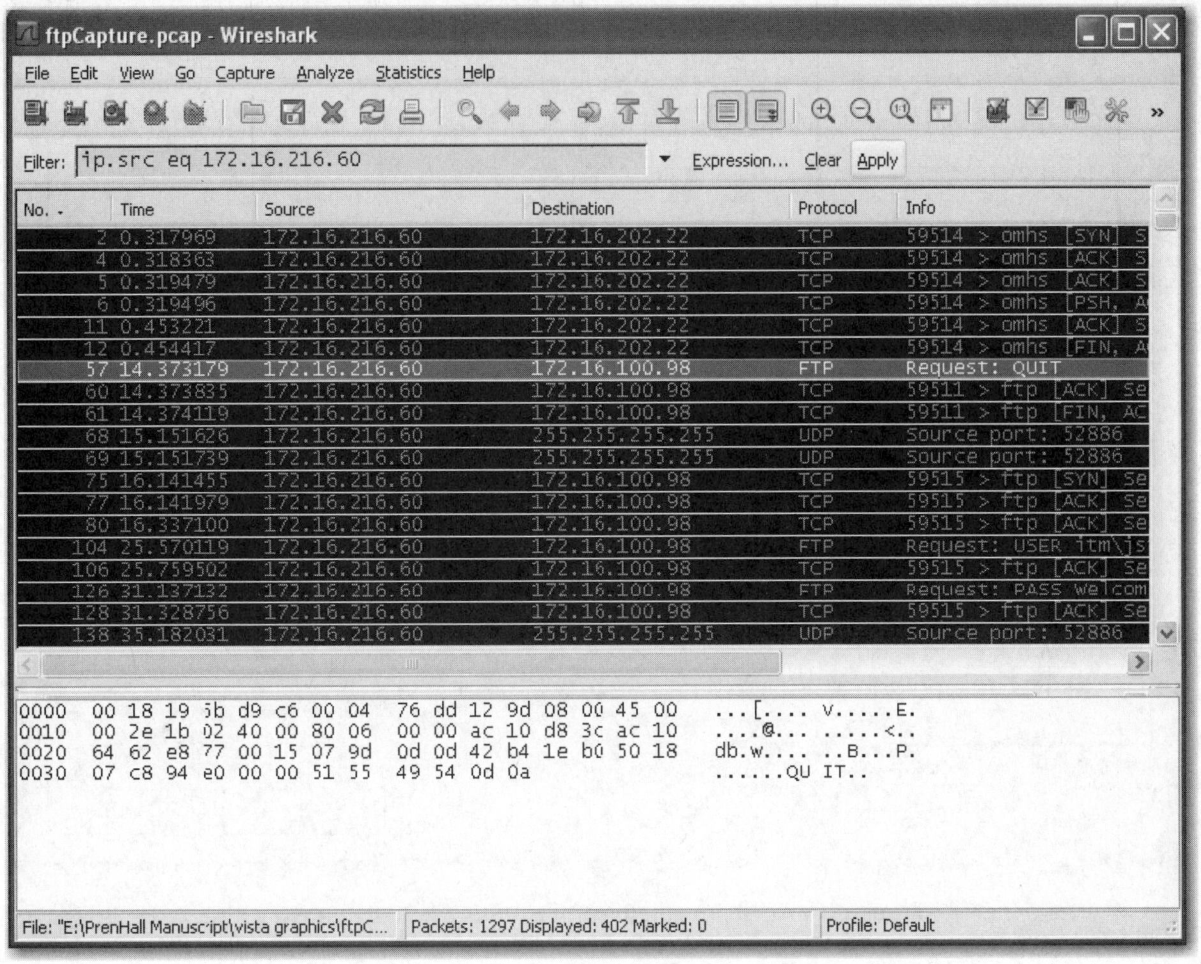

Figure 8: A display filter that uses a comparison operator

For a complete list of all available display filter operators click the **Help** option in the main Wireshark menu, select the *Manual Pages* option, and then click on the **Wireshark Filter** option (Figure 9).

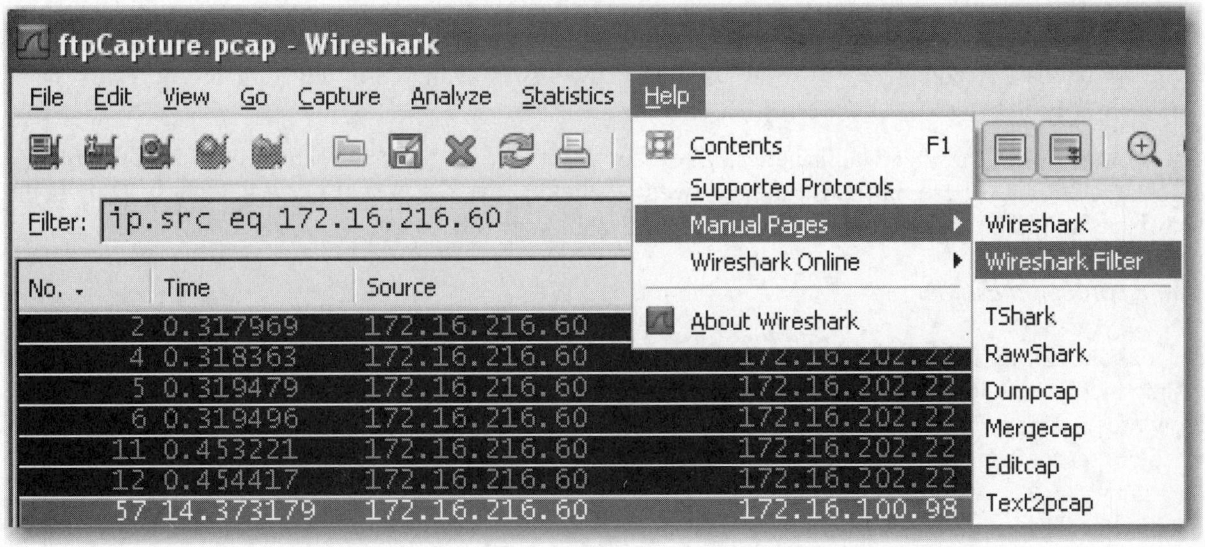

Figure 9: The *Help* menus for Wireshark Filters

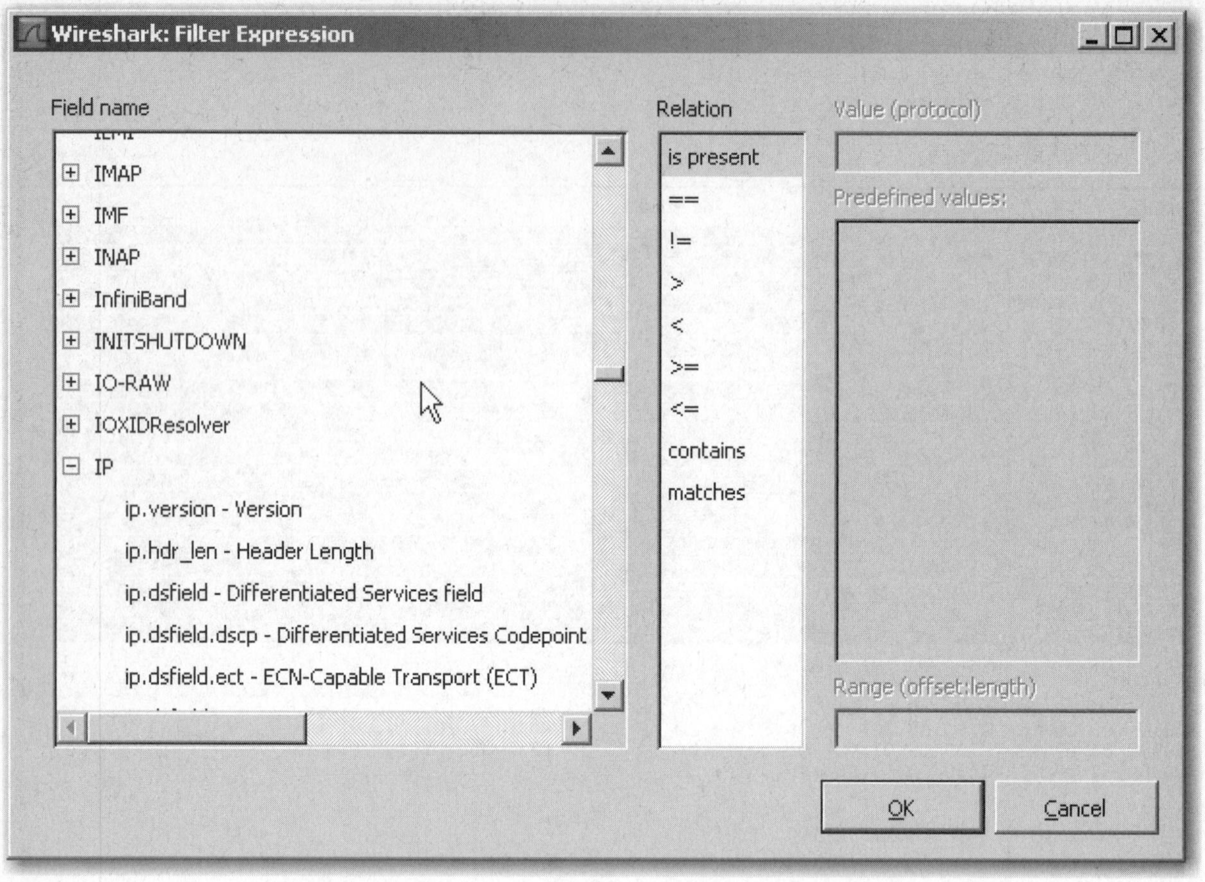

Figure 10: An abbreviated list of *display filter* keywords

Designing Display Filters

Display filter text strings can be as simple as a single keyword. They are seldom much more complex than a compound statement. In general these strings or clauses take the form of *keyword comparison-operator key-value*, where the *comparison operator* and *key-value* are optional components of the clause. Compound statements use logical operators (*and, or*) to link multiple clauses together. Creating a display filter is quite simple if you know which keywords are valid. Fortunately Wireshark provides a source for these keywords. A complete list of all possible keywords is available by clicking on the **Expression** button on the *Filter toolbar* (Figure 10).

The keywords are arranged alphabetically, except for the first eight. Each keyword has subfields associated with it. These subfields can be viewed by clicking the + *sign* next to the keyword. To hide the list of subfield keywords click the − *sign* next to the main keyword.

The Expression Builder

Besides providing a list of keywords, the *Expression builder* can also be used to create packet filters. Using the Expression builder involves a combination of selecting choices from a menu and typing keywords into the Filter text box. The Expression builder is accessed by clicking the **Expression** button on the Filter toolbar (Figure 11).

Figure 11: The Wireshark *Expression builder* toolbar choice circled

The three columns shown in the Expression builder dialog box allow you to select a *field name*, set up *a relationship*, and enter *a value* for the field name (Figure 10). This allows you to build very comprehensive filters. An example of how to use these features to build a display filter is shown in the next section.

Creating a Display Filter Using the Expression Builder

In this example we will build a simple filter that will display just those packets sent between two computers. This filter will be based upon the IP addresses of the two computers, because these addresses are directly associated with the IP packets sent between the two computers.

For our example we will focus on the packets sent between the web page server at *www.ibm.com* and your computer. To create this filter we need the IP addresses of these computers. To obtain the IP address of your computer, open a command window and use the *ipconfig* command to determine your computer's IP address (Figure 12).

The IP address for the IBM web server is the IP address associated with *www.ibm.com*. Typically you can determine this address by opening a command window and issuing an *nslookup* command for *www.ibm.com*. Unfortunately, many organizations block *nslookup* traffic for security reasons. Fortunately, Wireshark will allow us to use the URL, *www.ibm.com*, in the filter text.

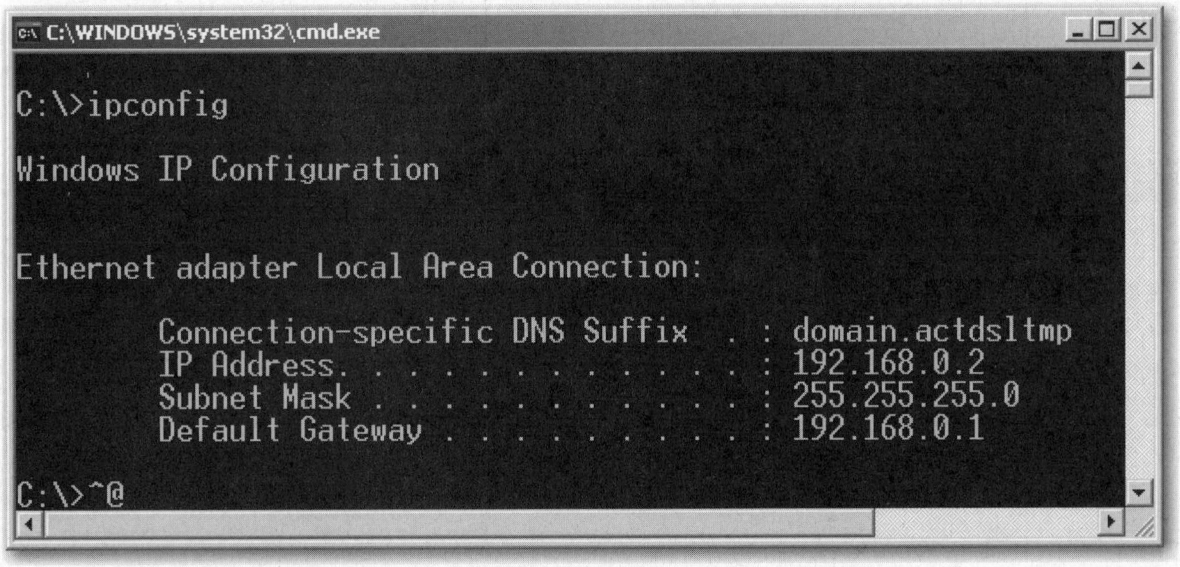

Figure 12: Using the *ipconfig* command to determine a computer's IP address

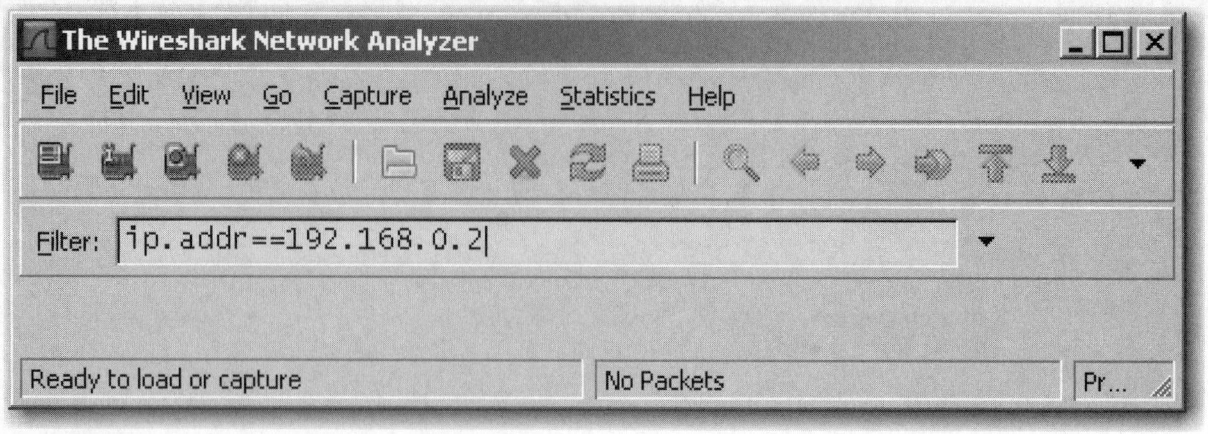

Figure 13: A display filter *clause* created using the *Expression* Builder

The general form of our display filter is *IP address equals **clientIPaddress** and IP address equals **serverHomepageURL***. In Wireshark, *ip.addr* is used to represent the expression *IP address,* == is used for *equals,* and && is used for *and.*

1. To begin building the filter, click the **Expression** builder button (Figure 13) on the **Filter** toolbar. Scroll down the list until you see the *IP* choice in the field column (entries in this column are in alphabetic order except for the first eight).

2. Click the + *sign* to expand the IP option. Select the **ip.addr** choice. In the *Relation* column select the == choice. Type the ***IP address*** of your computer in the *Value text box*. Click the **OK** button when you are done.

3. The filter will be applied to the captured packet data, and will be displayed in the Filter text box in the Filter tool bar (Figure 13). If you have not yet captured the data you can do so after you finish creating the filter.

4. To complete the filter statement we will use the clause just created as an example and type the remainder of the filter text. Type the following directly into the *Filter* textbox to change the clause into a compound statement: **&& ip.addr eq www.ibm.com**. Notice that we have used the *eq* comparison operator as an alternative to == sign.

5. As you type the filter text into the text box, it may change from red to green in color indicating when the filter expression is in error and when it is syntactically correct (Figure 14). Click the **Apply** button to filter the captured data.

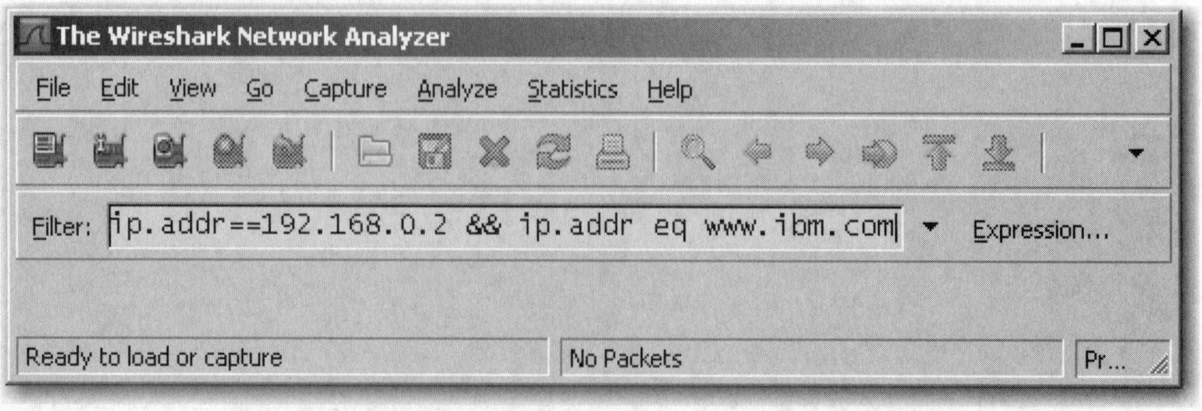

Figure 14: An example of a *compound display filter* statement

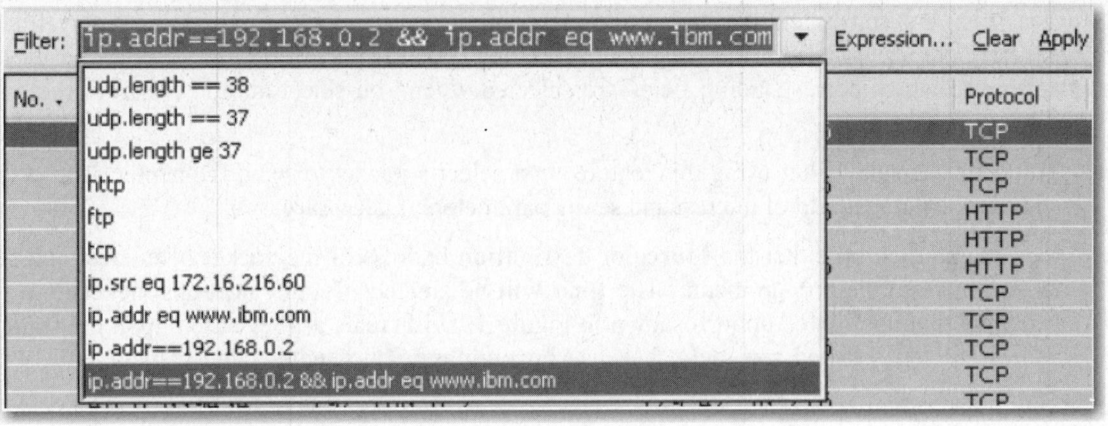

Figure 15: The *Filter drop-down* list displaying saved *display-filters*

6. Once you have applied a filter it will automatically be added to the drop-down list of filters which are displayed when you click the **down arrow** to the right of the **Filter text box** (Figure 15). This provides a convenient way to reapply a filter and reduces the effort involved in recreating or modifying the filter.

Using the Display Filter Shortcut Option

It is possible to create and apply a filter to an existing capture without typing a single key word. Short cut menus can be accessed by right-clicking on either the **source** or **destination** IP address of a given packet displayed in the Wireshark capture pane (Figure 16).

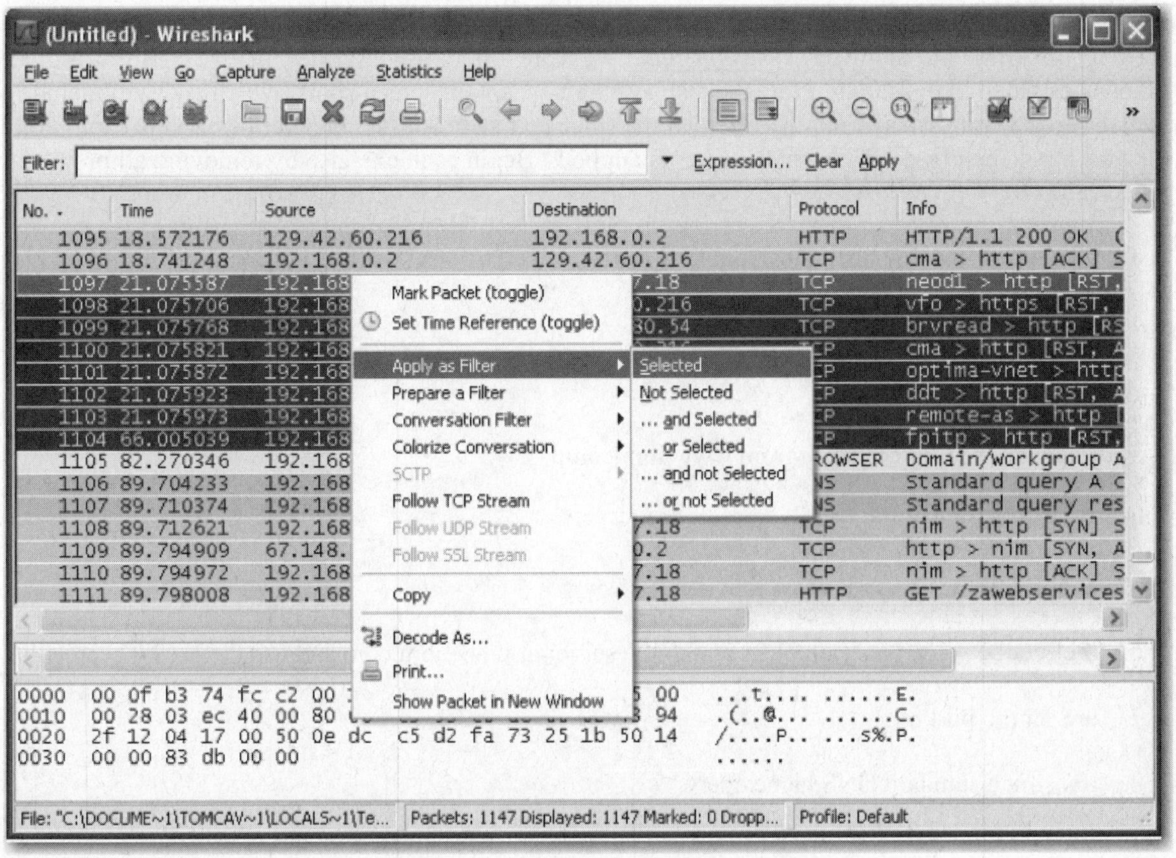

Figure 16: The *Filter pop-up* menus

This approach is very convenient because it allows you to use your mouse to create a display filter by simply selecting the criteria from the existing packet display. Display filters are created based upon which packet and which corresponding fields are selected when you select an address from the packet display window.

1. To create a display filter using this feature, first select a packet, expand the center pane options, and then select the field of interest and set its parameters if necessary.

2. Now, right-click on either the **source** or **destination** address of the packet of interest and select an option from the pop-up menu. The filter will be created if your selections make sense. For example, the highlighted options shown in Figure 16 will create a filter based upon the source IP address of the selected row only, because no options in the center pane had previously been specified.

3. After clicking on a *choice* in the shortcut menu the filter is applied automatically, and the filter text is displayed in the *Filter* text box.

4. To *remove* the filter and restore the display, click the **Clear** button on the Filter toolbar.

5. To *reapply* the filter click the **down arrow** next to the *Filter text box*, select the desired filter, and then click the **Apply** button.

6. More complex filters can be created by appending additional information to an existing filter as described earlier.

Exercises

Directions: Following the procedures outlined in this lab create a file containing packets captured while browsing the IBM site at **http://www.ibm.com**. Create filters as described below. Use any of the methods described in this lab to create the display filters. Capture screen shots (which you will include in your lab report) that display both the filter (in the filter text box) and the number of packets captured (in the status bar – see Figure 16) when the filter is applied. Begin each exercise by removing all previously applied filters.

Create filters that display only those packets that:

1. use the TCP protocol.

2. use the HTTP protocol.

3. request HTTP information from www.ibm.com.

4. are sent to your computer.

5. are sent to the server at www.ibm.com.

6. are sent between your computer and to the server at www.ibm.com and use the HTTP protocol.

7. are sent to port 80.

8. transmit a standard DNS name query.

Directions: For the following exercises first apply the filter you created in Exercise 3 (a filter to display HTTP traffic) to the raw data:

9. Which protocol is used by all packets in the filtered display?

10. What are the source port values for these packets? (Select at least two different packets before answering this question).

11. Which Transport Control Protocol flags are set?

12. What HTTP request type is specified?

13. What is the HTTP request version?

14. What version of the Internet Protocol is being used?

15. What is the IP header length in bytes?

16. Which IP flags are set?

17. What is the IP Time-to-Live value in seconds?

Submitting your Lab Report

Create a new page on your Google site and name it *Lab Twelve Report*. Copy questions 1 through 17 and their answers (including screen shots) to the Lab Twelve Report page.

LAB 13: ANALYZING TRANSPORT LAYER PROTOCOLS

OBJECTIVES

After completing this lab you should be able to do the following:

- ✓ Understand the differences between the UDP and TCP transport layer protocols

- ✓ Download files using the FTP and TFTP command-line file transfer utilities

- ✓ Compare and contrast the performance differences of FTP and TFTP

CONTENTS

HARDWARE, SOFTWARE, AND COMMUNICATIONS REQUIREMENTS FOR THIS LAB

- ➤ A Windows-based computer with Local Area Network access

- ➤ An Active Directory end-user account

- ➤ A remote server that supports FTP and TFTP services

- ➤ An end-user account for the FTP server (optional if the Anonymous account is available)

- ➤ Wireshark

USEFUL LINKS

- ➤ http://www.wireshark.org

LAB 13

Introduction

In this lab you will collect data to compare performance differences between the two Internet transport layer protocols, the *Transmission Control Protocol* (TCP) and the *User Datagram Protocol* (UDP). Data will be collected during the download of an arbitrarily large data file. Two different applications will be used for downloading data. The first application is the *File Transport Protocol* (FTP), which uses TCP as its transport layer protocol. The second is the *Trivial File Transport Protocol* (TFTP), which uses UDP as its transport layer protocol. You will use the Wireshark application to capture the packets that are transferred during the download sessions. You will also use the skills you learned in Lab 12 to create display filters to simplify the analysis of the data.

Transport Layer Protocols

UDP is a simple connection-less protocol used for exchanging files. UDP adds a small header to application data. The result is called a *UDP datagram*. When a UDP datagram is transmitted, the datagram is encapsulated with an IP header and datagrams are delivered using a best-effort mechanism.

TCP is more complex. TCP is a connection-oriented protocol. TCP clients establish logical connections (using a 3-way "handshake") to TCP servers before data transmissions take place. Once a connection is established, data can be transferred in both directions. *TCP segments* consist of a TCP header and a *payload* that contains application data. A sending application submits data to TCP as a single stream of bytes without indicating message boundaries in the byte stream. The sender decides how many bytes are put into a TCP segment. TCP ensures reliable delivery of data, using numerous mechanisms, including acknowledgements from TCP recipients, and controls the amount of data that a sender can transmit via two mechanisms, *flow control* and *congestion control.*

Part One: UDP-Based File Transfer

TFTP is a minimal protocol for transferring files without authentication. TFTP uses UDP for data transport. TFTP servers use port 69 and transfer data in 512 byte blocks. Each block must be acknowledged before another is sent.

In this section of the lab you will download a file named *large.d* (stored on a TFTP server connected to the lab network) to your computer. If you are working from off-campus you must connect to the lab network using the VPN software (See Appendix A for information regarding how to install and configure the VPN client software) before you can download the file.

TFTP File Transfer Procedures

1. Start the Wireshark application by clicking the **Start** button and selecting the **Wireshark** choice from the **All Program** menu (Figure 1).

2. Start a *Wireshark capture session* by clicking the **Interfaces** choice in the Capture menu (Figure 2). The *Capture Interfaces* dialog box appears. Click the **Start** button to the right of the description of the network interface that is connected to your network to start the capture session.

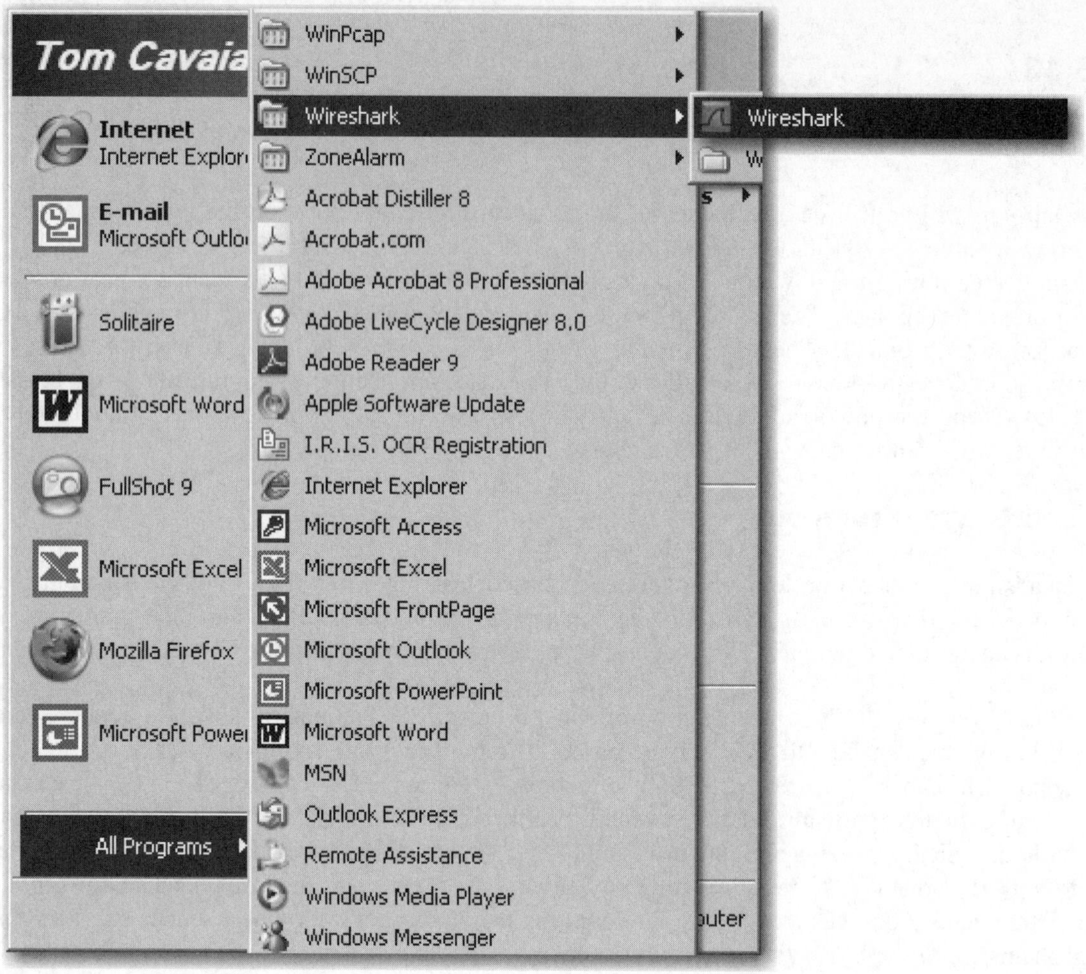

Figure 1: The *All Programs* menu displaying the Wireshark choices

3. Open a *command window* on your Windows desktop by clicking the **Start** button on the Window *Task Bar* and then clicking the **Run** option in the *System* menu (Figure 3).

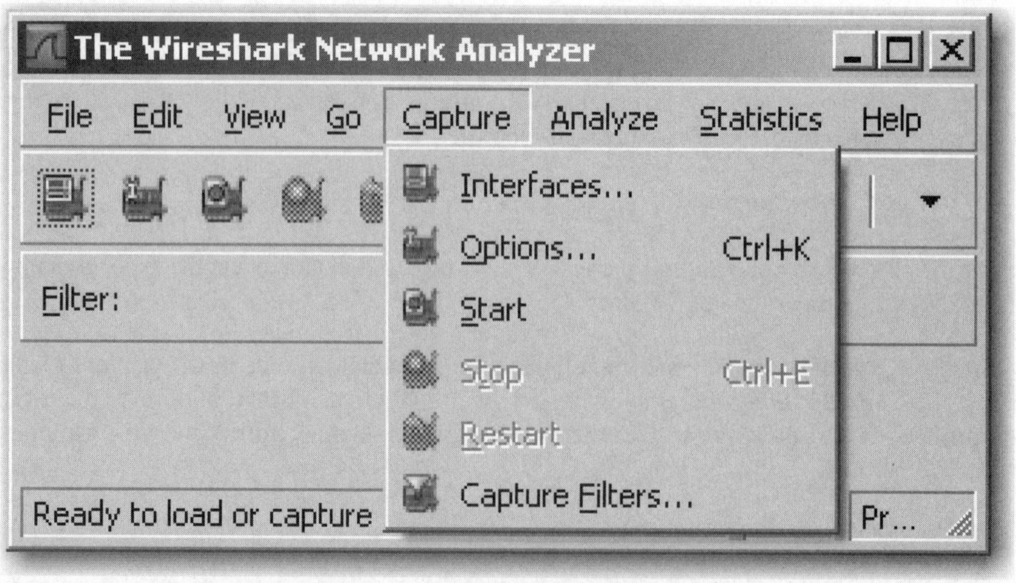

Figure 2: The *Wireshark Capture* menu displaying the *Interfaces* and other choices

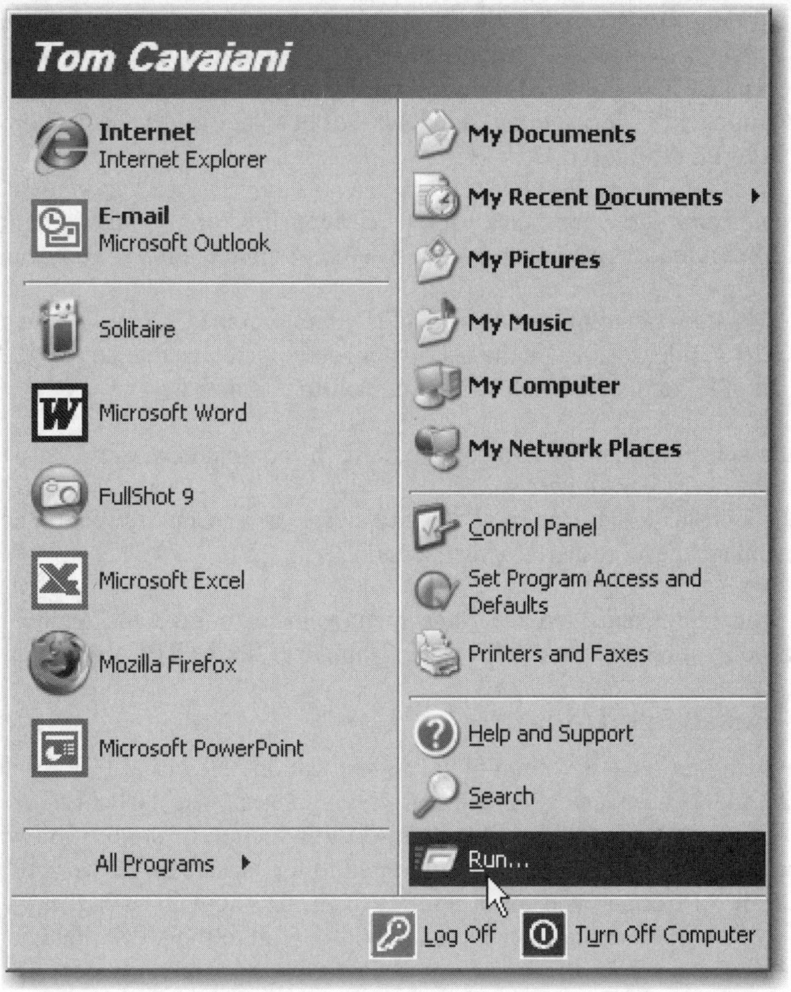

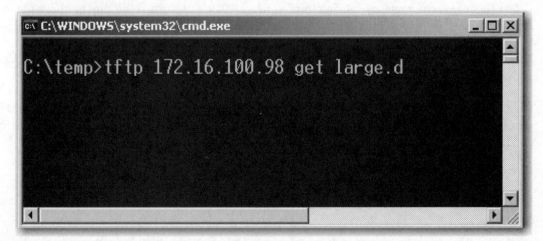

Figure 3: The Windows *System* menu showing the *Run* option

4. In the command window that appears type **tftp** *tftpServerIPaddress* **get large.d** and press the **Enter** key to start a TFTP session that will transfer the *large.d* file to your computer (Figure 4). Your instructor will supply you with an actual IP address for the tftp server. For this discussion we are using 172.16.100.98.

```
 C:\WINDOWS\system32\cmd.exe                          _ □ X

C:\temp>tftp 172.16.100.98 get large.d
```

Figure 4: A *command window* showing the *tftp download* command

Note 1: If you get a "Timeout Occurred" message, the firewall software on your computer is blocking the transfer. If you are using a Windows firewall, temporarily disable it by clicking Start – Control Panel – Security Center to change the firewall setting to OFF. If you are using a third party firewall, like ZoneAlarm, then right-click its icon on the Windows Taskbar and select the Shutdown option. After shutting down the firewall, repeat step 4.

Note 2: The tftp command downloads files to your current directory. Make certain that your current directory has been configured for reading and writing before issuing the *tftp get* command.

Note 3: Windows Vista does not allow you to save files directly to the C drive. If you are using Vista you must save your files to a folder located on the C drive or some other writable drive. Make certain that you change your destination folder location before issuing the tftp command.

5. When the download is complete type **exit** to close the command window.

6. Activate the Wireshark application window (if necessary). Click the **Stop** choice in the Capture menu to terminate the Wireshark capture session.

7. Click the **File** Menu and then the **Save** menu choice to save the temporary Wireshark file containing the captured network traffic data. Name this file **TFTPCapture.pcap**.

Part Two: TCP-Based File Transfer

FTP supports plain text file transfers with minimal authentication. FTP uses TCP for data transport. FTP servers use ports 20 and 21 to transfer segments of varying sizes. The TCP *sliding window protocol* is used to determine the number of bytes in a segment. In this section of the lab you will download a file named *large.d* that is stored on an FTP server connected to the classroom network to your computer. If you are working from off-campus you must connect to the lab network using the VPN software (See Appendix A for information regarding how to install and configure the VPN client software) before you can download the file.

FTP File Transfer Procedures

1. Start the Wireshark application by clicking the **Start** button and selecting the **Wireshark** choice from the **All Programs** menu (Figure 1).

2. Start a *Wireshark capture session* by clicking the **Interfaces** choice in the Capture menu (Figure 2). The *Capture Interfaces* dialog box appears. Click the **Start** button to the right of the description of the network interface that is connected to your network to start the capture session.

3. Open a *command window* on your Windows desktop by clicking the **Start** button on the Window *Task Bar* and then clicking the **Run** option in the *System* menu (Figure 3).

4. In the command window that appears type **ftp** *ftpServerIPaddress* and press the **Enter** key to start an FTP session (Figure 5). Your instructor will supply you with an actual IP address for the FTP server. For this discussion we are using 172.16.100.98.

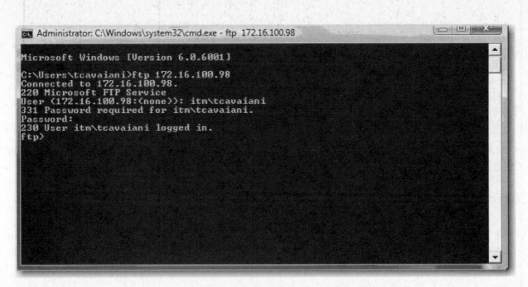

Figure 5: A command window displaying an FTP authentication dialog between client and server

Note 1: If you get a "Timeout Occurred" message, your firewall is blocking the transfer. Temporarily shutdown the firewall (See Note 1 page 128) and repeat step 4.

Note 2: The ftp command downloads files to your current directory. Make certain that your current directory has been configured for reading and writing before issuing the *ftp get* command.

Note 3: Windows Vista does not allow you to save files directly to the C drive. If you are using Vista you must save your files to a folder located on the C drive or some other writable drive. Make certain that you change your destination folder location before issuing the tftp command.

5. FTP requires that users authenticate to the server before they can download files. Enter ***DomainName\username*** and press the **Enter** key. (Your instructor will provide a value for the *DomainName*). For this demonstration we will use *itm* for the domain name. A password prompt appears. Enter your **password** and press the **Enter** key.

6. Type **get large.d** to download the *large.d* file to your computer. The server will return a message indicating that the file has been transferred (Figure 6).

Figure 6: A command window showing the FTP *get* command and a transfer complete message

7. Type **quit** ending the ftp session.

8. Type **exit** to close the command window.

9. Activate the Wireshark application window (if necessary). Click the **Stop** choice in the Capture menu to terminate the Wireshark capture session.

10. Click the **File** Menu and then the **Save** menu choice to save the temporary Wireshark file containing the captured network traffic data. Name this file **FTPCapture.pcap**.

Part Three: Data Analysis

Visual analysis of unfiltered packet captures can be overwhelming, simply because of the sheer volume of data that must be examined. As mentioned in Lab 12, Wireshark has tools that allow you to create *display filters* to hide unwanted packets. Four suggestions for creating display filters are provided below:

1. Create a display filter to eliminate all packets except those exchanged between sender and receiver. Use IP addresses to identify the client and server computers. The general syntax of such a filter is *ip.addr == clientIPaddress && ip.addr == serverIPaddress*.

2. Create filters to eliminate all protocols except the protocol of interest. For example, the filter *protocol = ftp-data* eliminates all packets that do not include FTP data.

3. Combine filters to refine the display. For example, combining the above two filters eliminates all non-FTP packets transferred between the two computers involved (Figure 8).

4. Check the status bar for packet counts. The Wireshark *status bar* displays both the total number of packets captured and the number of packets displayed as a result of filtering (Figure 7).

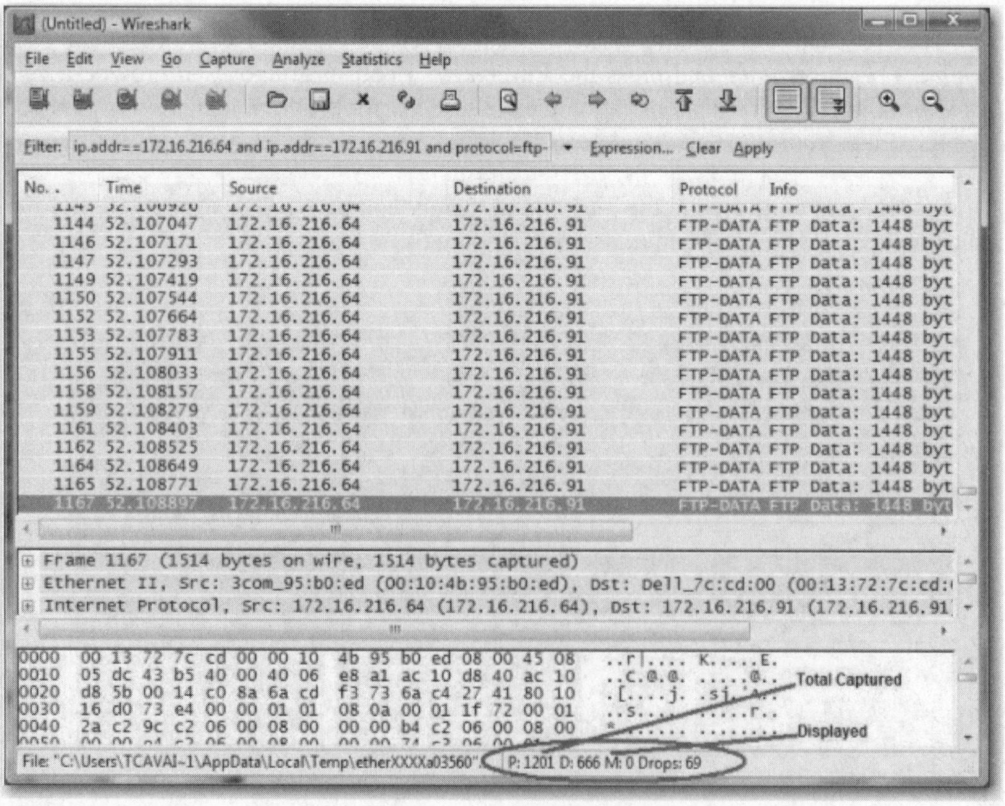

Figure 7: A *filtered* Wireshark packet capture displaying packets *captured* and *displayed*

130

Questions

Directions: For the following questions create screen captures that support your answers.

TFTP

1. How many packets are exchanged during the download of the large.d file? **Hint**: Create a filter that displays only those packets that use TFTP.

2. How many packets are data *acknowledgments*? **Hint**: TFTP acknowledgements are stored in the TFTP *opcode* field. Use the Expression builder to create the filter.

3. How many data-only packets are exchanged in the transfer of the large.d file? **Hint**: Use the Expression builder to set the TFTP opcode field value to data packet.

4. How many control packets (non-data and non-acknowledgements) are exchanged in the transfer of the large.d file? **Hint**: Create a display filter that displays packets that are not TFTP acknowledgements or data packets.

5. How many acknowledgements does TFTP send for each data packet sent?

6. How long in seconds does it take to download the file using TFTP?

FTP

1. How many packets are exchanged in the download of the large.d file?

2. How many data-only packets are exchanged in the download of the large.d file?

3. How many control packets (non-data and non-acknowledgements) are exchanged during the download of the large.d file?

4. How many acknowledgements are sent during the download of large.d? Is it possible to provide a definitive answer for this question? Which protocol acknowledges the receipt of data transmitted?

5. How long in seconds does it take to download the file using FTP (do not count the time it takes to authenticate to the FTP server).

6. Based upon the times determined previously in these exercises, which method, FTP or TFTP, takes more time to download large.d?

7. Under what conditions would it take less time to transfer a file using TFTP? with FTP?

8. Create a filter that displays packets that use the FTP protocol only. Review the *info* column in the top panel in the Wireshark application window. Do you see any readable alphabetic characters?

9. Consider your answer to question 8. Do you see any potential problems in using FTP to transfer confidential information such as passwords?

10. Were you aware that FTP transmitted data in plain text format prior to using Wireshark?

Submitting your Lab Report

Create a new page on your Google site and name it *Lab Thirteen Report*. Copy questions all questions and their answers (include screen shots) to the Lab Thirteen Report page. Attach the FTPCapture.pcap and TFTPCapture.pcap files to your report.

LAB 14: SECURITY POLICIES

OBJECTIVES

After completing this lab you should be able to do the following:

- ✓ Describe basic security policy concerns

- ✓ Download a sample security policy document from a highly trusted Internet source

- ✓ Customize a security policy template

CONTENTS

HARDWARE, SOFTWARE, AND COMMUNICATIONS REQUIREMENTS FOR THIS LAB

- ➤ A Windows-based computer

- ➤ Access to the Internet

USEFUL LINKS

- ➤ **http://www.sans.org/resources/policies/**

LAB 14

Introduction

Every organization needs a set of formally stated guidelines regarding acceptable behaviors and required procedures as they relate to the use of computer hardware, software, and company data by its employees. This set of guidelines is called a *security policy*. Such a policy will assure that the organization's assets are secure and that any breech of security is properly handled. This lab will provide you with an opportunity to gain a basic understanding of the components of a security policy and how you might customize a security policy template to fit the needs of your organization.

Part One: Security Policy Basics

1. Logon to your computer and double-click the **Internet Explorer icon** on the Windows *Desktop* or in the *Start* Menu.

2. Enter the URL **http://www.sans.org/resources/policies/** into IE's **Locator** text box and click the **Go to** button or press the **Enter** key.

3. The *SANS Institute Security Policy Project* home page appears (Figure 1).

4. **Click** the **Need a Primer on Security Policies?** link located in the right-hand column.

5. The *Policy Primer* page appears (Figure 2).

Figure 1: The SANS Institute Security Policy Project home page

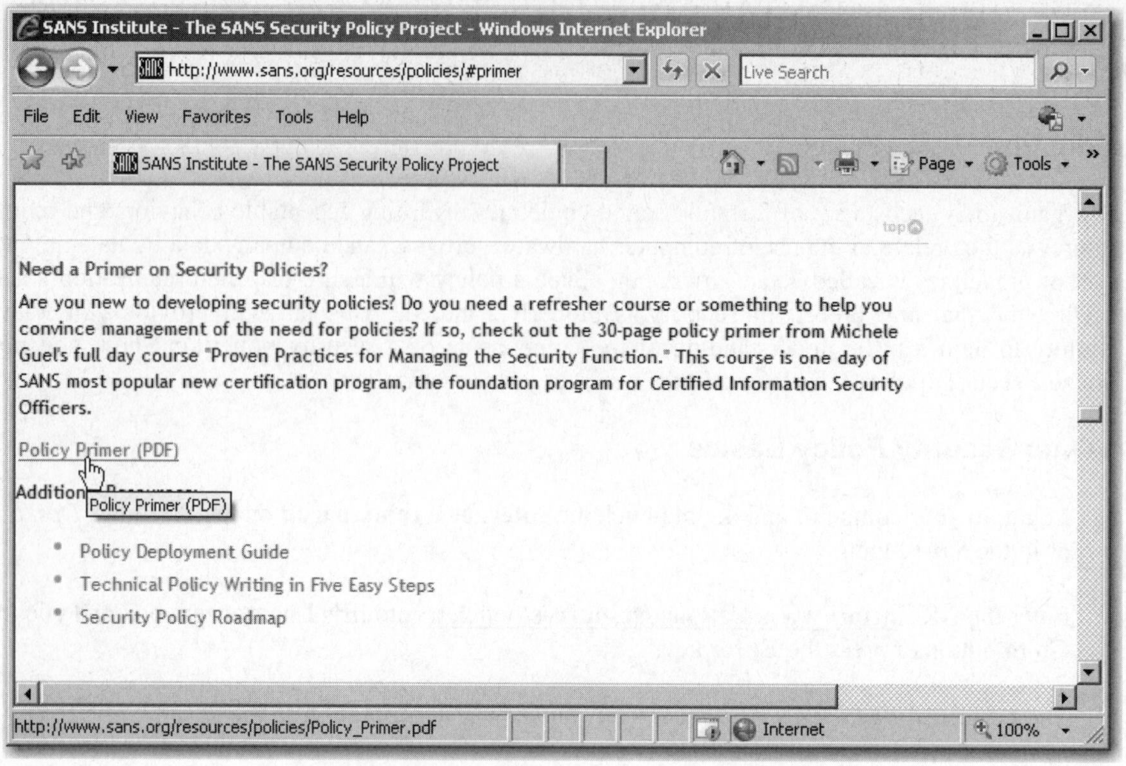

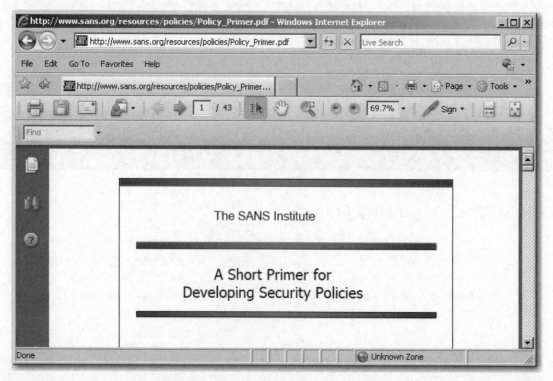

Figure 2: The *SANS Policy Primer* page

6. This page includes a short description of the *Policy Primer (PDF)*. Click the **Policy Primer** link to open the *Policy Primer*. The Policy Primer title page appears (Figure 3).

Figure 3: The *Policy Primer* title page

Review the contents of the Policy Primer and answer the following questions:

Questions

1. What is a security policy?

2. How does a standard differ from a guideline?

3. Give an example of a security policy guideline.

4. Explain the Why-What-How model for security policies.

5. What is the purpose of a policy impact assessment?

6. How does a procedure differ from a policy?

7. What processes would be outlined by a Password Management Procedure?

8. What is a guiding principle?

9. What highest level security principles regarding the key information assets and resources of an organization should every organization be concerned with?

10. Provide three examples of guiding principles.

11. List three events that would trigger a change to a company's security policy.

12. Describe the components of the Security Policy Life Cycle.

13. What are the titles of those who review security policy change requests?

14. What is an SME?

15. Why is it important for SMEs to review security policies?

16. Why should an organization's Legal and Human Resources departments review updated security policies and standards?

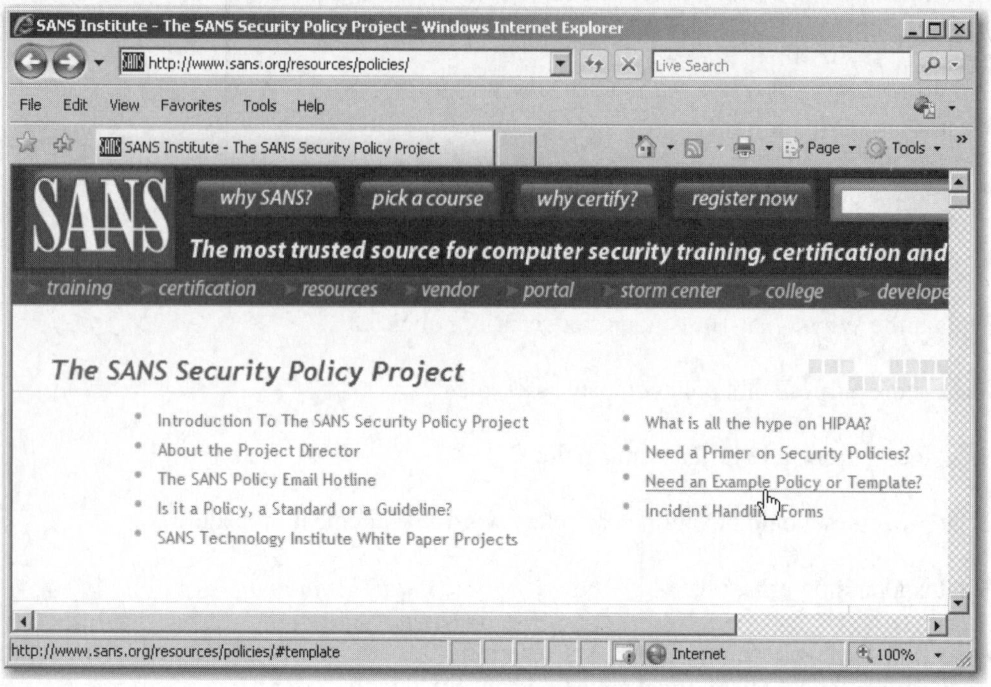

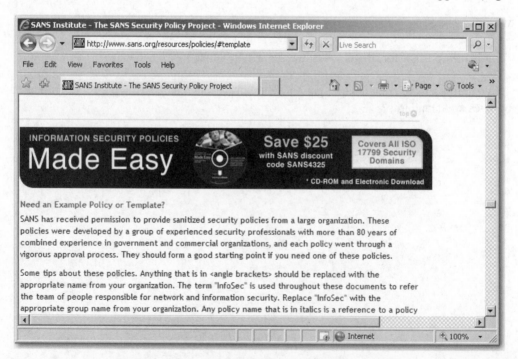

Figure 4: SANS home page with the *Need an Example Policy or Template?* link selected

Part Two: Customizing a Security Policy Template

1. Return to the SANS home page. Click the **Need an Example Policy or Template?** link located in the right column (Figure 4).

2. A page describing the security templates available from the SANS institute appears (Figure 5).

Figure 5: The SANS *Security Policy Project* page

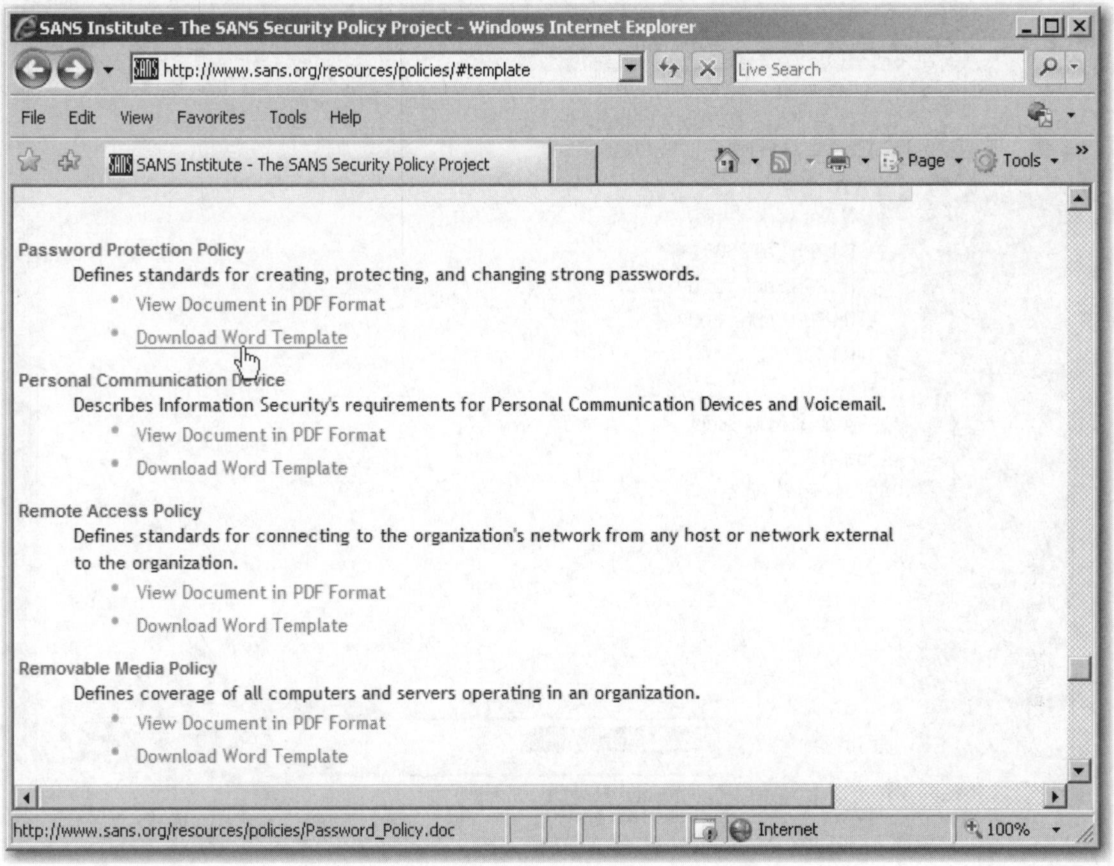

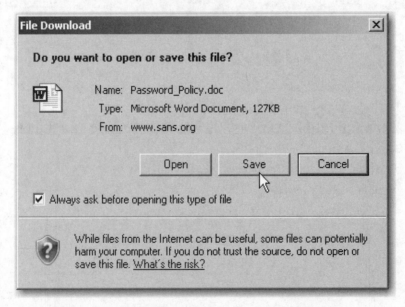

Figure 6: The SANS *Security Policy Project* page displaying the *Password Protection Policy* template and other template options

3. Read the information on this page and then scroll down this page until you see the *Password Protection Policy* template link. Click the **Download Word template** link (Figure 6).

4. The *File Download* dialog box appears (Figure 7). Click the **Save** button.

Figure 7: The Windows *File Download* dialog box

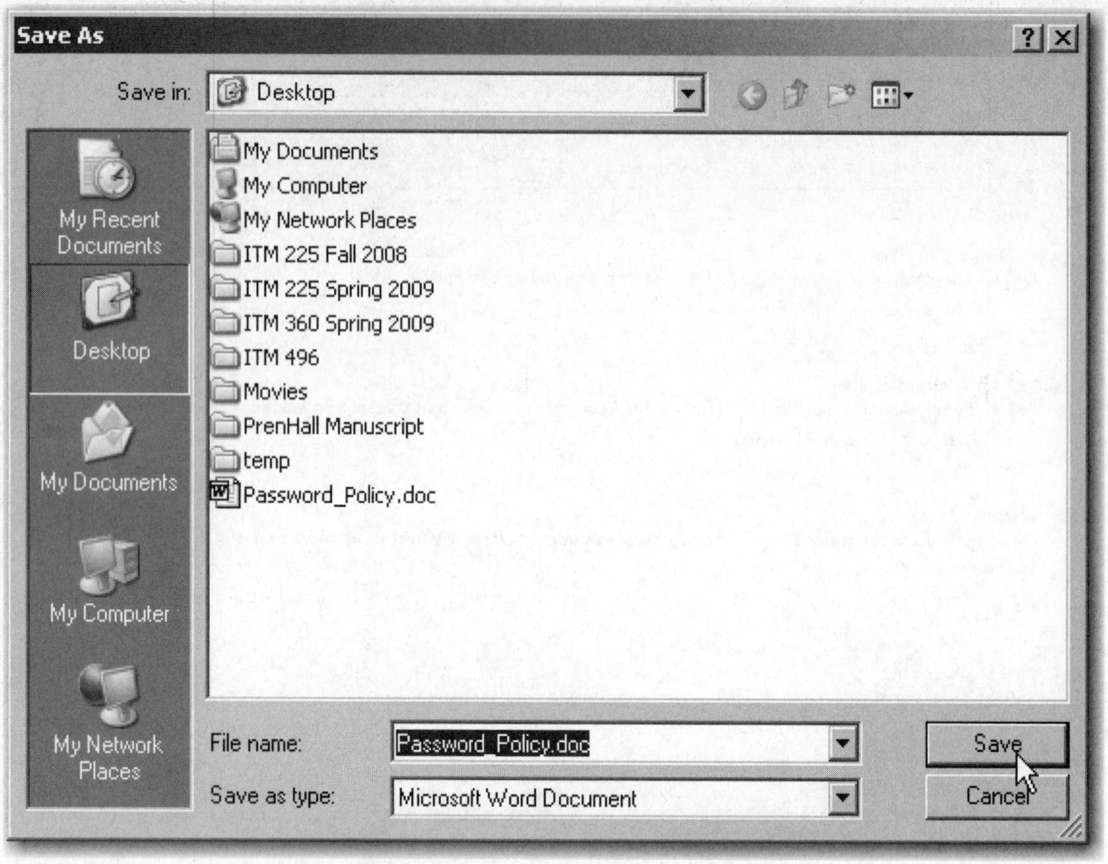

Figure 8: A Windows *Save As* dialog box

5. A Windows *Save As* dialog box appears (Figure 8). Click the **Save** button to save a copy of the *Password_Policy.doc* file to your Windows Desktop. The *Download complete* dialog box appears (Figure 9). Click the **Close** button on the title bar of the dialog box to continue.

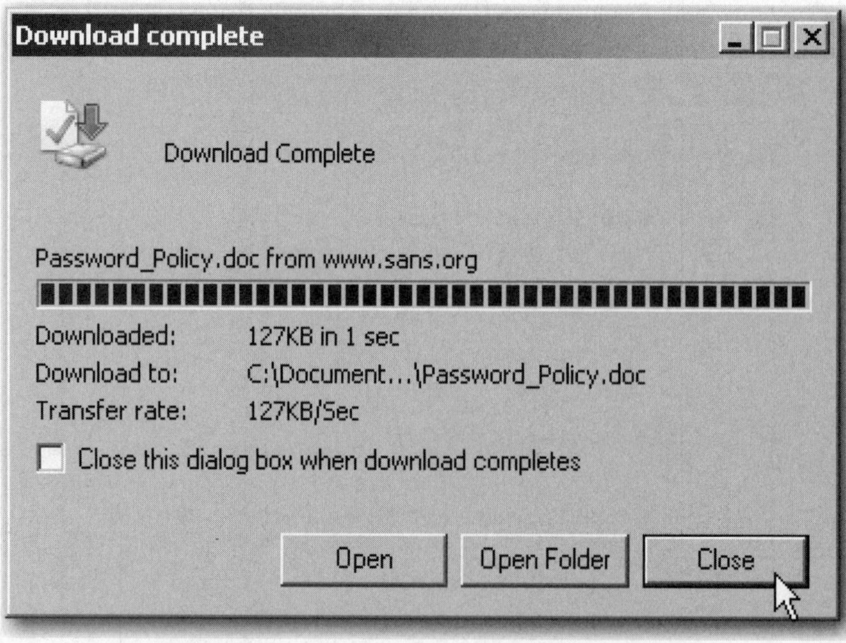

Figure 9: The *Download complete* dialog box

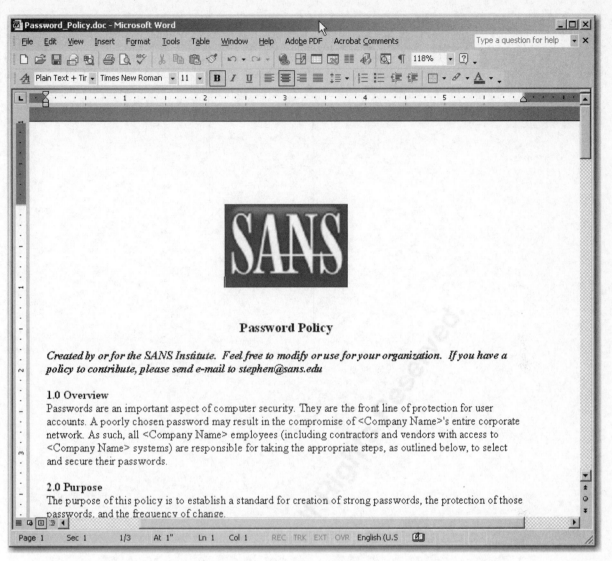

Figure 10: The first few lines of the SANS *Password Policy* template

6. Click the **Close** button on the Internet Explorer title bar to close IE. Locate the **Password_Policy.doc** file icon on your desktop and double-click the icon to open the file (Figure 10).

7. Read the document to become familiar with the guidelines and procedures that pertain to a company password security policy.

Questions

1. The Password Policy template contains numerous references to *<Company Name>*. Create a name for a fictitious organization and replace all occurrences of the *Company Name* tag with the name of the fictitious organization.

2. Does the password you use to access your organization's network meet the requirements for a "strong" password as described in this document?

3. If not, why not?

Submitting your Lab Report

Create a new page on your Google site and name it *Lab Fourteen Report*. Copy the questions in Parts One and Two and their answers to the Lab Fourteen Report page. Attach a copy of your modified *Password Policy* document to your lab report.

LAB 15: EVALUATING NETWORK PERFORMANCE

OBJECTIVES

After completing this lab you should be able to use the IT Guru Academic Edition Network Analyzer:

- ✓ to create simple simulation scenarios

- ✓ evaluate network performance on a simulated network

- ✓ display charts and graphs based upon simulated performance data

CONTENTS

HARDWARE, SOFTWARE, AND COMMUNICATIONS REQUIREMENTS FOR THIS LAB

- ➢ A Windows-based computer

- ➢ Access to the Internet

USEFUL LINKS

- ➢ http://www.opnet.com/university_program/itguru_academic_edition/

LAB 15

Introduction to IT Guru

This lab introduces you to a simulation program that you can use to learn more about the variables that affect network performance. The simulation program used in this lab is the academic edition of the IT Guru OPNET network simulator (See Appendix G for instructions describing how to download and install the software and activate the software license). IT Guru lets you measure and compare *load* and *delay* on both baseline and expanded versions of a simulated network. You will complete two tutorials in this lab: one to learn about the basic operation of the IT Guru software; and a second that describes the procedures required to create logical network scenarios, capture network performance data, and create output that will allow you to display performance differences in a meaningful way.

To start the IT Guru Academic Edition and complete the tutorials proceed as follows:

1. Click the **Start** button on the Windows Task Bar to display the *System* menu.

2. Click the **All** *Programs* option to display all menu choices.

3. Click the **OPNET IT Guru Academic Edition** choice to start the program (Figure 1).

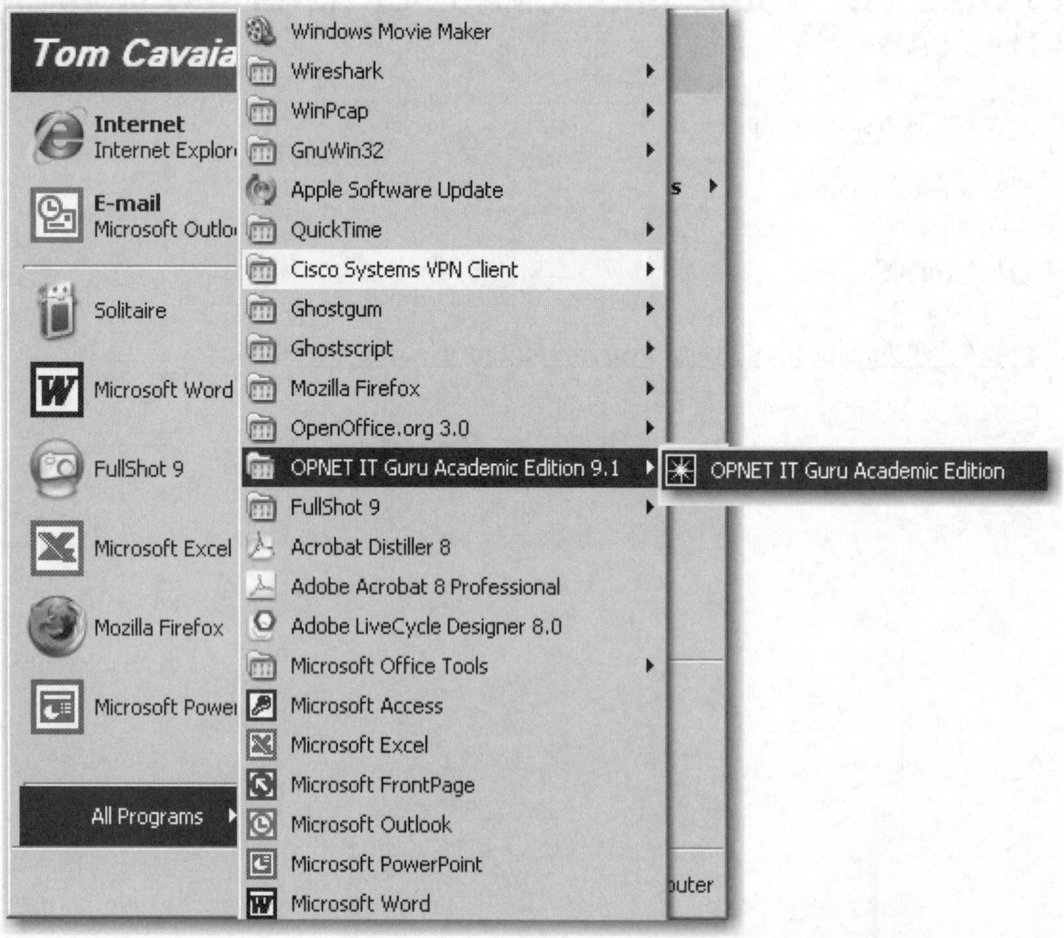

Figure 1: The OPNET IT GURU Academic Edition menu choices

4. A DOS window appears momentarily and then closes automatically. The OPNET *Restricted Use Agreement* dialog box appears.

5. Click the **I have read the SOFTWARE AGREEMENT...** button to accept the licensing agreement and continue. The *IT Guru Academic Edition* main application window appears. **Note**: If you click the **I DO NOT ACCEPT** button the program will terminate.

6. Click the **Help** choice on the menu bar. A dropdown menu appears. Click the **Tutorial** choice.

7. If *Adobe Acrobat Reader* is installed on your computer, then the *Tutorials* page appears.

8. If this page does not appear, download a copy of *Adobe Acrobat Reader* from the World Wide Web at **http://www.adobe.com/**, install it, and perform steps 6 and 7 again.

9. Complete both the **Introduction** and **Small Internetworks** tutorials. Consult the *Troubleshooting* link if you have difficulty obtaining the results indicated in the tutorials. Answer the following questions as you work through the tutorials.

Questions

1. List the four general steps that make up the workflow for IT Guru.

2. What is the main IT Guru staging area for creating a network simulation?

3. Briefly describe the IT Guru Workspace.

4. What action must you perform to display IT Guru Toolbar button tool tips?

5. What is the main goal of the testing to be performed in the Small Internetworks scenario?

6. What is the first step in creating a new network model?

7. Define a node.

8. Define a link.

9. What types of cables can be represented by IT Guru links?

10. Consider the following node/link model: 3C-SSII-1100-3300-4S-ae52-e48-ge3. How many Ethernet ports are represented by this model?

11. What procedure turns drag and drop object creation off?

12. What types of statistics can be collected during an IT Guru simulation?

13. What is the purpose of the repositories preference?

14. How much network activity, in minutes, is simulated by the Small Internetworks project?

15. What is the actual elapsed time, in seconds, for the baseline project when it runs on your computer?

16. What is the approximate maximum load value, in bits/sec, on the server for the baseline network, when its scenario is run on your computer?

17. After the baseline network reaches steady state, what is the value of the maximum delay in milliseconds?

18. What is the approximate maximum load value, in bits/sec, on the server for the expanded network, when its scenario is run on your computer?

19. In the expanded network maximum load graph window click the **down arrow** next to the text box labeled *As Is*. Select *time_average* form the list that appears. In your opinion does the expansion of the network add significant load to the network? Explain your reasoning.

20. Was there any significant change in Ethernet delay for the expanded network when the scenario is executed?

Submitting your Lab Report

Create a new page on your Google site and name it *Lab Fifteen Report*. Copy the answers to the questions to the Lab Fifteen Report page.

LAB 16: ELECTRONIC MAIL AND SMTP

OBJECTIVES

After completing this lab you should be able to do the following:

✓ Understand the basic SMTP command set

✓ Send a message to an SMTP server using SMTP commands

✓ Describe errors that might occur when connecting to an SMTP server or when sending messages to an SMTP server

CONTENTS

HARDWARE, SOFTWARE, AND COMMUNICATIONS REQUIREMENTS FOR THIS LAB

➢ A Windows-based computer

➢ Access to the Internet

➢ Access to an SMTP server

USEFUL LINKS

➢ **http://support.microsoft.com/kb/153119**

➢ **http://www.yuki-onna.co.uk/email/smtp.html**.

LAB 16

Introduction

This lab focuses on electronic mail and the *Simple Mail Transport Protocol* (SMTP). Electronic mail systems offer obvious speed advantages over traditional mail systems, allow users to send a single message to multiple recipients, and provide the opportunity for nearly instantaneous feedback upon receipt of a message. Such systems are based upon the SMTP protocol, one of the many protocols that belong to the TCP/IP protocol suite. SMTP supports a small command set. In this lab you will use these SMTP commands to send a message to an SMTP server. Although you would not normally send email this way, knowing these commands provides you with a means for troubleshooting problems that can occur on an SMTP server.

The Evolution of Electronic Mail

The concept of *electronic mail (e-mail)* predates internetworking. The first electronic mail systems were implemented on mainframe computers. Software running on the mainframe implemented the entire electronic mail system. Users had mainframe "mailboxes" and mail was "delivered" by moving messages from one mailbox to another. Mainframe e-mail systems supported local communication only. No infrastructure existed for sending mail to individuals not connected to the mainframe.

The first document describing an electronic mail protocol was RFC 196 published in 1971. It describes *A Mail Box Protocol* designed to send documents to remote printers. In the mid-1970s development began on a more comprehensive method of implementing email using existing application-layer transfer protocols, such as the *File Transfer Protocol (FTP)*. In 1980 the *Mail Transfer Protocol (MTP)* was published. This protocol used both FTP and Telnet for transferring e-mail.

In 1981 the *Simple Mail Transfer Protocol (*SMTP*)* was published. SMTP described in detail how mail could be moved from one TCP/IP host to another without using file transfer methods like FTP. Although SMTP retains certain similarities to FTP, it is an "independent" protocol running over TCP. SMTP has become the defining standard for email *delivery* on the Internet supporting the transfer of plain text messages and more complex file formats such as MIME attachments.

The SMTP Command Set

Like FTP, all SMTP commands are sent as plain ASCII text over a TCP connection established between the client and the server. It is helpful to know the basics of this command set so that you can better understand the underlying steps involved in sending email and because these commands provide a means for troubleshooting problems between mail clients and SMTP servers.

Command Syntax

The basic syntax of an SMTP command is *command-code [parameter]*

When parameters are used they follow the command code and are separated from it by a space. For example, the *HELO* command is specified with the command code, a space, and then the domain name of the SMTP sender. Table 1 provides a list of the SMTP commands used in this exercise and brief descriptions of each.

Table 1: The SMTP Command Set

Command	Parameters	Description
HELO	Sender's domain name	Initiates the SMTP session
MAIL	FROM: *message originator*	Specifies message sender
RCPT	TO: *recipient's mailbox*	Specifies message recipient
DATA	None	Message data is entered one line at a time followed by a carriage return. The last line of the message must be a *single period* followed by a carriage return
QUIT	None	Terminates the session and delivers message

Connection Establishment and Termination

Figure 1 illustrates the steps involved in transferring a message from an SMTP sender to receiver.

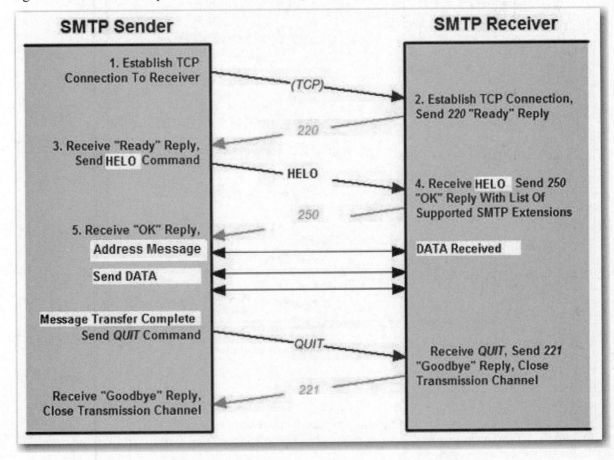

Figure 1: Steps involved in SMTP message transfers

Procedures

To send a message to the SMTP server using telnet[1] proceed as follows[2]:

1. Click the **Start** button on the Windows *Task Bar* to display the *Start* menu (Figure 2).

2. Click the **Run** option in the Start menu to display the *Run* dialog box (Figure 3).

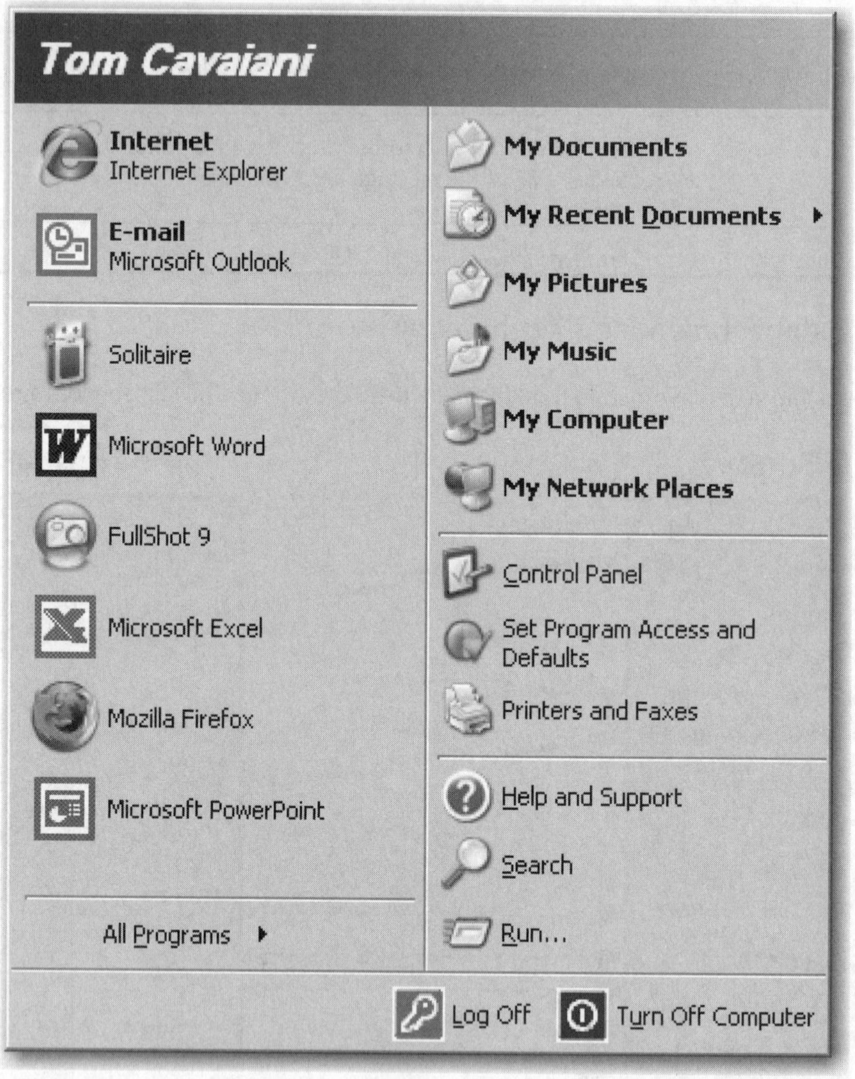

Figure 2: The Windows *System* menu

---

[1] If you are using Windows Vista for this exercise, you must first activate the *telnet client* software. See Appendix B for the details. As an alternative you can use *putty.exe* to start a telnet session (see Appendix F for installation details for putty.exe).

[2] If you are working from off-campus you must first connect to the lab network using the Cisco VPN client (See Appendix A for details on installing and configuring the Cisco VPN client software).

Figure 3: The Windows *Run* dialog box

3. Type **cmd** in the *Open textbox* (Figure 3). Click the **OK** button.

4. A command window appears (Figure 4). Type **telnet** followed by the **SMTP Server IPAddress** followed by a space and the number **25**, the SMTP port number. Your instructor will provide an IP address for the SMTP server. For this demonstration 172.16.100.98 is being used. Press the **Enter** key to continue.

5. Press the ALT and PrintScreen keys at the same time to capture an image of the command window. Paste this image into a Word document. Do this after each command you enter, so that you will have the images required for the report you will be creating for this lab.

6. You will see a message indicating that you are connected to the SMTP server[3]. You are now ready to send a message.

Figure 4: A command window showing a sample telnet command needed to connect to a SMTP server

---

[3] If you are having trouble connecting to the server, ping the SMTP server's IP address to test for connectivity.

7. Use the *Helo:* command to initiate your session (capture and paste the image)[4].

8. Use the *Mail From:* command to identify yourself as the sender (capture and paste the image).

9. Use the *Rcpt to:* command to identify the recipient of your message (capture and paste the image).

10. Issue the *Data* command followed by the content of your message (capture and paste the image).

11. Terminate your message by pressing the **Enter** key, typing a **period**, and then pressing the **Enter** key a second time (capture and paste the image).

12. Use the *Quit* command to end your session (capture and paste the image).

Exercise[5]

Follow the procedures above to send a message to an SMTP server using telnet and SMTP commands. Use the information shown below for the parameters required by the SMTP commands.

- Mail server name – *provided by your instructor*

- SMTP port – 25

- Sender email address – your email address

- Recipient email address – your instructor's email address

- Message data – Your full name and a list of the commands and parameters you used to accomplish the following:

  - ✓ Establish your session
  - ✓ Send the message
  - ✓ Terminate the session

Submitting your Lab Report

Create a report that includes the images you captured while completing the above exercise. Clearly label each image to indicate to which step in the exercise it pertains. Create a new page on your Google site and name it *Lab Sixteen Report*. Copy or attach your report to this page.

---

[4] Be aware that telnet is a terminal emulation program that sends every keystroke to the SMTP server. Typographical errors are not handled at all by telnet. If you make a typographical error and attempt to correct it by backspacing, telnet sends a non-printing backspace character to the SMTP server, which will include this character in the command string. Obviously this will cause the command to be misinterpreted by the SMTP server and it will return an error message. To avoid such errors be very deliberate when typing the commands and their parameters or create a text file that you can use for copying and pasting commands to the command line interface.

[5] Specific step-by-step instructions for this exercise can be found at either of the following locations: **http://support.microsoft.com/kb/153119** or **http://www.yuki-onna.co.uk/email/smtp.html**.

APPENDICES

APPENDIX A

INSTALLING AND CONFIGURING A VPN

Your organization's network is probably protected by a firewall that denies access to unauthorized users that may attempt to access it via the Internet. To secure their network many organizations require that authorized users access it using a *virtual private network* or *VPN*. A VPN is a secure tunnel through the Internet from a user's remote location to the campus network. Your network administrator can supply you with special VPN software that will allow you to set up a VPN on your computer. This appendix includes step-by-step instructions for installing and configuring Cisco's VPN client software on a Windows computer.

Installing the Cisco VPN Client Software

Registered users who hold a valid *Technical Support Services Agreement (TSSA)* with Cisco can download the latest VPN client software from the *Support* page of the Cisco site on the World Wide Web at **http://www.cisco.com/en/US/support/index.html**. You can register at no charge, but will probably need to depend upon your organization for the TSSA. Therefore the following instructions assume that you have obtained a copy of the Cisco VPN client software from your network administrator who has copied the software to a CD for your use. To install the Cisco VPN Client software proceed as follows:

1. Insert the CD containing the Cisco VPN installation files into the CD-ROM drive on your computer. Click on the **Start** button on the Windows *Task Bar* and then click the **My Computer** option (Figure 1). The *My Computer* dialog box appears. A list of system drives and folders is shown in the right-hand pane (Figure 2).

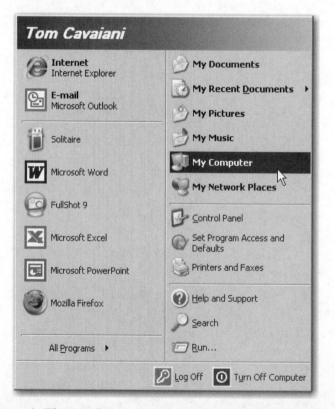

Figure 1: The *My Computer* option in the Windows *Start* menu

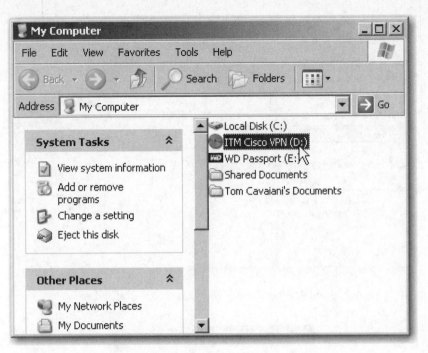

Figure 2: The *My Computer* dialog box listing available resources

2. Double-click the **Cisco VPN** icon (Figure 2). A dialog box displaying the Cisco VPN client installer executable file appears (Figure 3). Double-click the **installer executable file** icon (in this case it is labeled **vpnclient-win-msi-5.0.03.0560-k9.exe**) to begin installing the software. A dialog box prompting you to unzip these files appears (Figure 4). The installation files must be extracted (decompressed) before the installation process can begin. Click the **Unzip** button to continue.

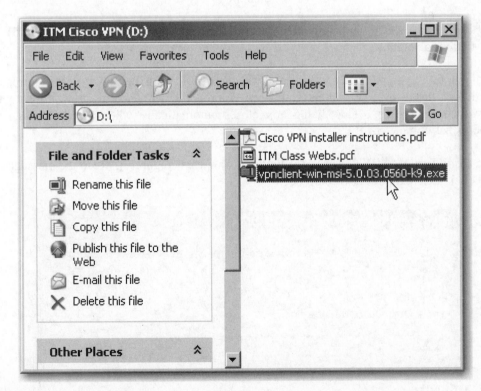

Figure 3: A dialog box displaying *Cisco VPN files* required for installing the VPN client software

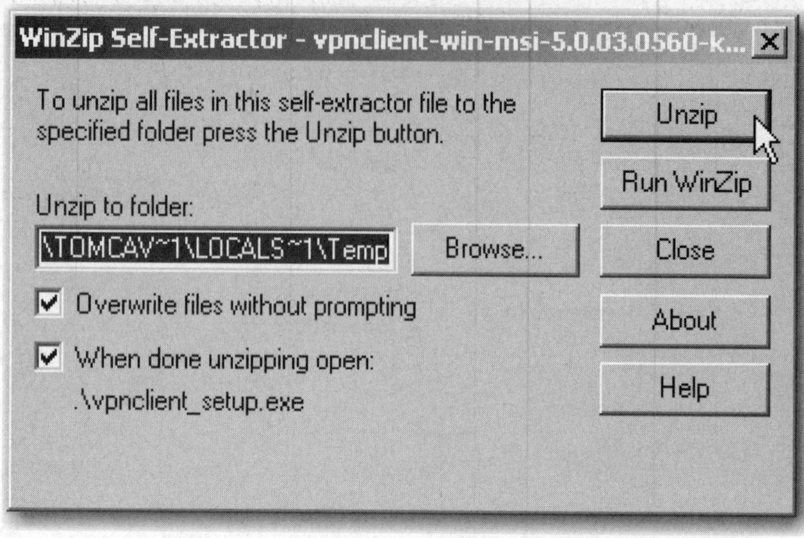

Figure 4: The *WinZip Self-Extractor* dialog box

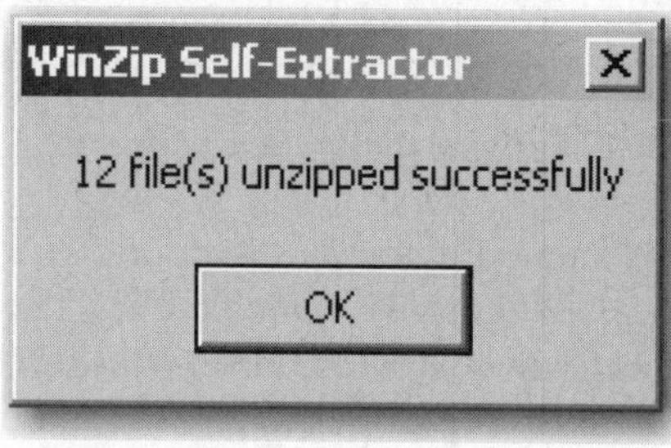

Figure 5: The WinZip Self-Extractor message box indicating that the files have been successfully unzipped

3. A message box appears indicating that the files were successfully extracted (Figure 5). Click the *OK* button to continue.

4. A dialog box appears briefly to indicate that the installer is gathering system information that is needed to install the VPN client software. A progress bar, as well as the time remaining, is displayed (Figure 6). This dialog box closes automatically when the information gathering process has completed.

5. The *Cisco Systems VPN Client Setup* dialog box appears (Figure 7). Read the messages displayed and click the **Next** button to continue.

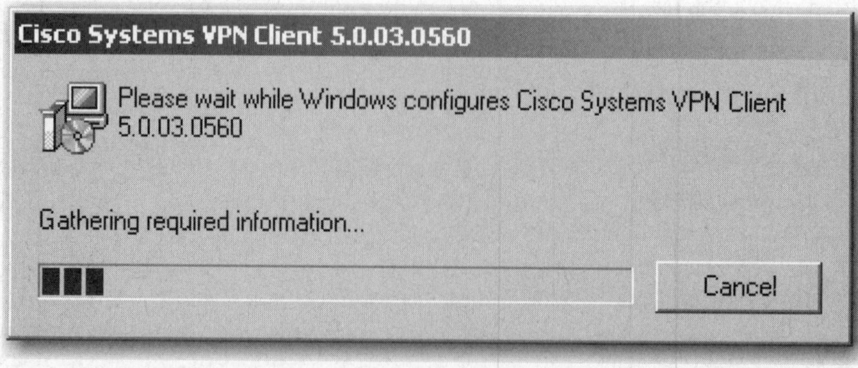

Figure 6: The Cisco VPN Client dialog box indicating that the installation information is being collected

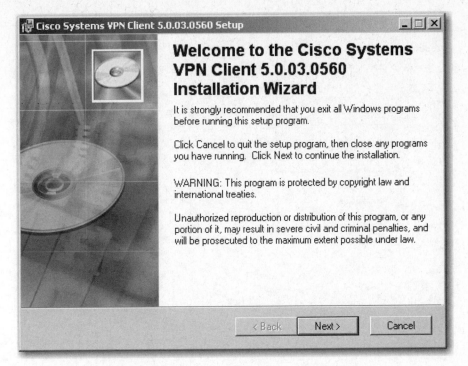

Figure 7: The Cisco *VPN Client Setup* dialog box

6. The *License Agreement* dialog box appears (Figure 8). Read the agreement. If you agree with its terms click the **I accept the license agreement** radio button to activate the *Next* button. (If you click the **Cancel** button the installation procedure will terminate.) Click the **Next** button to continue. The *Destination Folder* dialog box appears (Figure 9). You may click the *Browse* button to select a different location for this folder. It is recommended that you accept the default. Click the **Next** button to continue.

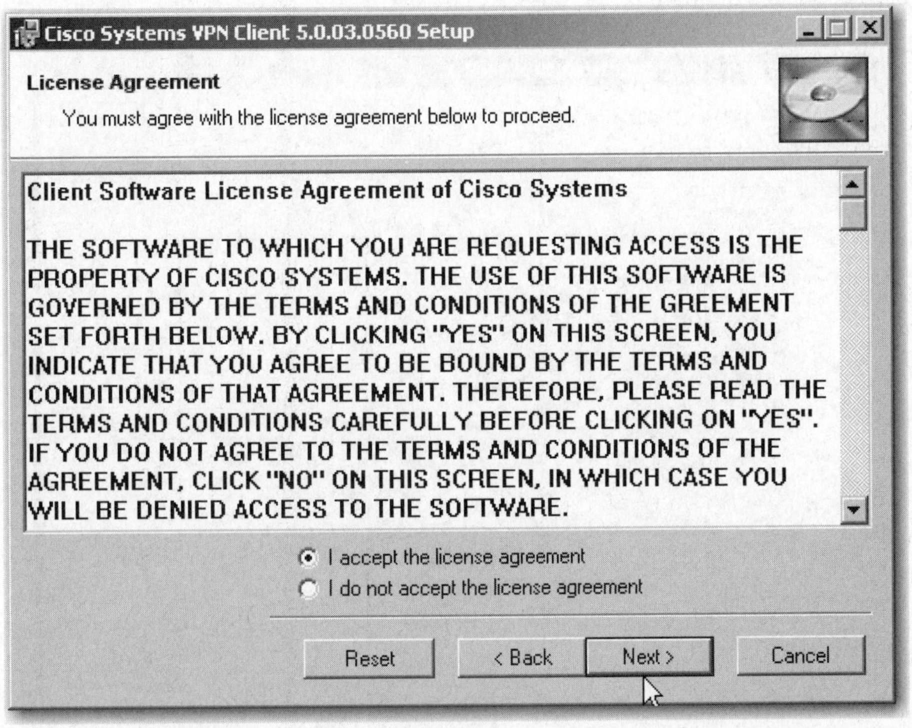

Figure 8: The VPN Client *License Agreement* dialog box

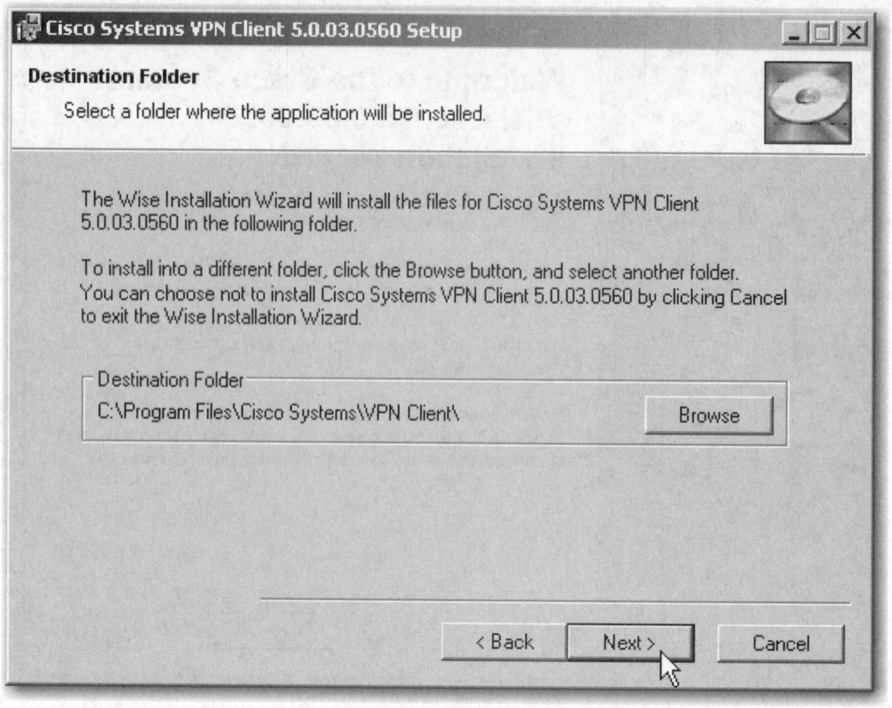

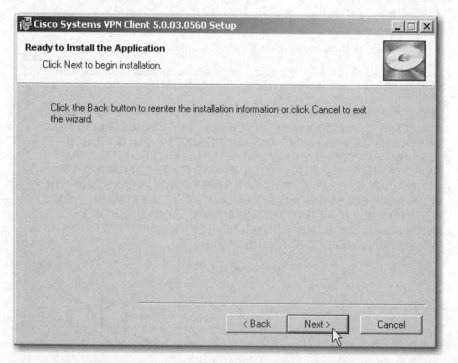

Figure 9: The Cisco VPN Client *Destination Folder* dialog box

7. The *Ready to Install the Application* dialog box appears (Figure 10). Click the **Next** button to install the VPN software. A dialog box indicating features are being installed appears. Messages will be displayed in this dialog box indicating the progress that is being made (Figure 11). When installation of the VPN software is complete this dialog box automatically disappears.

8. When installation is complete, the dialog box shown in Figure 12 appears. Click the **Finish** button to close this dialog box.

Figure 10: The Cisco VPN Client *Ready to Install the Application* dialog box

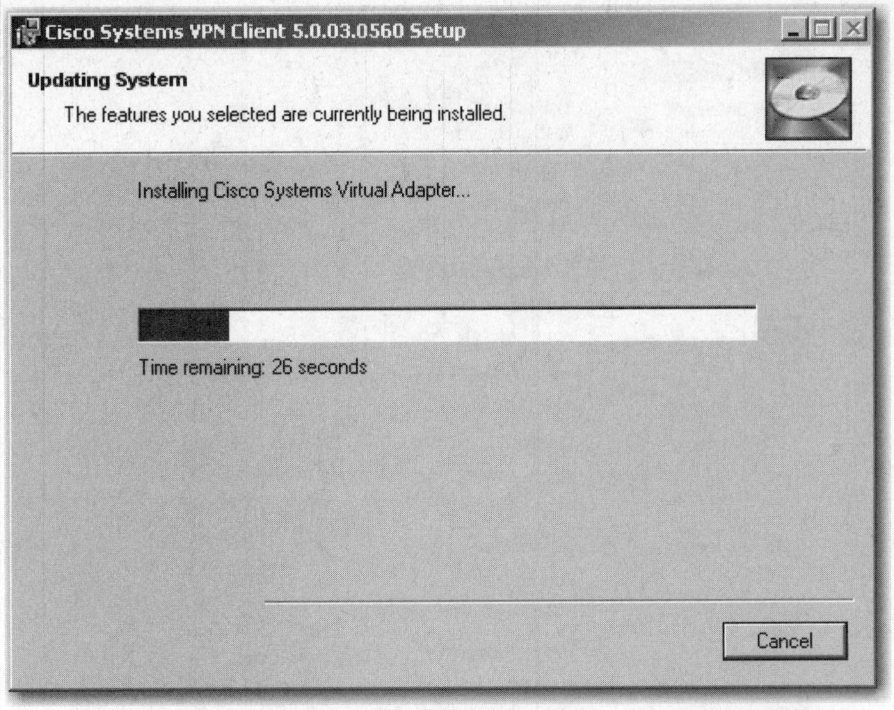

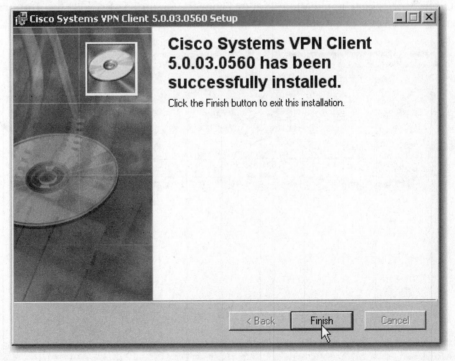

Figure 11: The Cisco VPN Client *Updating System* dialog box

9. The next step in the installation process is to import the *VPN Profile*. This file has a *pcf* extension and is stored on the installation CD. You must import this file while running the *Cisco VPN client* program. To start the *Cisco VPN client* program, click the Windows **Start** button and then click the **All Programs** option in the *Start* menu. Locate the **Cisco VPN Client option** in the menu (Figure 13).

Cisco Systems VPN Client
5.0.03.0560 has been
successfully installed.

Click the Finish button to exit this installation.

< Back   Finish   Cancel

Figure 12: The Cisco VPN client dialog box indicating the VPN client software has been successfully installed

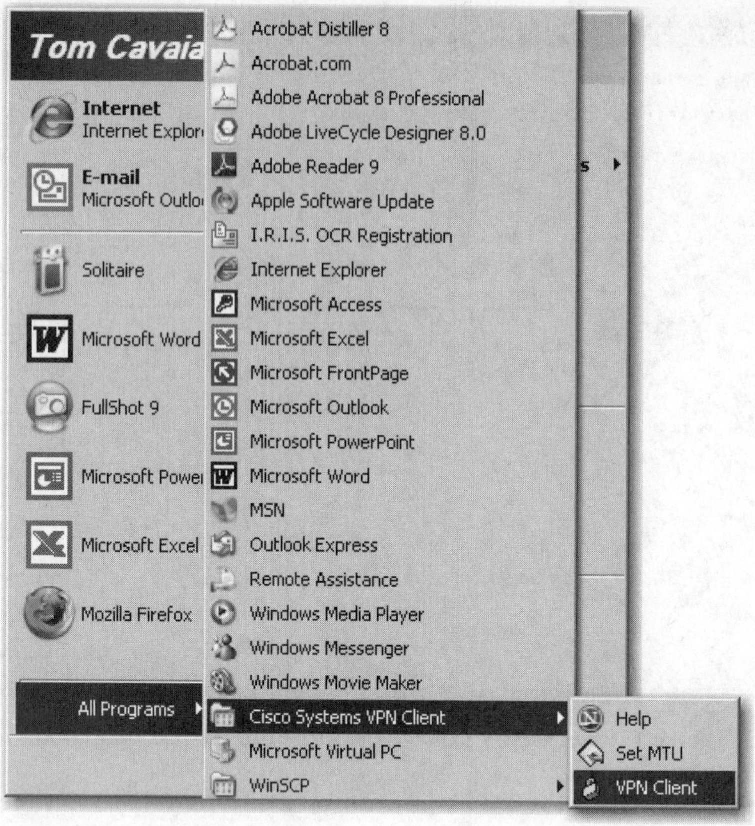

Figure 13: The *Cisco VPN Client* choices in the *All Programs* menu

10. Double-click the **VPN Client** menu choice to start the VPN client program.

11. The Cisco VPN client application window appears (Figure 14). Click the **Import** icon in the toolbar to continue.

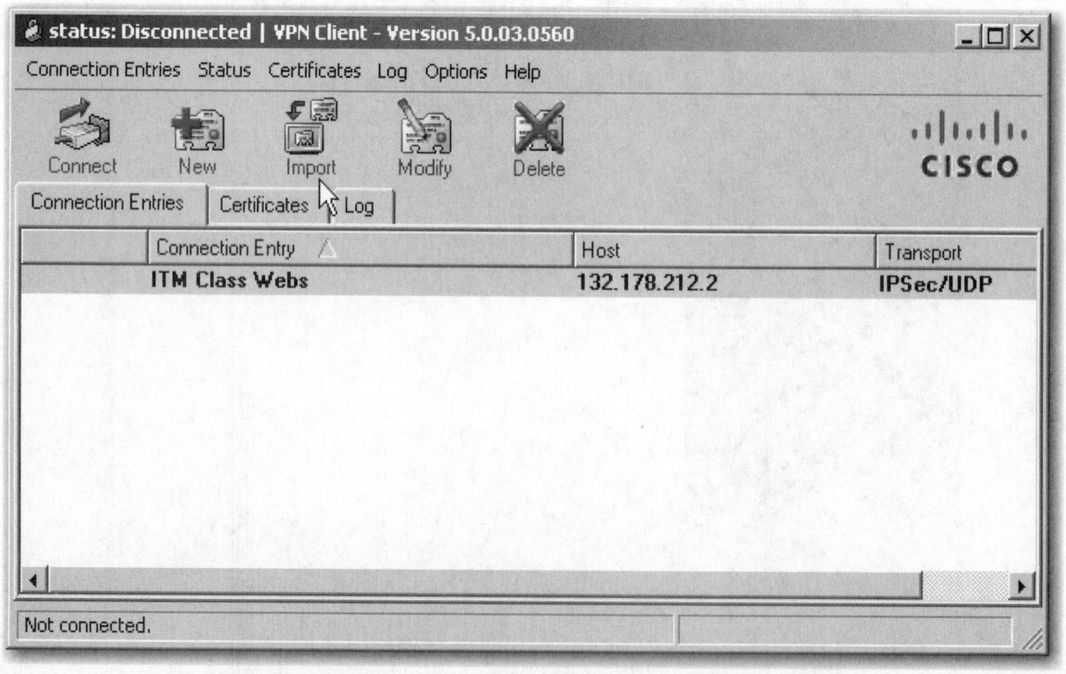

Figure 14: The Cisco VPN Client application window

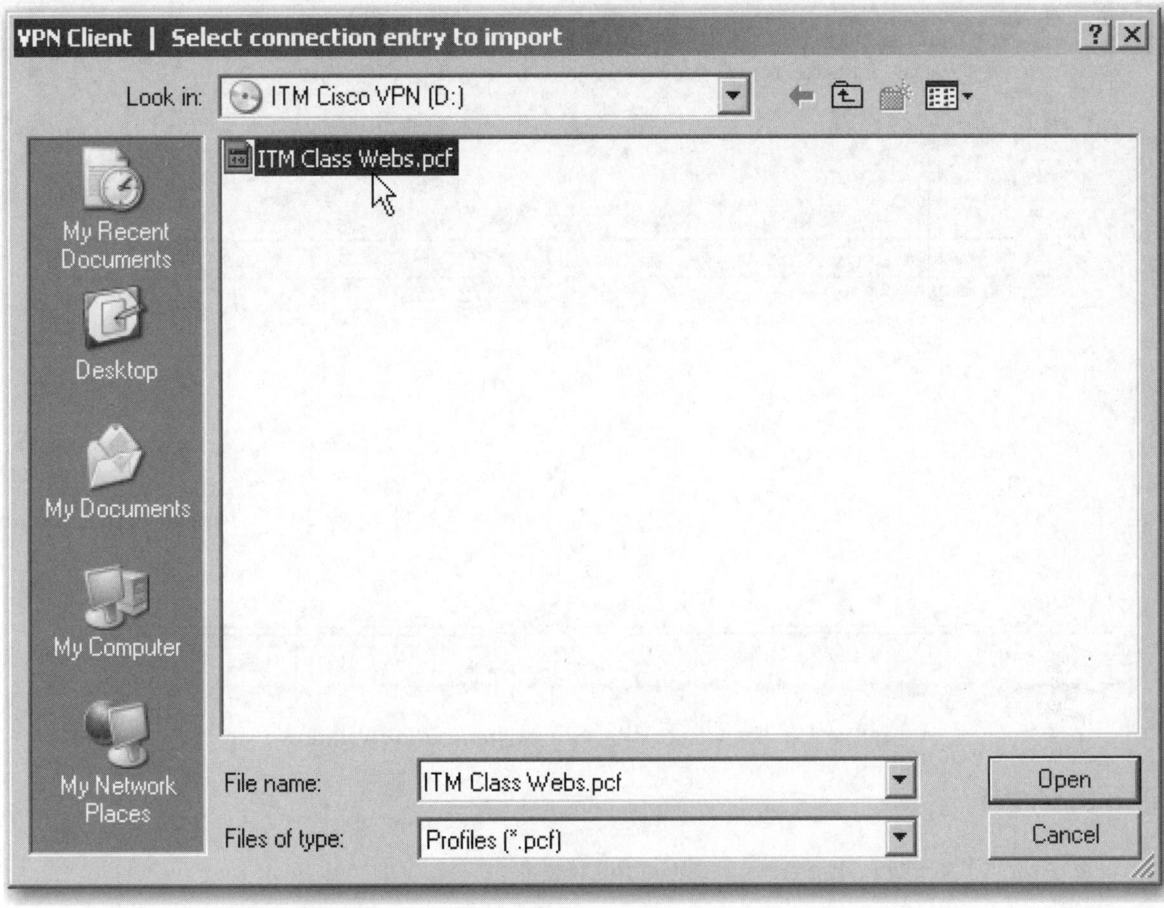

Figure 15: The *Select connection entry to import* dialog box

12. The *Select connection entry to import* dialog box appears (Figure 15).

13. Select the *profile* (in this case the ITM Class Webs.pcf file) and then click the **Open** button. If the *profile* is not shown, click the **Look in** text box's **drop-down arrow** to select the CD-ROM drive that contains it.

14. A dialog box indicating the profile was successfully imported appears (Figure 16). Click the **OK** button to close the dialog box.

15. The VPN client software is ready to use.

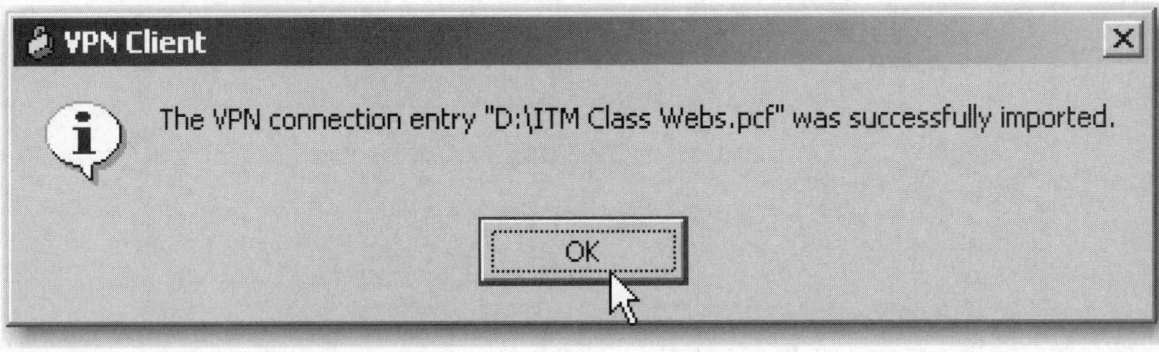

Figure 16: The VPN Client dialog box indicating the Class Webs file was successfully imported

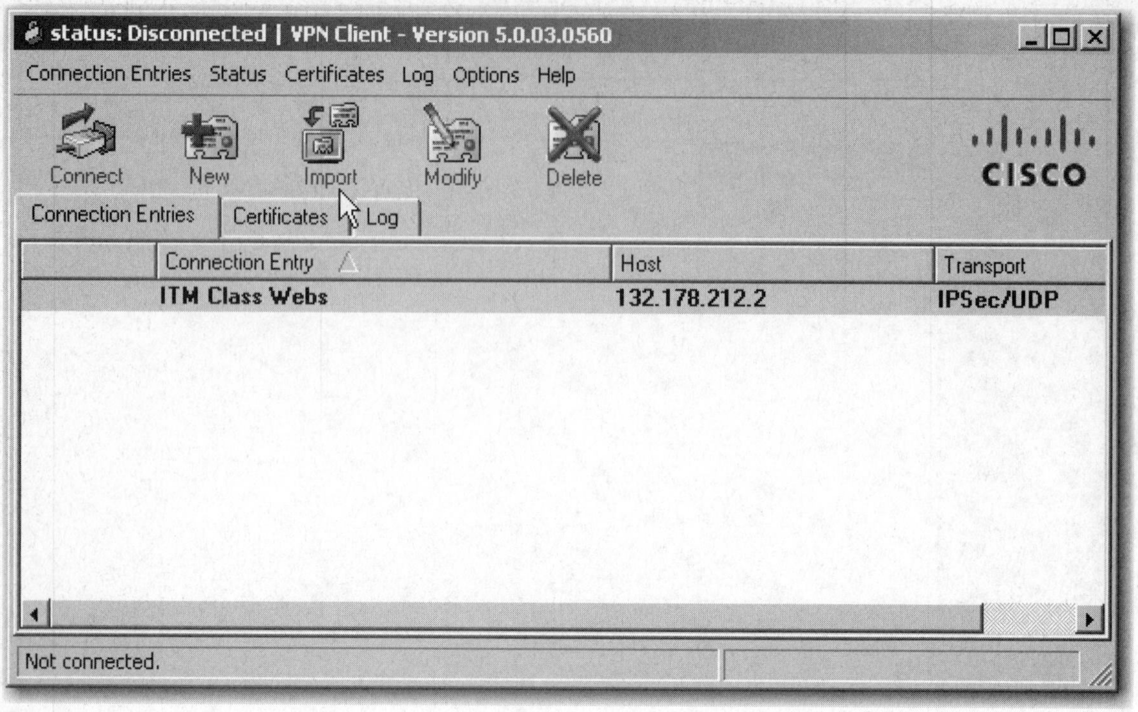

Figure 17: The Cisco VPN Client *Application* Window

Using the VPN

To use the Cisco VPN client software proceed as follows:

1. Start the Cisco VPN Client as described in step 10 above. The *Cisco VPN Client* splash screen will appear briefly. The *Cisco VPN client* application window will appear (Figure 17) after the splash screen disappears.

2. Click on the **Connect** icon to open the *VPN Client User Authentication* dialog box (Figure 18). Enter your **username** and **password** and click the **OK** button.

3. Once you have successfully authenticated to the network a *yellow lock icon* will appear at the right-hand end of the Windows Task Bar (Figure 19). This icon indicates that you are connected to the network. You can now run network applications from your home computer.

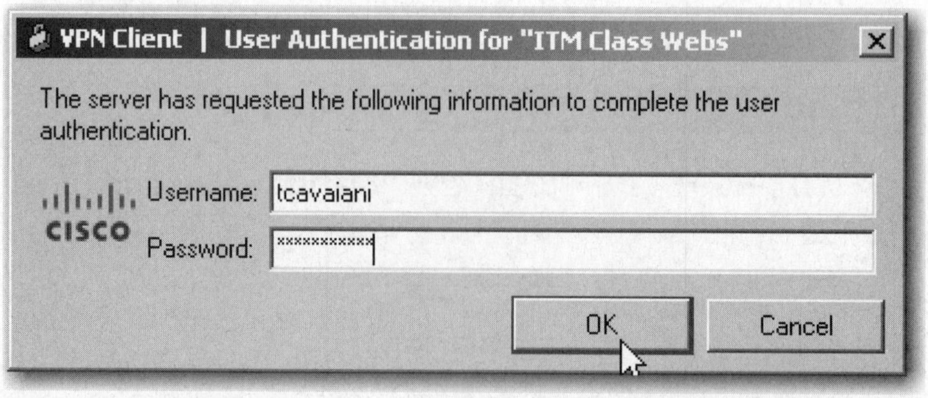

Figure 18: The VPN Client *User Authentication* dialog box

Figure 19: The VPN Client *lock* icon that is displayed on the Windows Task Bar

Authenticating to the Network

If you need to authenticate to a *Windows server* on your campus network from your remote location, you will first need to run the VPN client software as described above. Once you have established a VPN connection then you will need to run the *Remote Desktop Connection* software available as an accessory program in Windows. The following steps outline this procedure.

1. Click the **Start** button on the Windows Task Bar. The Windows *Start* menu appears (Figure 20).

2. Select the **All Programs** choice to display a list of choices.

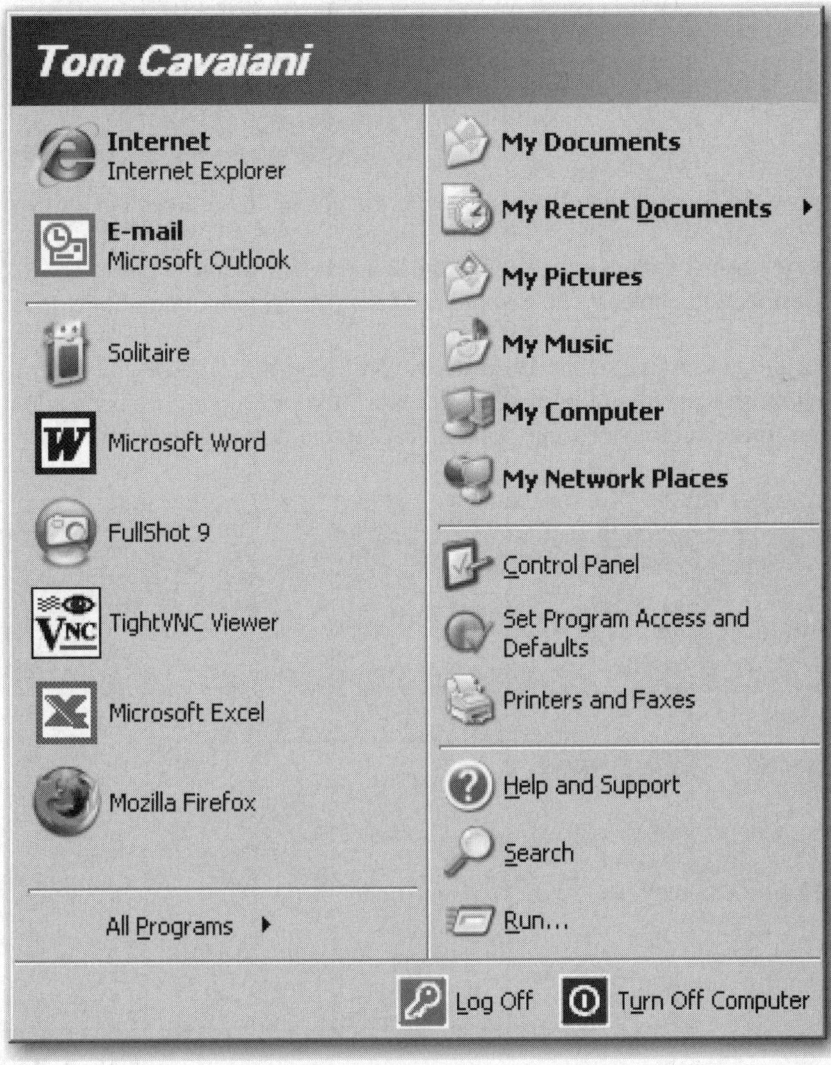

Tom Cavaiani

Internet Internet Explorer	My Documents
E-mail Microsoft Outlook	My Recent Documents ▶
Solitaire	My Pictures
Microsoft Word	My Music
FullShot 9	My Computer
TightVNC Viewer	My Network Places
Microsoft Excel	Control Panel
	Set Program Access and Defaults
Mozilla Firefox	Printers and Faxes
	Help and Support
	Search
All Programs ▶	Run...

🔑 Log Off   ⭘ Turn Off Computer

Figure 20: The Windows *Start* menu that is displayed when the *Start* button is clicked

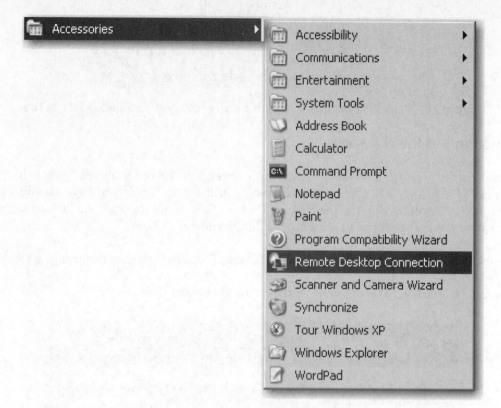

Accessories	►		

Accessories ►

- Accessibility ►
- Communications ►
- Entertainment ►
- System Tools ►
- Address Book
- Calculator
- Command Prompt
- Notepad
- Paint
- Program Compatibility Wizard
- Remote Desktop Connection
- Scanner and Camera Wizard
- Synchronize
- Tour Windows XP
- Windows Explorer
- WordPad

Figure 21: The *Remote Desktop Connection* choice in the *Accessories* menu

3. Select the **Accessories** choice to display the *Accessories* menu (Figure 21). Click the **Remote Desktop Connection** choice. The *Remote Desktop Connection* dialog box appears (Figure 22).

4. Enter either the **host name** or the **IP address** of the server to which you want to connect. Your network administrator will provide these addresses if your account has been authorized to connect to the server from a remote location. Click the **Connect** button to continue.

Remote Desktop Connection

Remote Desktop
Connection

Computer: `172.16.100.21` ▼

User name: ITM\tcavaiani

You will be asked for credentials when you connect.

[Connect]   [Cancel]   [Help]   [Options >>]

Figure 22: The *Remote Desktop Connection* dialog box

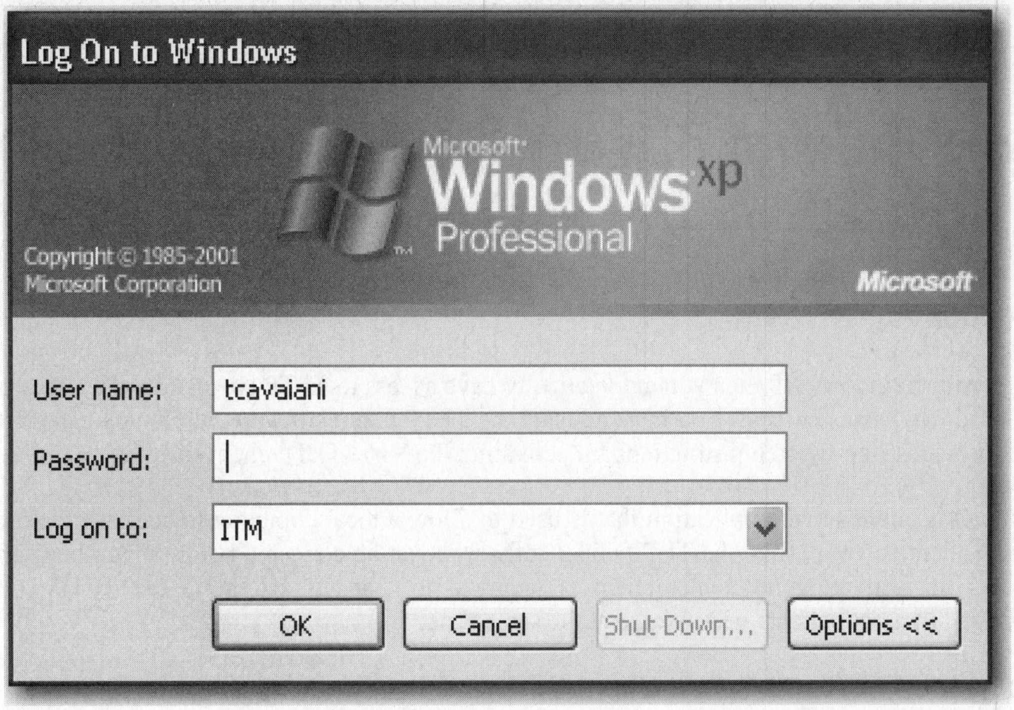

Figure 23: A Windows XP *Log On to Windows* dialog box that displays after the *Remote Desktop Connection* software has connected to the campus server

5. A *Log On to Windows* dialog box appears. Enter your **User name** and **Password** into their respective textboxes. Change the **domain name** in the *Log on to:* text box if necessary. Click the OK button to log on to the server.

APPENDIX B

CONFIGURING CLIENT SOFTWARE IN WINDOWS VISTA

Introduction

If you are using Windows XP then you automatically have access to TFTP client software. This is not the case in Windows Vista. In Vista you must activate the TFTP client software before you can use it. This appendix provides step-by-step instructions for activating the Vista TFTP client software.

Note: *Telnet* is client/server application that is used to allow a local computer to access a remote server. The Telnet client software, like the TFTP client software must be activated before it can be used. Since the process for activating the telnet client is identical to that for activating the TFTP client it is recommended that both clients be activated at the same time.

Installing the TFTP and Telnet Client Software in Windows Vista

1. Click the **Start** button on the Vista *Task Bar* to open the *Start* menu (Figure 1).

Figure 1: The *Vista Start* menu showing the *Control Panel* choice

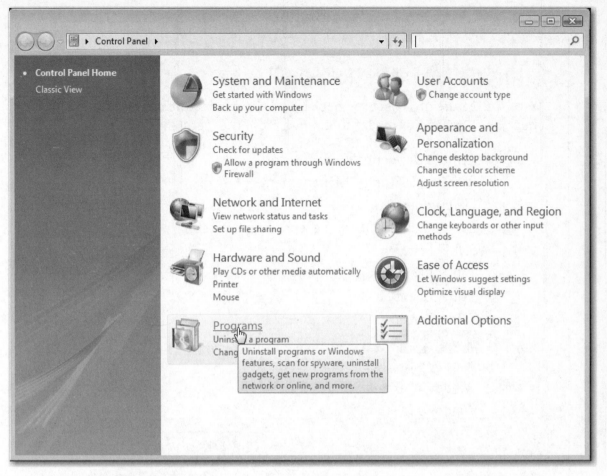

Figure 2: The Vista *Control Panel* dialog box with the *Programs* choice selected

2. Click the **Control Panel** option to open the *Control Panel* dialog box (Figure 2). Double-click on the **Programs** choice.

3. The *Control Panel – Programs* dialog box appears (Figure 3). Click on the **Turn Windows features on or off** option under the *Programs and Features* heading.

4. The Windows *Features* dialog box appears (Figure 4). Scroll down the list and check the box next to **TFTP Client** option. *Note*: You may also activate the **telnet client** at this time. Click the **OK** button to continue.

Figure 3: The *Control Panel-Programs* dialog box with the *Turn Windows features on or off* choice selected

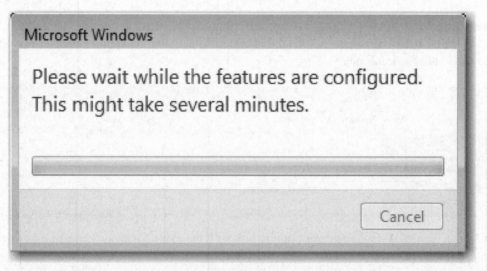

Figure 4: The Windows *Features* dialog box showing the *TFTP Client* and other options

5. It will take between 30 to 60 seconds to activate this feature. A dialog box (Figure 5) is displayed until this procedure is complete. Don't forget to close the *Control Panel* dialog box after the feature has been activated. You are now ready to use the Vista TFTP client.

Figure 5: Dialog box displayed while Vista activates the TFTP client software

166

APPENDIX C

RUNNING LINUX FROM A BOOT DISK

Introduction

Typically the Linux operating system is installed and run on a workstation. If you would like to learn more about Linux but do not have a spare computer or do not wish to install Linux on an existing computer, you have an alternative. Linux can be run from a bootable CD. This appendix discusses the procedures required to load and run the Knoppix distribution of Linux from the CD player on your computer.

The Knoppix software can be downloaded from the web and copied to a CD or DVD. The official Knoppix site is located at **http://www.knopper.net/knoppix/index-en.html**. This site explains what Knoppix is and how to obtain a copy either via a download or through a reseller. You will find a list of locations for downloading Knoppix at **http://www.knopper.net/knoppix-mirrors/index-en.html**. Resellers are available world-wide. You can locate a reseller at **http://www.knopper.net/knoppix-vendors/index-en.php**.

The bootable version of Knoppix is run entirely from either a CD or DVD and will have no affect on any system files installed on your computer. You simple insert the CD/DVD into a DVD player on your computer and then boot your computer. The Knoppix system files are copied into memory on your computer and used to run the operating system from the CD\DVD. When you have completed your Knoppix session you remove the CD\DVD from the player and reboot the computer to run the operating system installed on the computer.

How this Appendix differs from Lab 11

The information discussed in this appendix is very similar to that covered in Lab 11. The major differences are the distribution of Linux used — Knoppix here and Suse Linux in Lab 11— and the fact that Knoppix is running from a boot disk. The Knoppix interface and procedures are slightly different than those used in the Suse Linux distribution. Therefore the step-by-step instructions covered in the lab have been modified to reflect the differences in the Knoppix desktop interface and procedures. Except for these minor differences, the material covered in Lab 11 is identical to that covered in this appendix.

Running Knoppix

A bootable version of Linux is readily available from the Knoppix site on the World Wide Web. Consult Appendix C to learn more about obtaining a copy of a bootable Knoppix CD. To transform your computer into a Linux computer, simply insert the Knoppix CD into the CD player and restart the computer. If you have problems loading Knoppix from the CD, consult Appendix D.

Startup Screens

The Knoppix *Boot* window is the first screen to appear as files are loaded from the CD-ROM into computer memory. This window displays the Knoppix version number across the top of the screen and a message indicating that you must press the Enter key to start Linux from the CD. The message also indicates that you can terminate your session by removing the CD from its drive and restarting your computer to resume running the operating system installed on it.

Towards the bottom of the screen is another block message comprised of three lines of text. The first line indicates that you can press the F2 or F3 keys for help and boot options. The next displays the Linux Live CD version number, the URL to the Knoppix home page, and the product release date. A *boot* prompt is shown as the last line on this screen. Any special parameters that are required for loading Linux onto your system will appear after this prompt as you type them at the keyboard. An example of a boot parameter is "knoppix nodma". This boot parameter is required to suppress the error message "cannot find file system on CD". You will not know in advance which parameters are needed to make Linux run from the CD on your particular computer. Some trial and error may be required to determine the correct parameters. It is best to simply press the Enter key when initially loading Linux from the Knoppix Live CD and then record any error messages that are displayed. With the aid of the error message and a little searching on the web you should be able to find the appropriate parameter or parameters that are required to boot Knoppix from the CD. You may also consult Appendix D for more information regarding some of the more common error messages that are displayed and the boot parameters that are required to suppress these errors.

After you have determined which, if any parameters are required to get Knoppix to boot from the CD and have pressed the **Enter** key. a screen containing the familiar Linux penguin logo and a "Welcome to the KNOPPIX live GNU/Linux on CD!" message appears if the upper portion of your computer display screen. This graphic is followed by a line-by-line display of configuration messages that appear on the screen as information is loaded from the CD into memory on your computer. These messages will indicate which features are being installed and if the feature was successfully installed or not. For example, the network interface card on your computer will be configured with an IP address during this part of the installation process. If an IP address can be located and assigned to your computer's NIC, then a message indicating that this task was accomplished will be displayed. The configuration process will take a few minutes depending upon the amount of memory installed on your computer and the speed of your CPU.

When all devices have been configured this screen disappears and a dialog box displaying the progress of peripheral initialization appears. This dialog box displays the Knoppix version number towards the top of the window and a row of seven icons towards the bottom. The icons include a disk drive, wrench, a globe, a desk lamp, a monitor, a file folder, and the KDE logo, and represent different peripheral devices that require installation of device drivers to make them function correctly. Don't worry, none of these drivers will be installed on your computer's hard disk drive. Instead they are being installed on a "RAM disk" in computer memory that can emulate your computer's hard disk drive. This dialog box will disappear automatically after all peripheral devices have been initialized.

Preliminary Messages

You may see one or more preliminary dialog boxes during the boot process and that overlay the KDE desktop. One such dialog box is a language selection dialog box. Knoppix is available in German, Danish, Dutch, English, Spanish, French, Italian, Japanese, and Russian. The two-character country code abbreviations are shown on the language selection screen. Select your language choice from the available options by clicking on the appropriate country code. For example, you would click the *EN* abbreviation to run the English language version of Knoppix. After you have selected a language choice, the dialog box containing the language codes disappears.

The *What is Knoppix* dialog box appears after the language selection dialog box disappears. This page is a short presentation written by Klaus Knopper that describes the Live Knoppix CD and its features. Review the information in this dialog box to learn more about Knoppix and the features it supports. When you have finished reading this material, click the **Close** button on the right-hand end of the dialog box's title bar to close the dialog box.

Once these dialog boxes have been closed the KDE desktop will be fully visible. **Note**: Depending upon the resolution of your monitor you may need to scroll the screen to see the KDE task bar and desktop icons. If scroll bars are not displayed, moving the display is accomplished by positioning the mouse pointer on the appropriate window boundary and moving the mouse pointer in the direction you want to scroll the window.

The KDE Desktop

The *KDE Desktop* is available on most, if not all, Linux distributions. The KDE desktop has a similar look and feel to that of MS Windows. The desktop contains icons that can be clicked to run applications and a taskbar that contains a Start button and other icons that can be used to display different menus. Using the KDE desktop environment simplifies common file management activities. Creating new files and folders, copying and pasting files from one folder to another, and saving and retrieving existing files are just a few examples of the file management activities that can be accomplished.

The KDE Taskbar

The KDE taskbar is the bottom row that appears on the KDE desktop. It includes icons that, when clicked, display menus or dialog boxes that provide an interface to the available file management and system configuration functions available in Linux. The taskbar also displays the current date and time. Descriptions of the KDE taskbar icons and their purpose are listed below:

- *KDE Start button* — clicking this button displays a menu with an extensive set of options.

- *Program Configuration* (Penguin) — clicking this icon displays a menu for configuring network and Internet utilities, service utilities, shell interfaces, and setting the root password.

- *Window Management* — clicking this icon provides options for resizing the current window

- *Show Desktop* — clicking this icon displays the current KDE desktop

- *Home Directory* — clicking this icon displays files and folders in Knoppix home directory.

- *Terminal Program* — clicking this icon opens a command line interface window.

- *Web browsers* — icons for two web browsers, Konqueror and Weasel, are provided.

- *Open Office* — this icon provides access to a suite of office applications that includes a word processor, spreadsheet, presentation graphics, and other office applications.

Configuration

The *KDE Start button* and *Program Configuration* icons can provide most, if not all, the options required to configure your system from the desktop. The *KDE Start* button displays a menu system when clicked. This menu is quite extensive and provides access to numerous applications that can be used for configuring your desktop, as well as configuring your system settings. Some of the applications available include development environments, editors, emulators, games, graphics programs, on-line help, browsers to access to the Internet, a search feature, and applications for viewing system settings.

The *Program Configuration* icon provides access to specific tools for configuring selected system settings and services. When the icon is clicked a menu system with choices for system configuration, network/Internet, services, utilities, root shell, and setting the root password is displayed. Most of these choices have additional options that are displayed in submenus. For example, selecting the *Network/Internet* choice in the main menu displays a submenu with a *Network card configuration* choice that can be clicked to display a dialog box with options for changing the IP address on your computer or having it selected automatically using DHCP.

File Management

Files and folders are easily created. You may create files and folders in the Knoppix Home directory or on the hard disk or external disk drives attached to your own computer. Icons on the Knoppix Desktop provide access to your computer's disk drives. To create a folder, proceed as follows:

1. Click the **Home** icon on the KDE toolbar.

2. A dialog box displaying the files and folders in the user's Home directory appears.

3. Move the mouse pointer to the **white-space** in the *folder* pane of the dialog box and right-click.

4. A pop-up menu appears. Click the **Create New** choice in the menu.

5. A submenu appears. Click the **Folder** choice.

6. A *New Folder* dialog box appears. Type a *name* in the *Enter folder name* text box and click the **OK** button to create the new folder.

7. Creating a new file is similar to creating a folder. First right-click in the **white-space** of the folder where you want to save the file. A pop-up menu appears. Click the **Create New** choice.

8. A submenu appears. Click either the **Text File** or **HTML File** choice. The *Enter text filename* dialog box appears.

9. Type a *name* in the *Enter text filename* text box. Click on **OK** button to create the file.

Right-clicking a file icon opens a pop-up menu that includes numerous options. These options include *Cut*, *Copy*, *Paste*, *Move to trash* (delete), and Rename. You can also use you mouse to drag and drop files from one folder to another.

Viewing and Changing File Permissions

1. Right-click the icon of the file whose permissions you would like to change.

2. A pop-up menu appears. Click the **Properties** option.

3. A *Properties* dialog box for the selected file appears.

4. Click the **Permissions** tab to view the permissions for that file. Click one of the **down arrows** to display a list of permission settings. Click the new permission to modify the setting.

5. Click the **OK** button to finalize the change.

Browsing the web

The *Konqueror* and *Weasel* browsers can be accessed via the icons located on the KDE taskbar. These browsers provide access to the World Wide Web. Simply click the browser's **icon** to begin using it.

1. Click the **KDE Start** button. The *Start* Menu appears.

2. Click the **Logout** option to end your session.

3. A confirmation dialog box appears.

4. Click the **Confirm** button to end your session.

Exercises

Create the files specified in the following exercises in your Home directory.

1. Create a new folder and name it *Lab C*.

2. Open the Lab C folder.

3. Create the following files: *A.txt, B.txt,* and *C.txt*.

4. Capture and save a snapshot of these files. ***Note***: Press the *Print Screen* button on the keyboard to create a snapshot of a screen. Snapshots are copied to the clipboard. When working on ITM Linux, you will need to paste them into the Windows *Paint* program before you can view and save them. In Knoppix, a convenient *Save As* dialog box will appear, after you press the *Print Screen* button to create a snapshot.

5. Modify A.txt so that its contents are as follows: *This is a plain text file. Its name is A.txt.*

6. Close A.txt and save the changes.

7. Create a new *Open Document Drawing* by clicking on the *Open Office* icon on the *KDE* taskbar.

8. Open the drawing file by clicking *New* in the *File* menu. Select the *Open Office Draw file type*.

9. Create a *green Smiley face* and a *red rectangle*.

10. Capture and save a snapshot of this file.

11. Save the changes and close the file.

12. Rename the drawing *Smile* and move it to the Lab C folder created in step 1.

13. Change the *Permissions* for B.txt to *Read and Write* for all groups.

14. Capture and save a snapshot showing the modified permissions.

15. Create a new folder in the Lab C folder called *Special files*.

16. Move *C.txt* to the *Special files* folder.

17. Capture and save a snapshot of this folder.

18. Rename *B.txt* to *List.txt*.

19. Open a terminal window and send a listing of the files in the *Lab C folder* to *List.txt*. **Hint**: Open a terminal window by clicking the task bar icon. Change your directory to Lab C if necessary. Use the redirection option (discussed in Lab 10) to send a listing of the files in the Lab C folder to the List.txt file. **Note**: file or directory names that include spaces must be enclosed in double quotes (" ").

20. Capture and save a snapshot of the Lab C folder. Create a report that contains all the snapshots you captured while performing the above procedures. Copy this report to a new page on your Google site using the *FireFox* browser. (*Note*: Unfortunately Konqueror, the default browser in Knoppix, does not fully support file transfers to Google pages). If the *FireFox* browser is not available, copy the file to a thumb drive and then transfer it to your Google site using a Windows browser. Name the Google page Lab C. *Note*: To copy an image to your Google page you must use the *Insert* option available in *Edit* mode.

21. Close all dialog boxes and terminate your session.

APPENDIX D

TROUBLESHOOTING KNOPPIX

This appendix provides information for solving some of the more common problems that may occur when loading Knoppix onto your computer from a bootable DVD.

Knoppix Boot Screen Does Not Appear

If the Knoppix boot window does not appear, restart your computer again and change the BIOS settings on your computer so that the DVD player is the first boot device. BIOS settings can be accessed by pressing either the **F2** or **DEL** keys on your keyboard after the monitor displays the startup screen when you power-on your computer. Once the BIOS menu appears, look for the *Boot* option. Click the **Boot** option to display a list of bootable devices. Make the DVD the first bootable device and save the changes (usually be pressing F10).

Knoppix Boot Screen Goes Black During Boot Process

If the Knoppix boot screen appears, but goes black when you press the **Enter** key, restart your computer and type *knoppix pci = nommconf* at the boot prompt and press the **Enter** key.

Cannot Find CD Error Message

If the Knoppix boot screen appears and the system begins to initialize devices, but fails with a message like "cannot find file system on CD" or hangs and displays a message like "looking for CD in: /dev/hdc", restart your computer and type **knoppix nodma** at the boot prompt and press the **Enter** key.

Mouse Does Not Work

If the Knoppix mouse pointer appears in the center of the Knoppix window, and your Windows mouse pointer is still functional when you move the mouse, restart Knoppix and type **Knoppix i8942.noloop** at the boot prompt. This problem typically occurs if you are running Knoppix on a *virtual* machine.

CD Configuration Issues

If you are still not able to boot from the DVD open the **Device Manager** in Windows and disable digital playback for CD audio. Proceed as follows:

1. Click the Windows **Start** button to open the *Start* menu (Figure 1).

2. Right-click the **My Computer** option to display the *Properties* dialog box.

3. Click on the *Manage* option. The *Computer Management* dialog box appears (Figure 2).

4. Click on the **Device Manager** option.

5. A list of devices appears in the right pane.

6. Click the + sign next to *DVD/CD-ROM drives* option to expand this option.

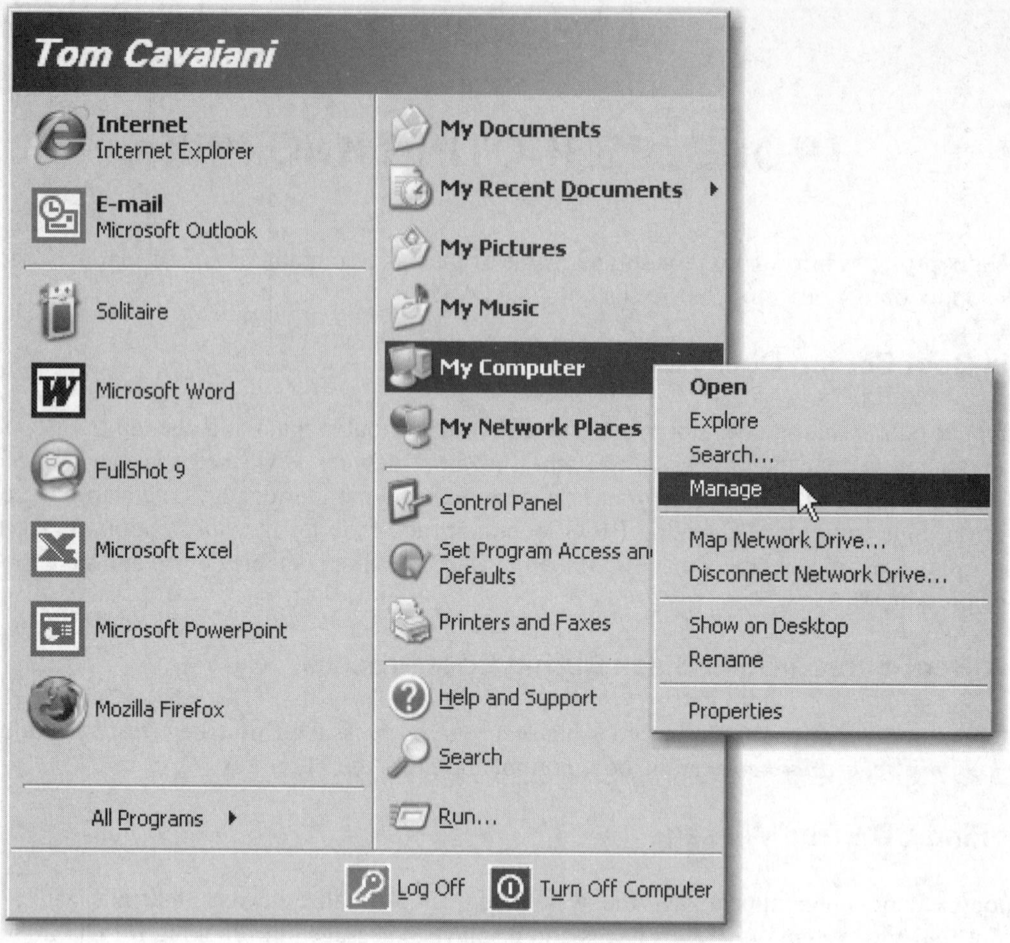

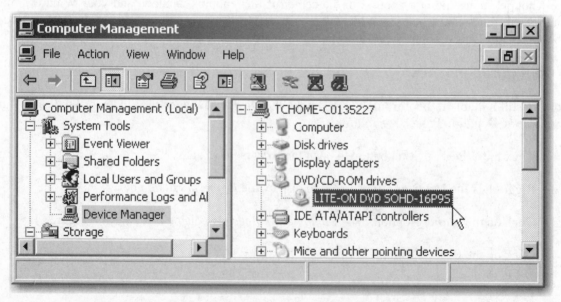

Figure 1: The *My Computer* pop-up menu with the *Manage* option selected

7. Right-click the named **DVD/CD-ROM drive** shown below the *DVD/CD-ROM drives* icon (Figure 2) to display the *Properties* pop-up menu (Figure 3).

Figure 2: The *Computer Management* dialog box showing a DVD device

174

Figure 3: The DVD/CD-ROM drives pop-up menu with the *Properties* option selected

8. Click the **Properties** tab (Figure 3). In the dialog box that appears click on the **Enable digital CD audio for this CD-ROM device** to clear the checkbox (Figure 4). This will disable digital playback for CD audio.

LITE-ON DVD SOHD-16P9S Properties

| General | Properties | DVD Region | Volumes | Driver | Details |

These settings determine the way in which Windows uses this CD-ROM for playing CD music.

CD Player Volume

Low ———————————————————— High

Digital CD Playback

You can have Windows use digital instead of analog playback of CD audio. This feature may not work with all CD-ROM devices, disable if you are having problems with CD audio.

☑ Enable digital CD audio for this CD-ROM device.

OK   Cancel

Figure 4: The *Properties* dialog box for a specific DVD device

APPENDIX E

INSTALLING WIRESHARK

Introduction

This appendix covers downloading, installing, and configuring Wireshark. Wireshark is an open-source protocol analyzer that can be used for capturing network traffic for troubleshooting and packet analysis purposes. You can download it free of charge and the download site is easy to find by performing a simple Google search. For your convenience the URL for Wireshark's home page, **http://www.Wireshark.org/download.html**, is provided here.

Downloading Wireshark

To download Wireshark on your computer proceed as follows:

1. Open Internet Explorer and enter the above URL into its *Locator* text box. Click the **Go to** button. The Wireshark home page appears (Figure 1). Scroll down this page until you see a list of stable Wireshark releases (Figure 2). Click the **Windows Installer** choice.

Figure 1: *The Wireshark* home page

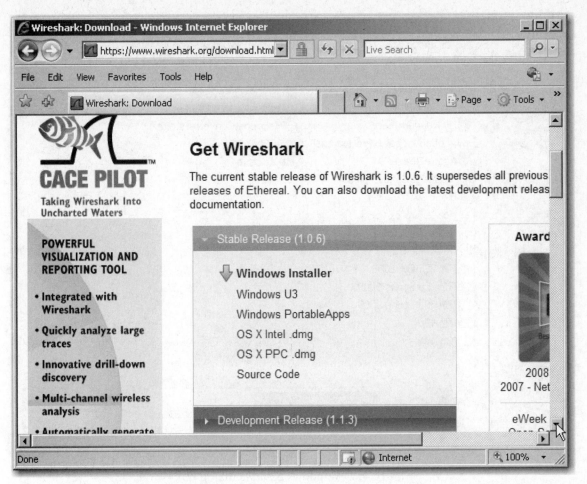

Figure 2: The more popular Wireshark platforms and associated download sites

2. The Windows *File Download – Security Warning* dialog box appears (Figure 3). If you want to know more about the risk of downloading this file click the **What's the risk** link.

3. Click the **Save** button to continue. A Windows *Save As* dialog box appears (Figure 4).

Figure 3: The Windows *File Download – Security Warning* dialog box

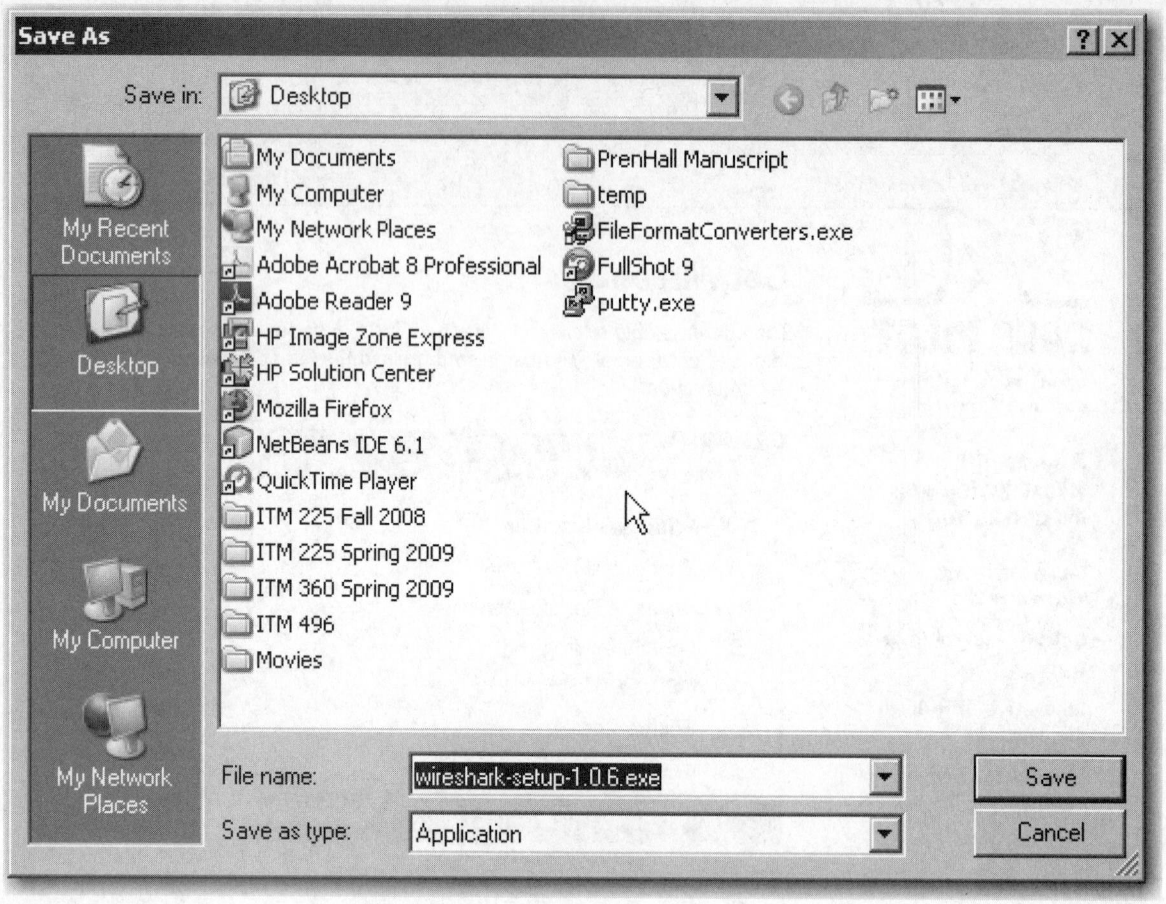

Figure 4: A Windows *Save As* dialog box

4. Click the **Save** button to download the Wireshark installation file to your computer. A *download progress* dialog box appears (Figure 5). This dialog box will display the amount of time left before the download is complete. A dialog box indicating that the download is complete eventually appears (Figure 6). Click the **Close** button to continue.

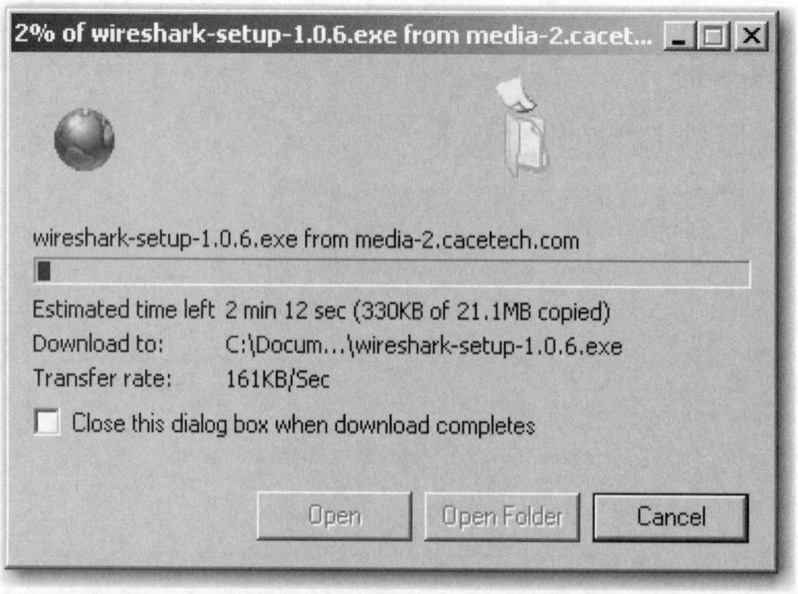

Figure 5: A dialog box displaying download progress

Download complete

Download Complete

wireshark-setup-1.0.6.exe from media-2.cacetech.com

Downloaded:	21.1MB in 2 min 23 sec
Download to:	C:\Docum...\wireshark-setup-1.0.6.exe
Transfer rate:	151KB/Sec

☐ Close this dialog box when download completes

[Run] [Open Folder] [Close]

Figure 6: The *Download complete* dialog box

Installing Wireshark

5. A Wireshark setup icon has been downloaded to your desktop (See Figure 7). Double-click this **icon** to begin installing Wireshark. The *Open File – Security Warning* dialog box appears (Figure 8). If you want to know more about digital signatures and security click the **How can I decide what software to run?** link. Click the **Run** button to open the Wireshark Setup Wizard (Figure 9).

wireshark-setup-1.0.6.exe

Figure 7: The Wireshark setup icon

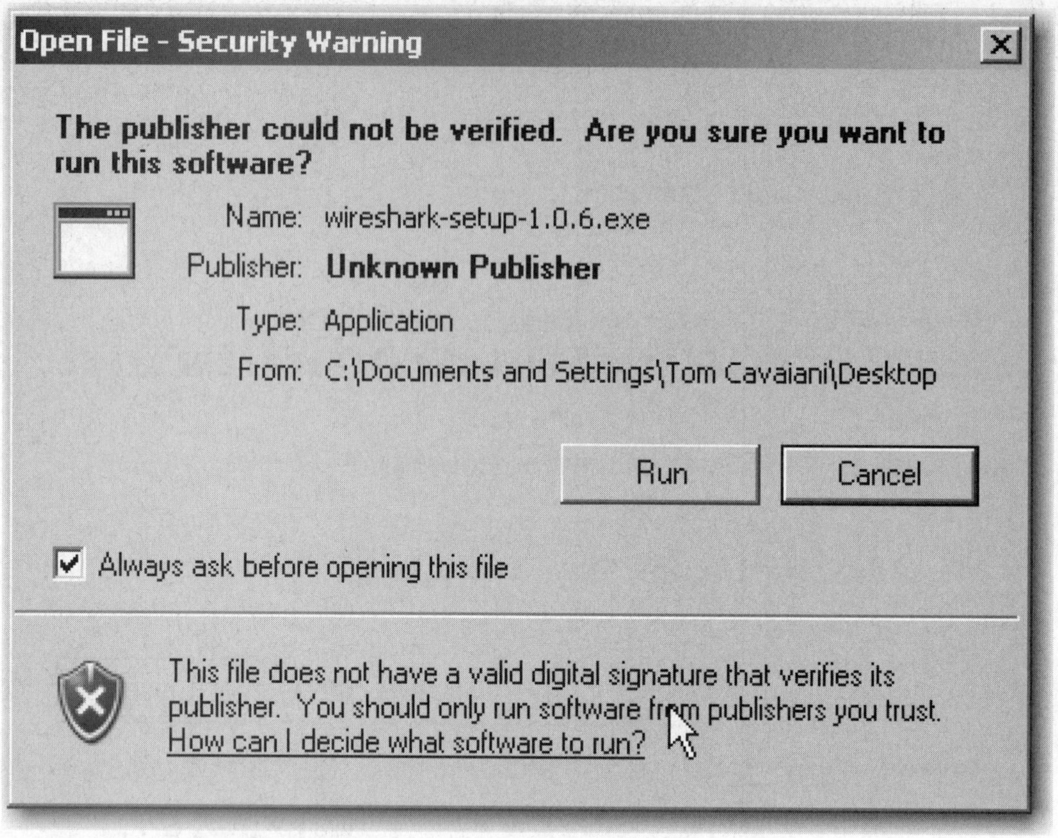

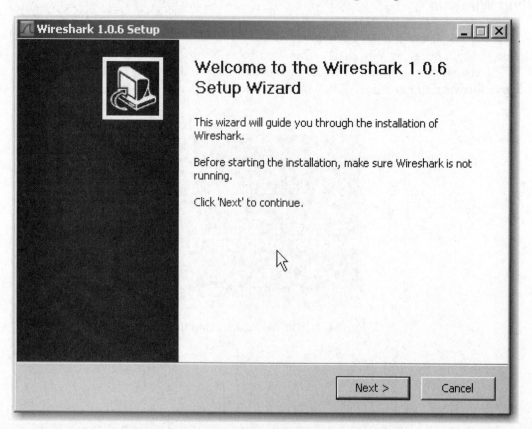

Figure 8: The *Open File – Security Warning* dialog box

Figure 9: The Wireshark *Setup Wizard* dialog box

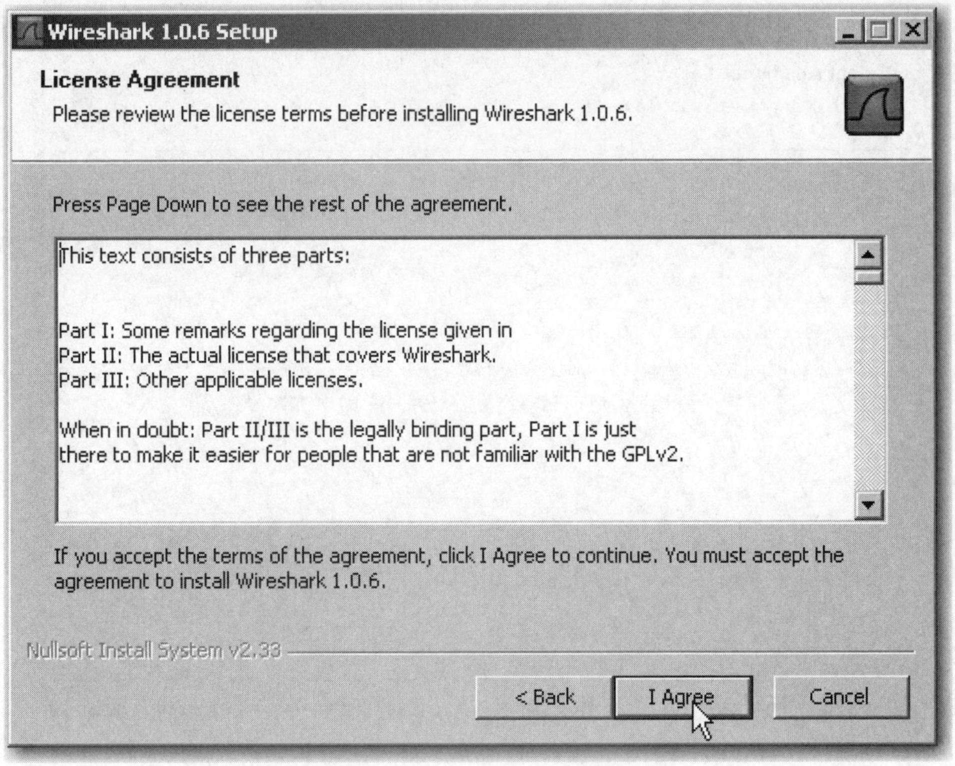

Figure 10: The Wireshark *License Agreement* dialog box

6. Click the **Next** button to continue. The Wireshark *License Agreement* dialog box appears (Figure 10). Read the agreement and click the **I Agree** button to continue. If you click the **Cancel** button the installation process will be terminated.

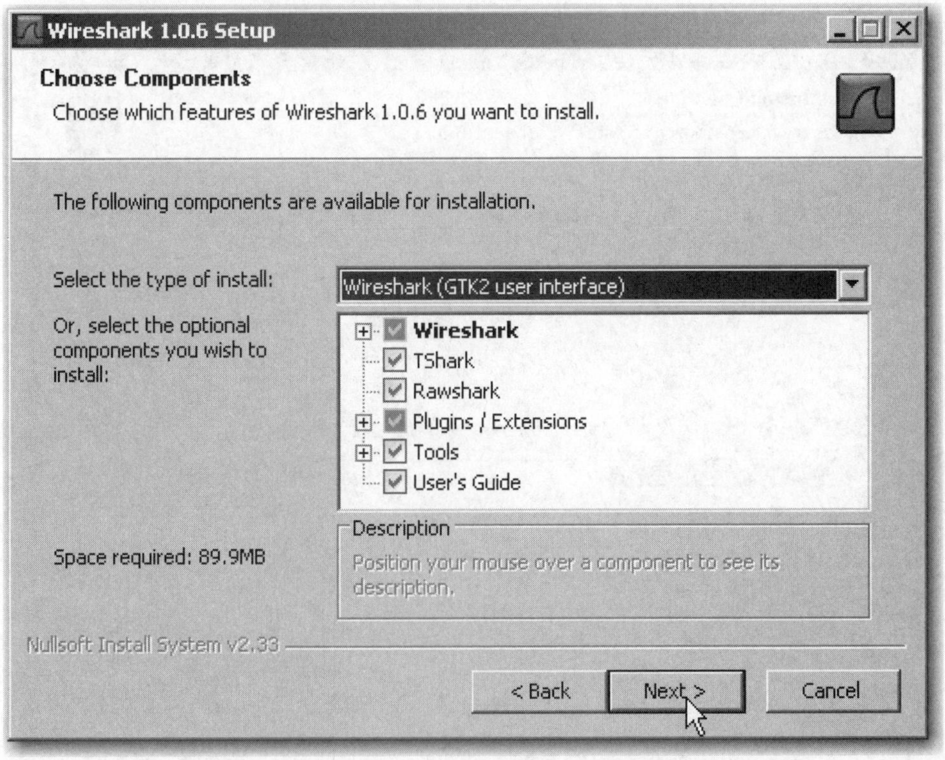

Figure 11: The *Choose Components* dialog box

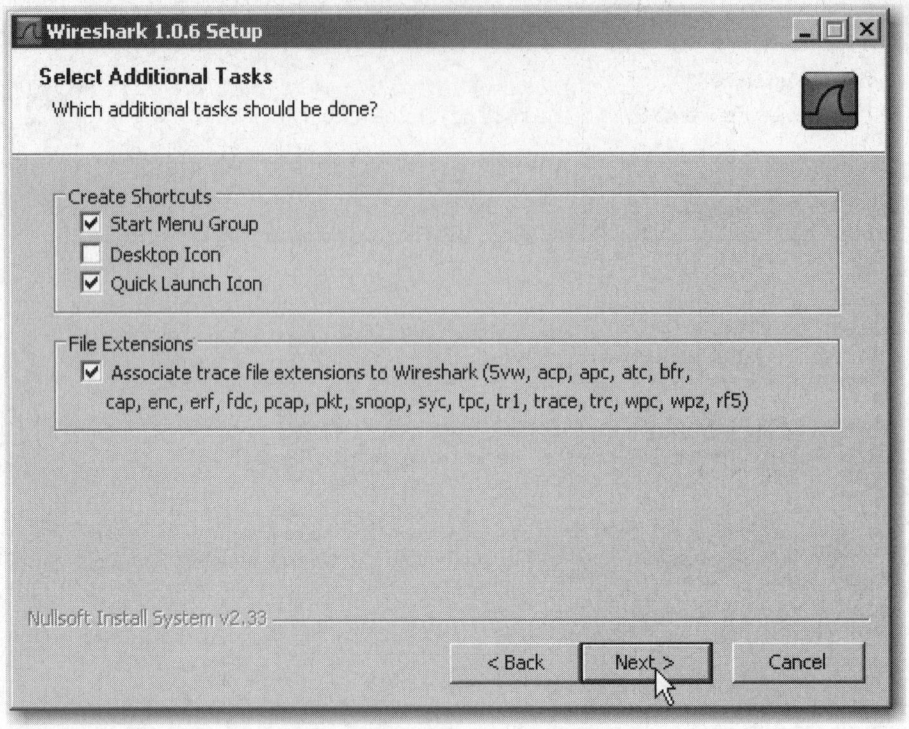

Figure 12: The *Select Additional Tasks* dialog box

7. The *Choose Components* dialog box appears (Figure 10). Click the Next button to accept the default settings and continue. The *Select Additional Tasks* dialog box appears (Figure 12).

8. If you would like to add a desktop icon for Wireshark, click the **Desktop Icon** check box. Click the **Next** button to continue. The *Choose Install Location* dialog box appears (Figure 13).

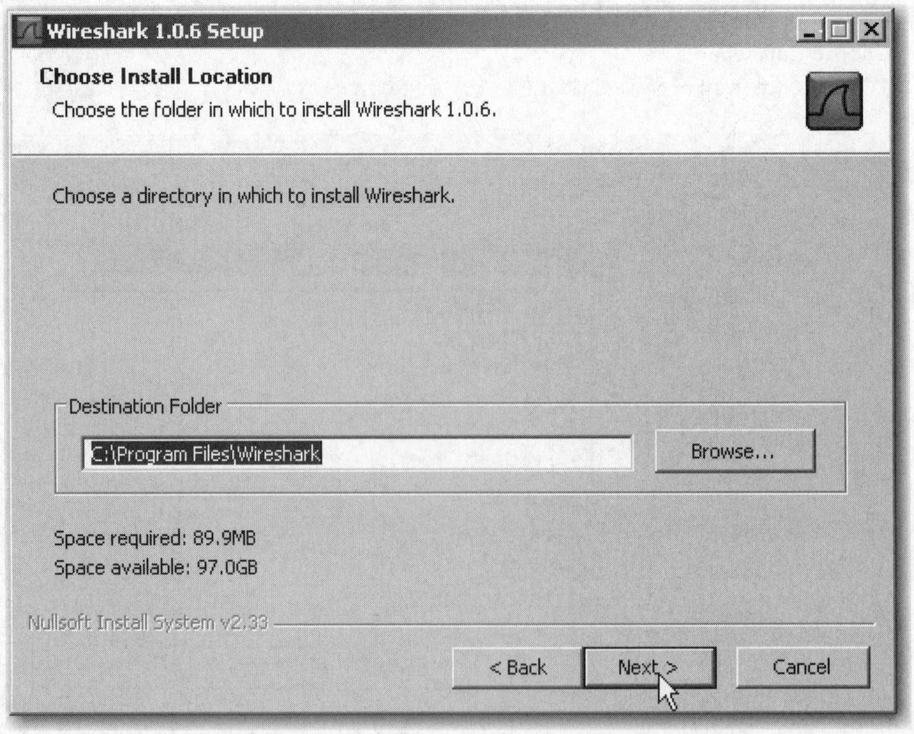

Figure 13: The *Choose Install Location* dialog box

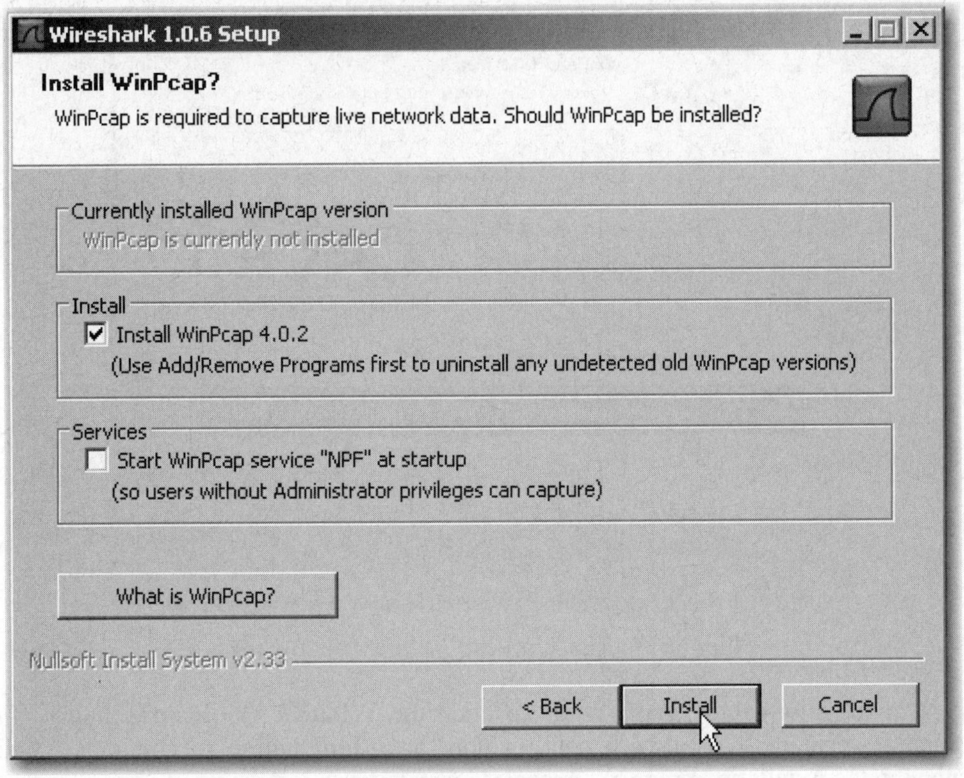

Figure 14: The *Install WinPcap?* dialog box

9. You may click the **Browse** button to specify another location. It is recommended that you accept the default location. Click the **Next** button to continue. The *Install WinPcap?* dialog appears (Figure 14).

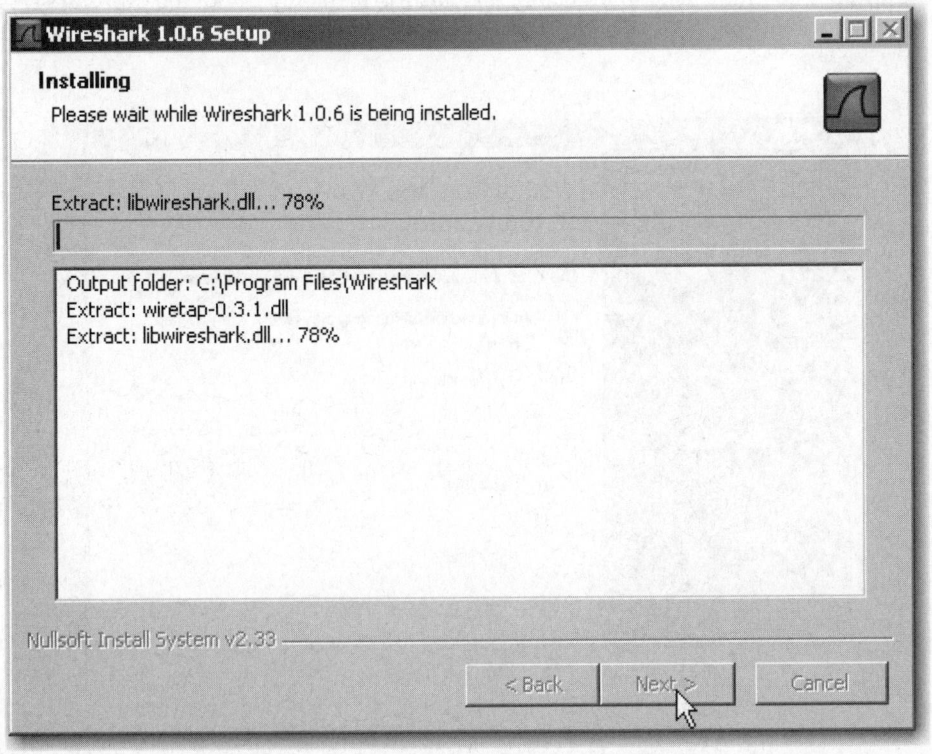

Figure 15: A dialog box showing installation progress. Files must be extracted before being installed.

Figure 16: The WinPcap *Installer* dialog box

10. To get more information about WinPcap click the **What is WinPcap?** button. WinPcap is required to capture live network data. Click the *Install* button to continue. A dialog box displaying the installation progress appears (Figure 15).

11. After all files are installed the Next button is activated. Click the **Next** button to continue. The WinPcap *Installer* dialog box appears (Figure 16).

12. This dialog box is essentially a "splash screen". No actions are required other than to click the **Next** button to continue. The WinPcap *Setup Wizard Welcome* dialog box appears (Figure 17).

Figure 17: The WinPcap *Setup Wizard Welcome* dialog box

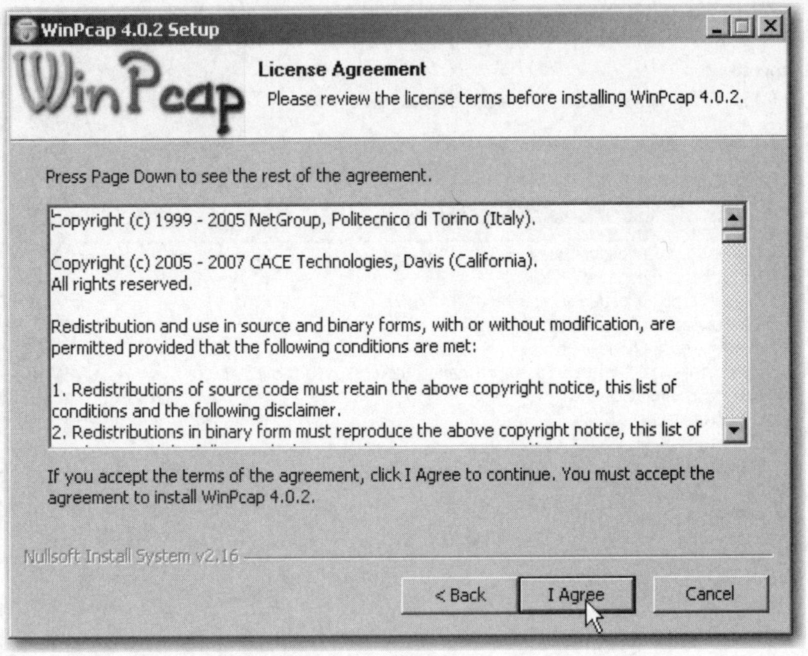

Figure 18: The WinPcap *License Agreement* dialog box

13. No action is required except to read the messages and click the **Next** button. The *WinPcap License Agreement* dialog box appears (Figure 18).

14. Read the terms of the agreement and click the **I Agree** button. Clicking the **Cancel** button terminates the installation process. A dialog box displaying installation progress appears (Figure 19).

15. After all files are installed the Next button is activated. Click the **Next** button to continue. A dialog box showing installation progress appears. Additional Wireshark files are being installed.

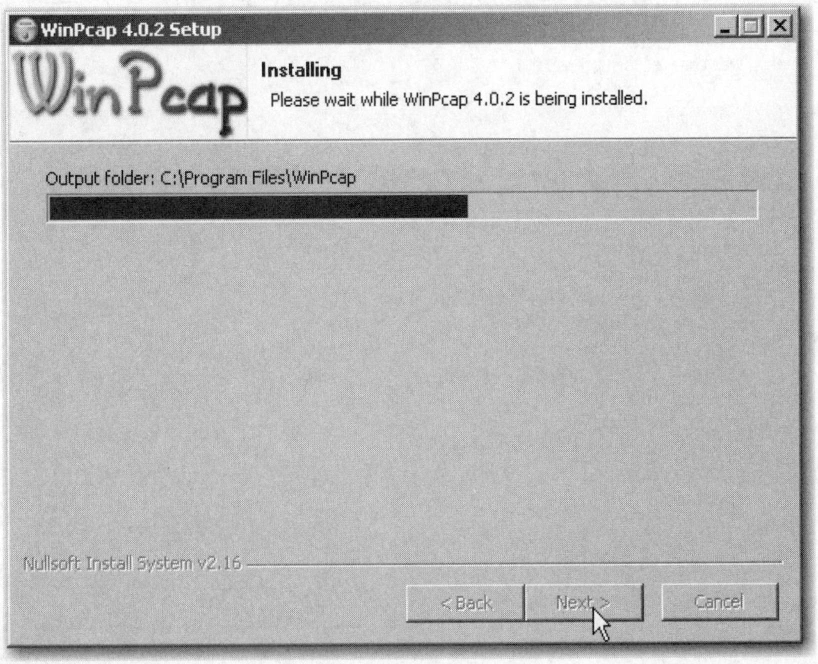

Figure 19: The WinPcap *Installing* dialog box showing installation progress

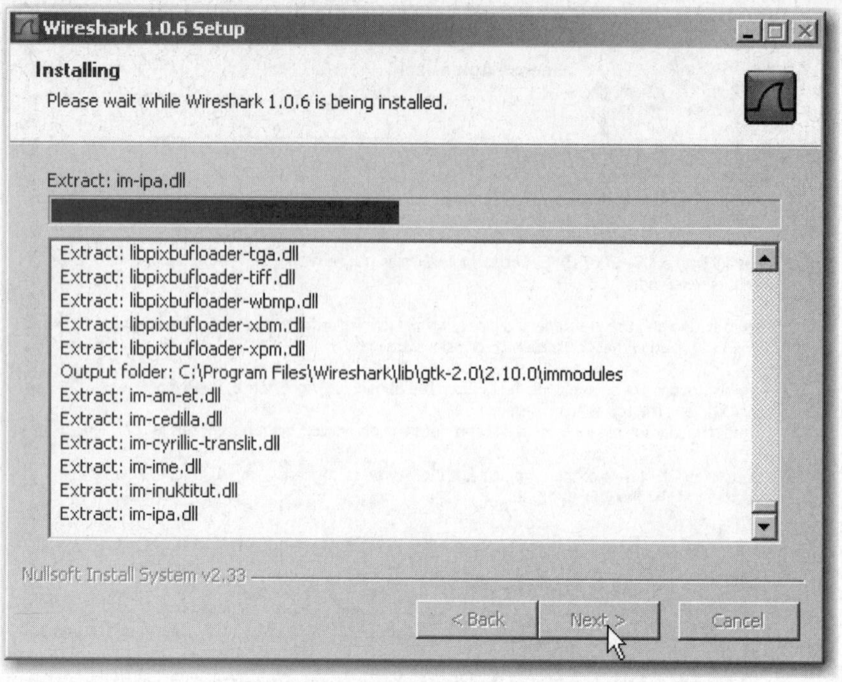

Figure 20: The Wireshark dialog box confirming that the setup wizard has completed installation of the WinPcap and Wireshark software

16. After all files are installed the Next button is activated and the *Installing* heading changes to *Installation Complete*. Click the **Next** button to continue.

17. Two dialog boxes indicating that the installation is complete will be displayed (Figures 22 and 23). Click the *Next* button in the first and the *Finish* button in the second dialog box to complete the installation of both Wireshark and WinPcap.

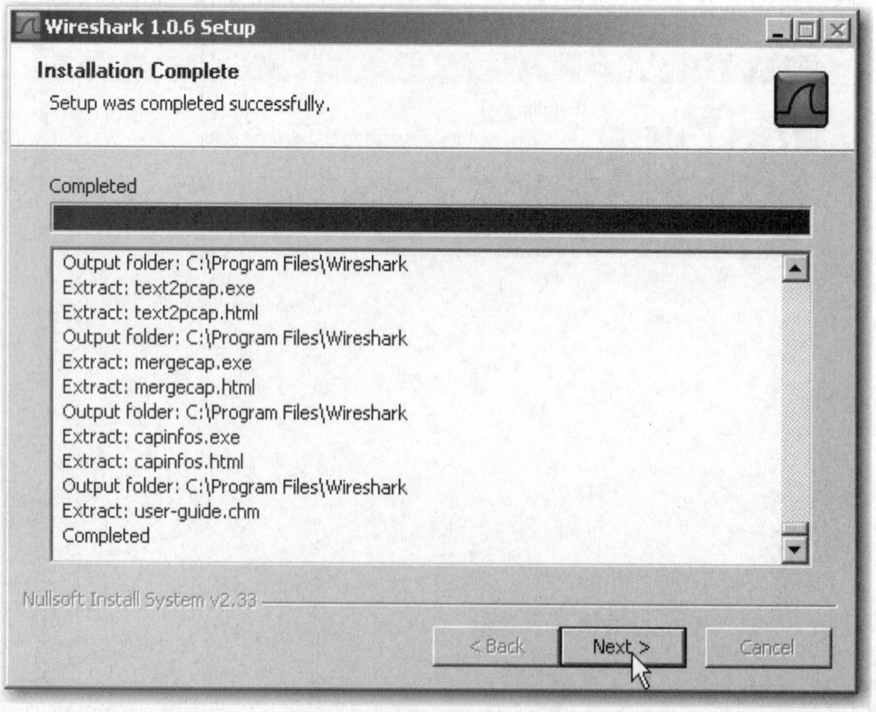

Figure 21: A dialog box indicating that installation procedures have been completed

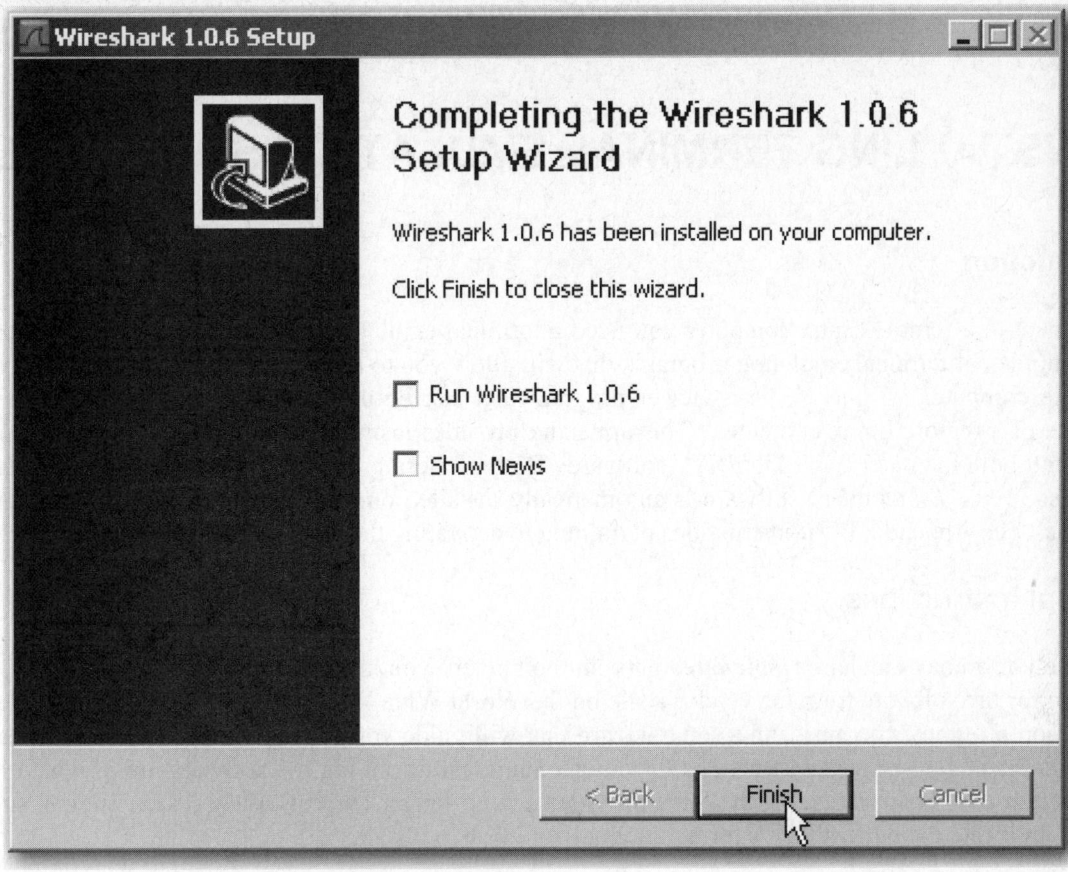

Figure 22: The *Wireshark Setup Wizard* dialog box indicating that Wireshark has been installed and is ready to run

18. A final *Wireshark Setup Wizard* dialog box appears indicating that Wireshark has been installed on your computer and is now ready to use.

APPENDIX F

INSTALLING TERMINAL EMULATION SOFTWARE

Introduction

To connect to a remote Linux computer you need a terminal emulation program. *PuTTY* and *Telnet* are two examples of terminal emulation programs that will allow you to access the command-line interface of a remote computer. *TightVNC* is a viewer program that can be used to access the graphical desktop interface of a remote Linux computer. This appendix provides instructions on how to obtain, download, and install both the *puTTY* and *TightVNC* software. Both of these programs are freeware, so no licensing fee is required. *Telnet* client software is automatically installed on Windows operating systems, except for Vista. See Appendix B for instructions pertaining to activating the Vista Telnet client software.

General Instructions

To install terminal emulation software on your computer, you must first download the installation program for the software from the vendor's site on the World Wide Web. After you have downloaded the installation program, you must run a setup wizard that will guide you through the installation process. A complete set of step-by-step instructions for downloading and installing the software are provided in the next section of this appendix. If the links provided are no longer current, use a search engine, such as Google, to locate the current URLs for the product you wish to install.

Part One: Downloading and Running the PuTTY Executable File

PuTTY is an open source terminal emulation program that also supports file transfers. PuTTY is easily accessible, can be downloaded quickly, and requires no installation. The following section describes the steps required to transfer puTTY from its site on the World Wide Web to your computer.

1. Open **Internet Explorer** by double-clicking its icon on the Windows desktop or in the Windows Start menu (Figure 1).

2. Type **http://www.google.com** in Internet Explorer's *Locator* text box and click the **Go to** button to the right of the Locator text box (Figure 2).

3. The Google home page appears.

4. Type **putty** in the Google *Search* text box.

5. A dropdown list of options, including a putty download option, appears (Figure 2).

6. Click this choice and then click the Google Search button.

Figure 1: The Internet Explorer icon

Figure 1: The Google homepage showing a list of choices that might appear when the key word *putty* is typed into the locator text box

7. The *PuTTY Download Page* appears (Figure 3). A list of puTTY files is displayed. Scroll down to see the download options (Figure 4).

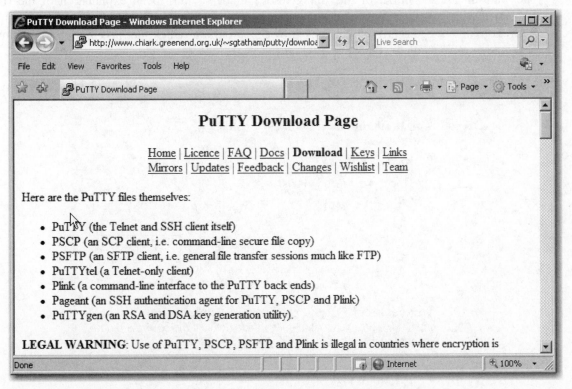

Figure 2: The *PuTTY Download Page* showing the puTTY file choices

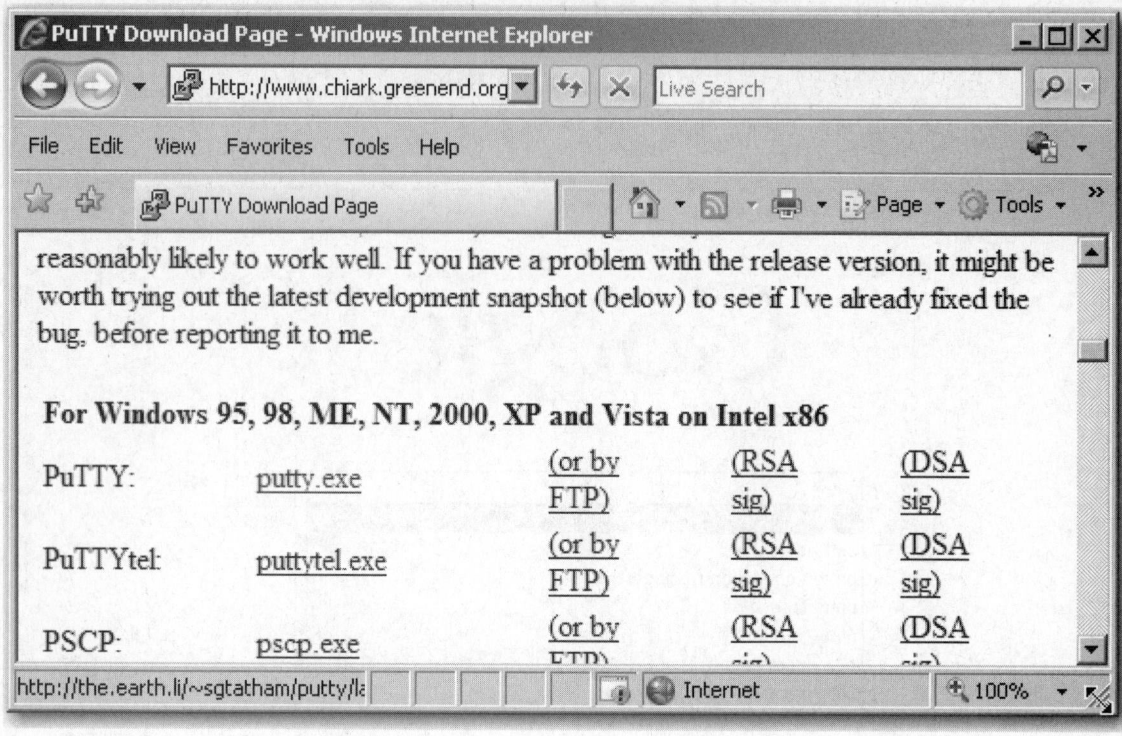

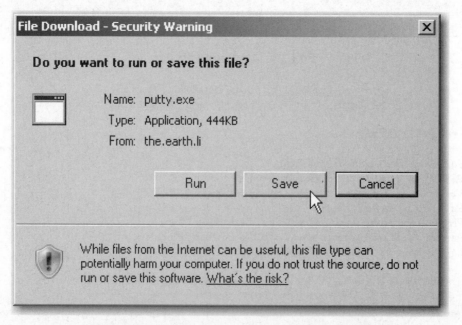

Figure 4: The puTTY download options for the Windows platform

8. The puTTY files are available for different computer platforms (Windows, Linux, Mac, etc). We will download the Windows version of puTTY (Figure 4). Click on the **puTTY.exe** link. The *File Download – Security Warning* dialog box appears (Figure 5).

9. The warning at the bottom of this dialog box includes a link to an explanation of the risks associated with downloading this file. You may click the **What's the risk?** link if you want to learn more about the security threats posed by this program. Click the **Save** button to continue. A Windows *Save As* dialog box appears (Figure 6).

Figure 5: The *File Download – Security Warning* dialog box

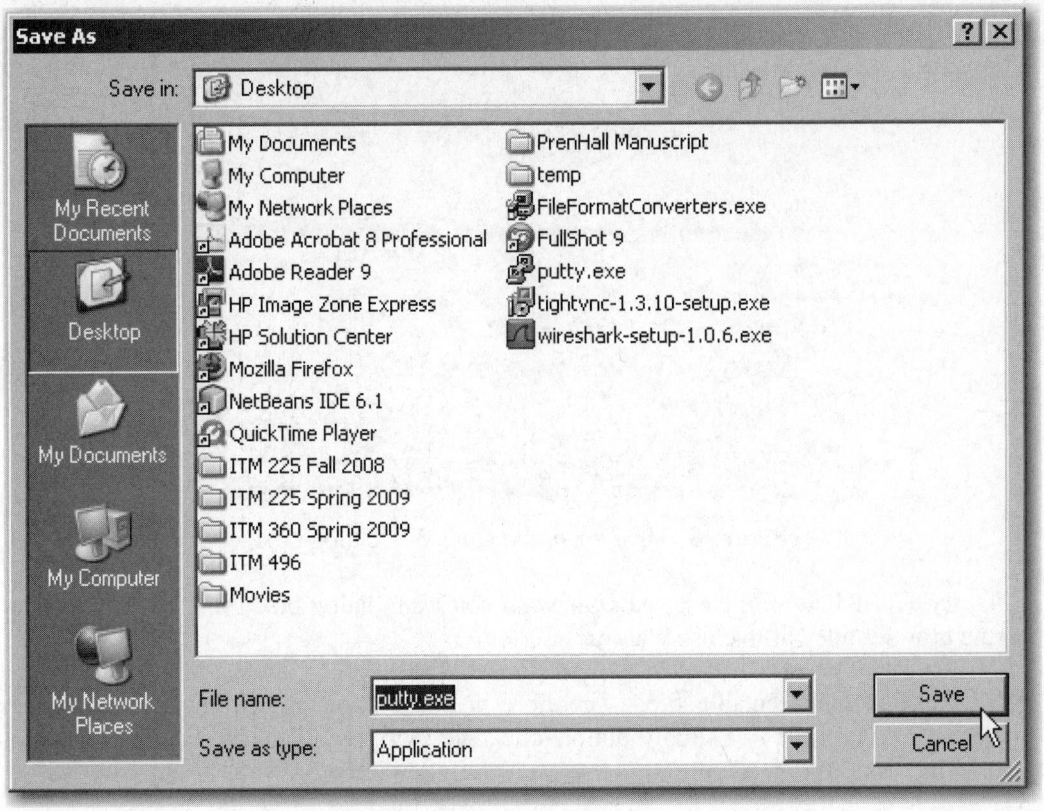

Figure 6: A Windows *Save As* dialog box

10. Accept the default save location (the Desktop) by clicking the **Save** button. A download progress dialog box will appear (Figure 7).

11. The progress screen indicates how much time is left until the download is complete. Since puTTY.exe is a small file, the download will complete in a matter of seconds. When complete, the *Download complete* dialog box appears (Figure 8).

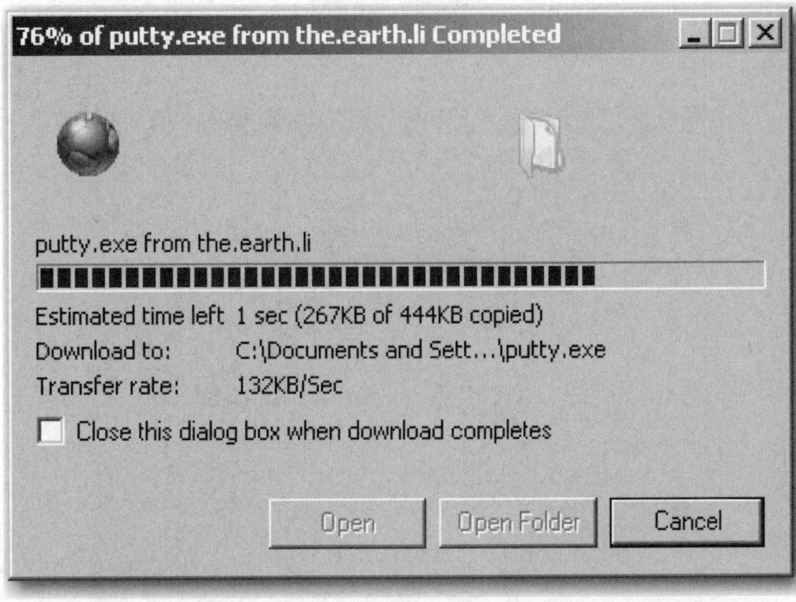

Figure 7: A dialog box showing progress made while downloading the puTTY installation file

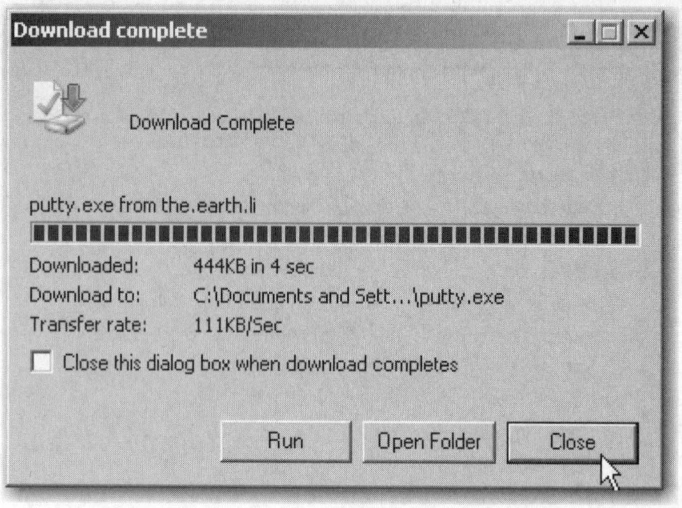

![Download complete dialog box showing Download Complete, putty.exe from the.earth.li, progress bar full, Downloaded: 444KB in 4 sec, Download to: C:\Documents and Sett...\putty.exe, Transfer rate: 111KB/Sec, checkbox "Close this dialog box when download completes", buttons Run, Open Folder, Close]

Figure 8: The *Download Complete* dialog box

12. Click the **Close** button to close the *Download complete* dialog box. Also click the **Close** button on the browser title bar to close your browser.

13. PuTTY.exe is an executable file. Therefore no installation procedure is required to run the software. To use puTTY, simply double-click the *putty.exe icon* that has been downloaded to your Windows Desktop (Figure 9).

14. The *Open File-Security Warning* dialog box appears (Figure 10) because putty.exe does not have a valid digital signature. Click the **link** shown towards the bottom of the dialog box to obtain details. If you do not want to see this dialog box again click the **Always ask before opening this file** checkbox to clear it. Click the **Run** button to continue.

Figure 9: The putty.exe desktop icon

![Open File - Security Warning dialog box. Text: "The publisher could not be verified. Are you sure you want to run this software?" Name: putty.exe, Publisher: Unknown Publisher, Type: Application, From: C:\Documents and Settings\Tom Cavaiani\Desktop. Buttons Run, Cancel. Checkbox checked "Always ask before opening this file". "This file does not have a valid digital signature that verifies its publisher. You should only run software from publishers you trust. How can I decide what software to run?"]

Figure 10: The *Open File-Security Warning* dialog box

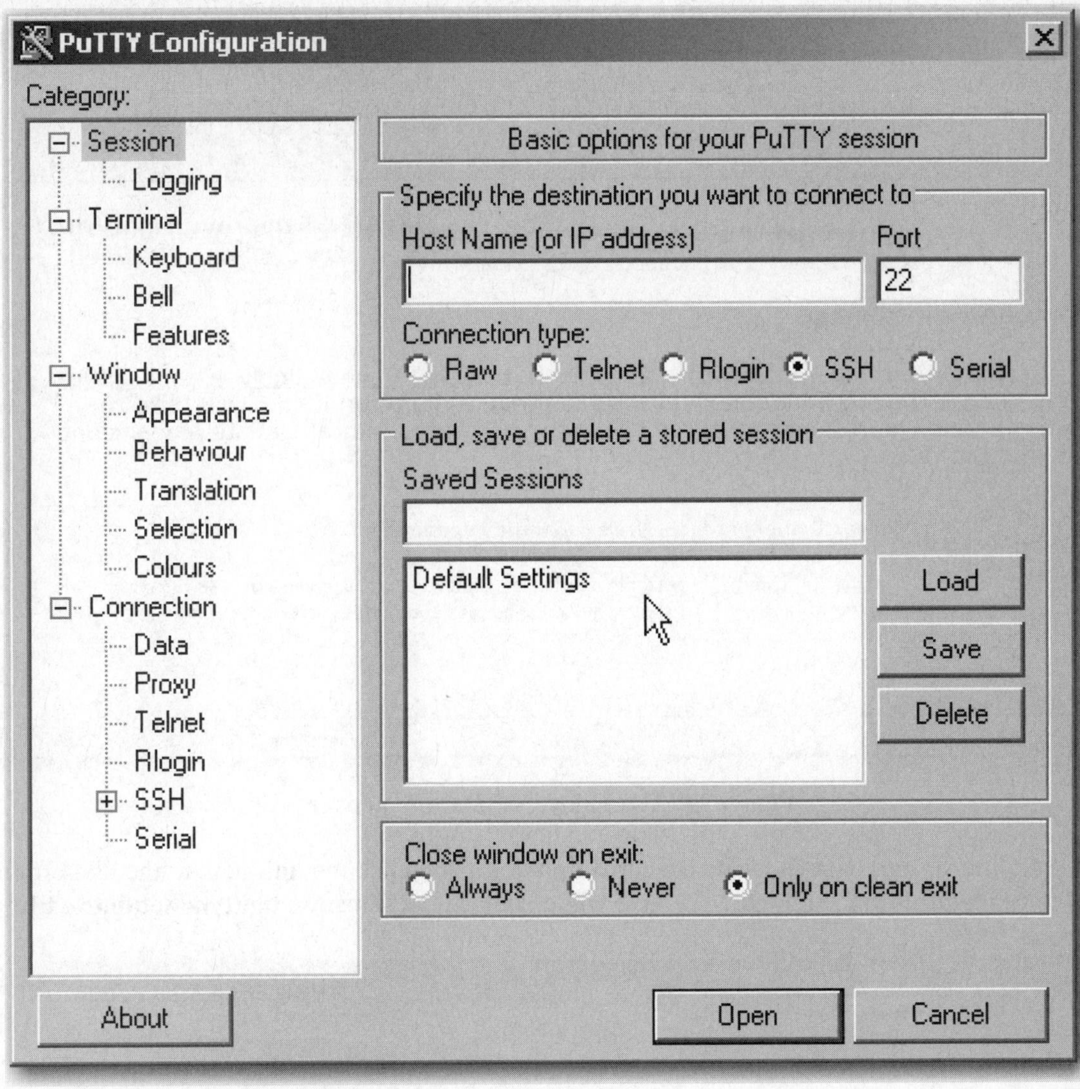

Figure 10: The puTTY *Configuration* dialog box

15. The *puTTY Configuration* dialog box appears (Figure 11). This dialog box contains locations for the remote computer's host name or IP address, the *Connection type* (raw, telnet, rlogin, SSH, or serial) and the *Port number* associated with the *Connection* type. Enter these **values** and click the **Open** button to connect to the remote computer.

Part Two: Downloading and Installing Tight VNC

This section describes how you can download and install the Tight VNC viewer on your computer. To download and install the software proceed as follows:

1. Open Internet Explorer by double-clicking the desktop icon (Figure 1).

2. Enter the following URL into Internet Explorer's locator text box: **http://www.tightvnc.com/download.html**.

3. Click the **Go to** button.

4. The *TightVNC download* page appears (Figure 11).

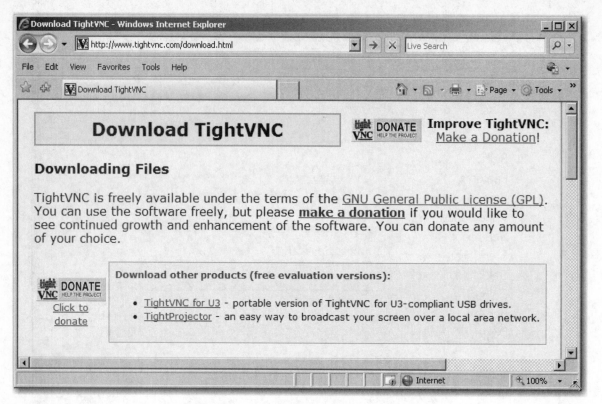

Figure 11: The TightVNC *Download* page

5. Scroll down this page to locate the correct platform and click the **link** next to the platform name to begin the download (Figure 12). We will download the Windows **tightvnc setup.exe** file.

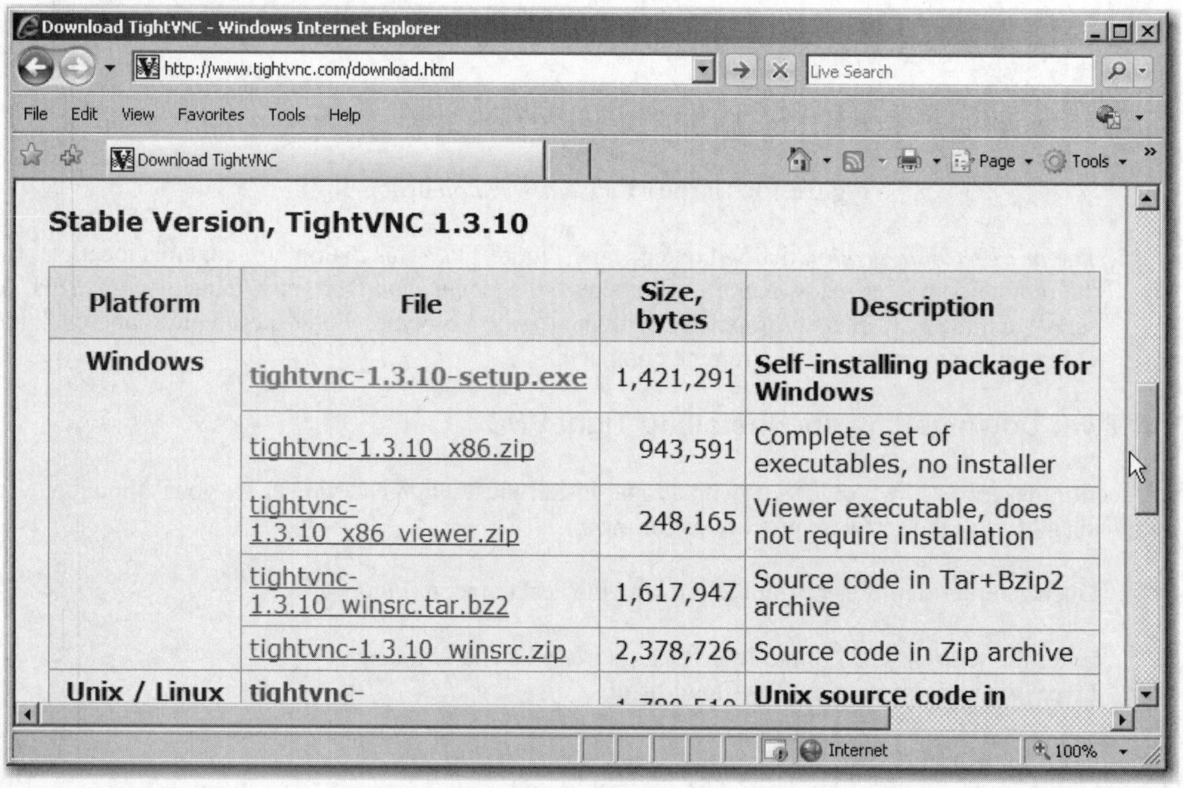

Stable Version, TightVNC 1.3.10

Platform	File	Size, bytes	Description
Windows	tightvnc-1.3.10-setup.exe	1,421,291	**Self-installing package for Windows**
	tightvnc-1.3.10_x86.zip	943,591	Complete set of executables, no installer
	tightvnc-1.3.10_x86_viewer.zip	248,165	Viewer executable, does not require installation
	tightvnc-1.3.10_winsrc.tar.bz2	1,617,947	Source code in Tar+Bzip2 archive
	tightvnc-1.3.10_winsrc.zip	2,378,726	Source code in Zip archive
Unix / Linux	tightvnc-		**Unix source code in**

Figure 12: The TightVNC download page displaying options for the *Windows* platform

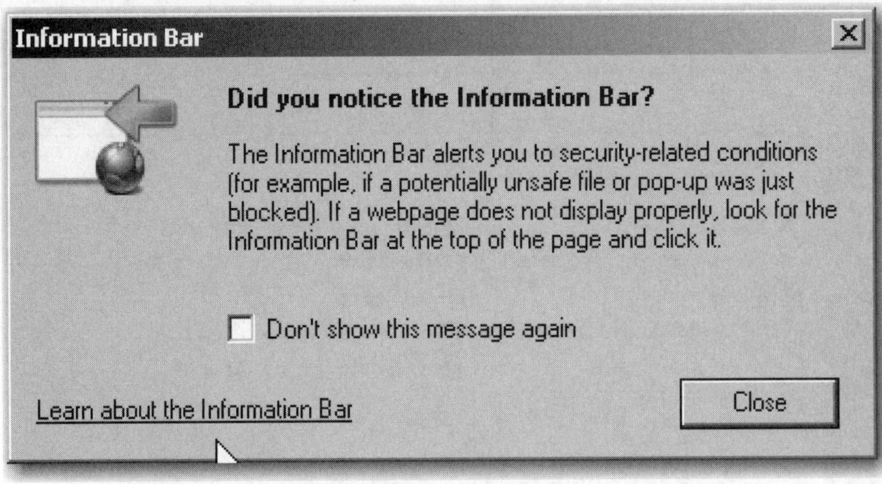

Information Bar
Did you notice the Information Bar?
The Information Bar alerts you to security-related conditions (for example, if a potentially unsafe file or pop-up was just blocked). If a webpage does not display properly, look for the Information Bar at the top of the page and click it.
Don't show this message again
Learn about the Information Bar
Close

Figure 13: The Windows *Information Bar* dialog box

To help protect your security, Internet Explorer blocked this site from downloading files to your computer. Click here for options...
Download File...
What's the Risk?
More information

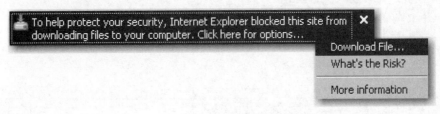

Figure 14: The pop-up menu that is displayed when right-clicking on the *Information Bar* on the download page

6. The *Information Bar* dialog box appears (Figure 13). A warning pertaining to unsafe files is displayed. The message also directs your attention to the *Information Bar* at the top of the screen. Click the **Close** button to close the dialog box. You will now have an unobstructed view of the download window and the Information Bar (Figure 14).

7. Clicking the **Information Bar** displays a pop-up menu. To learn more about the risks of downloading files from the Internet click the **What's the Risk** pop-up menu choice. Click the **Download File** option to download the file. The *File Download-Security Warning* dialog box appears (Figure 15).

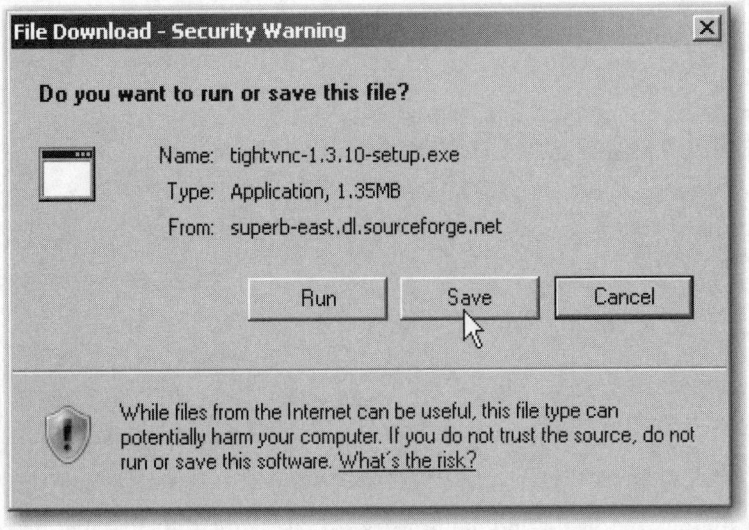

File Download - Security Warning
Do you want to run or save this file?
Name: tightvnc-1.3.10-setup.exe
Type: Application, 1.35MB
From: superb-east.dl.sourceforge.net
Run
Save
Cancel
While files from the Internet can be useful, this file type can potentially harm your computer. If you do not trust the source, do not run or save this software. What's the risk?

Figure 15: The Windows *File Download-Security Warning* dialog box

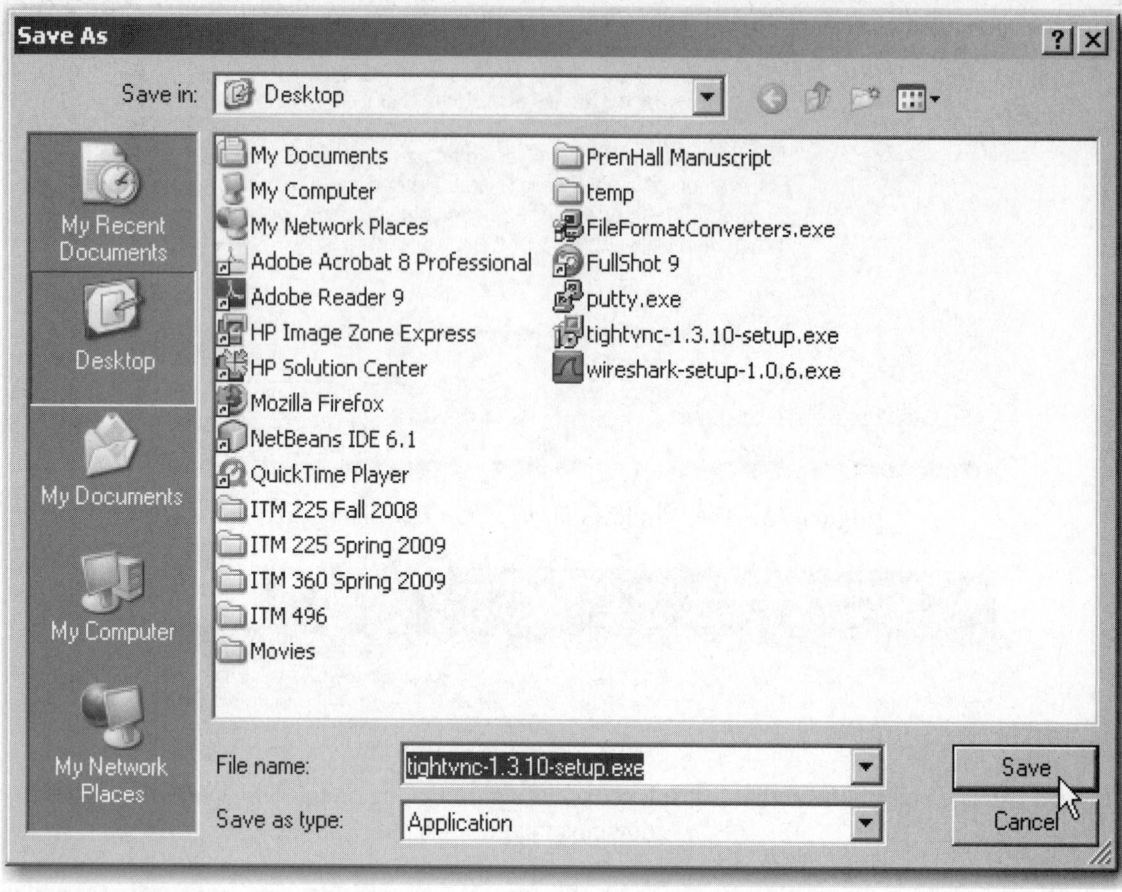

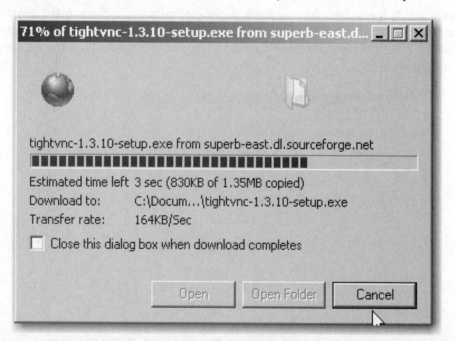

Figure 16: The Windows *Save As* dialog box

8. Click the **Save** button to download the setup file to your computer. A *Save As* dialog box appears (Figure 16). Click the **Save** Button to save the file to your Windows Desktop.

Figure 17: A dialog box displaying the progress of the TightVNC installation file download

Download complete ⬜ □ ✕

🗎 Download Complete

tightvnc-1.3.10-setup.exe from superb-east.dl.sourceforge.net

███

Downloaded:	1.35MB in 9 sec
Download to:	C:\Docum...\tightvnc-1.3.10-setup.exe
Transfer rate:	154KB/Sec

☐ Close this dialog box when download completes

[Run] [Open Folder] [Close]

Figure 18: A dialog box indicating that the download of the *TightVNC installation file* has completed

9. A *download progress* dialog box will appear (Figure 17). The amount of time left before the download is complete will be displayed and gradually diminish to zero.

10. When the download is complete a *Download complete* dialog box appears (Figure 18). Click the **Close** button to continue.

11. You are now ready to install the TightVNC viewer on your computer. Locate the *TightVNC setup.exe* file icon (Figure 19) either on the desktop or the download location you selected earlier.

12. Double-click the **setup** icon to begin the installation process. The *Open File-Security Warning* dialog box appears (Figure 20).

13. A warning indicating that this file does not have a valid digital signature is displayed in this dialog box. You can click the **How can I decide what software to run?** link to learn more about digital signatures and whether or not you want to install this file on your computer. If you click the **Cancel** button the installation procedure will be terminated. Click the **Run** button to continue.

14. The *Setup TightVNC* dialog box appears (Figure 21). Click the **Next** button to continue.

Figure 19: The *TightVNC setup* icon

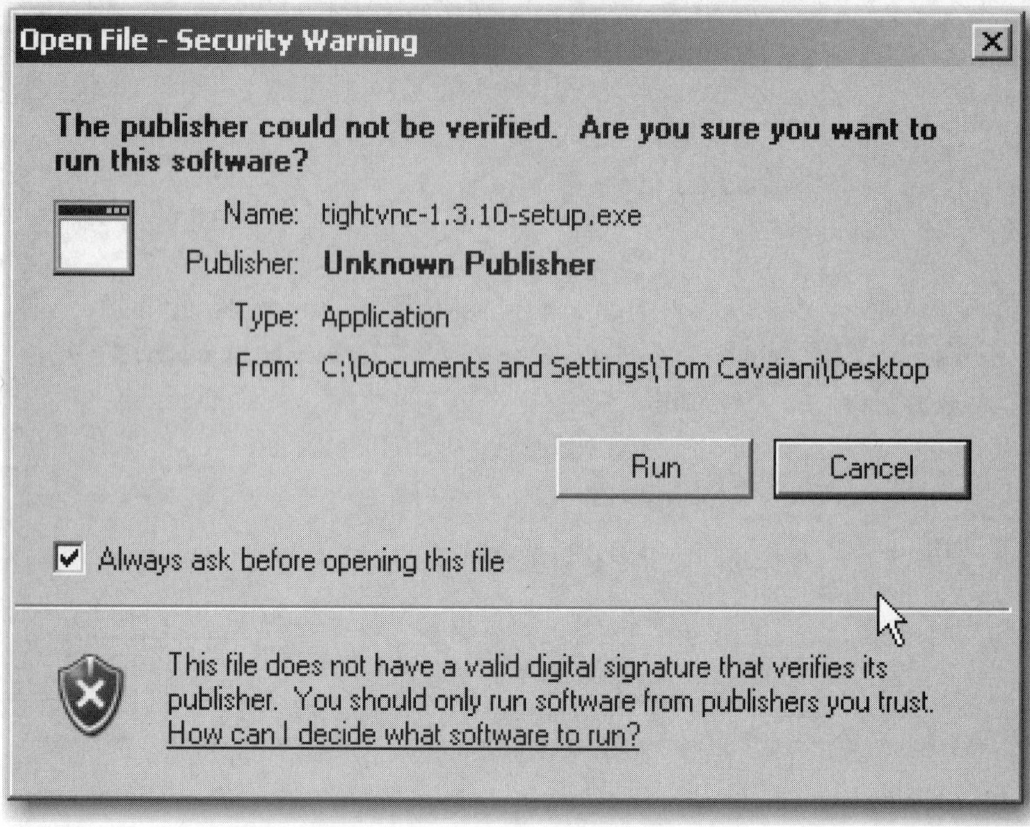

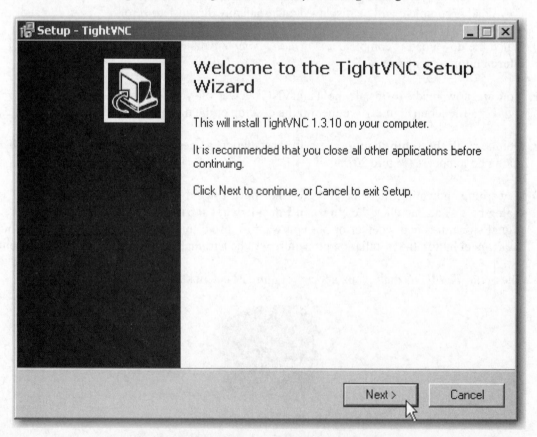

Figure 20: The *Open File-Security Warning* dialog box

Figure 21: The *Setup – TightVNC* dialog box

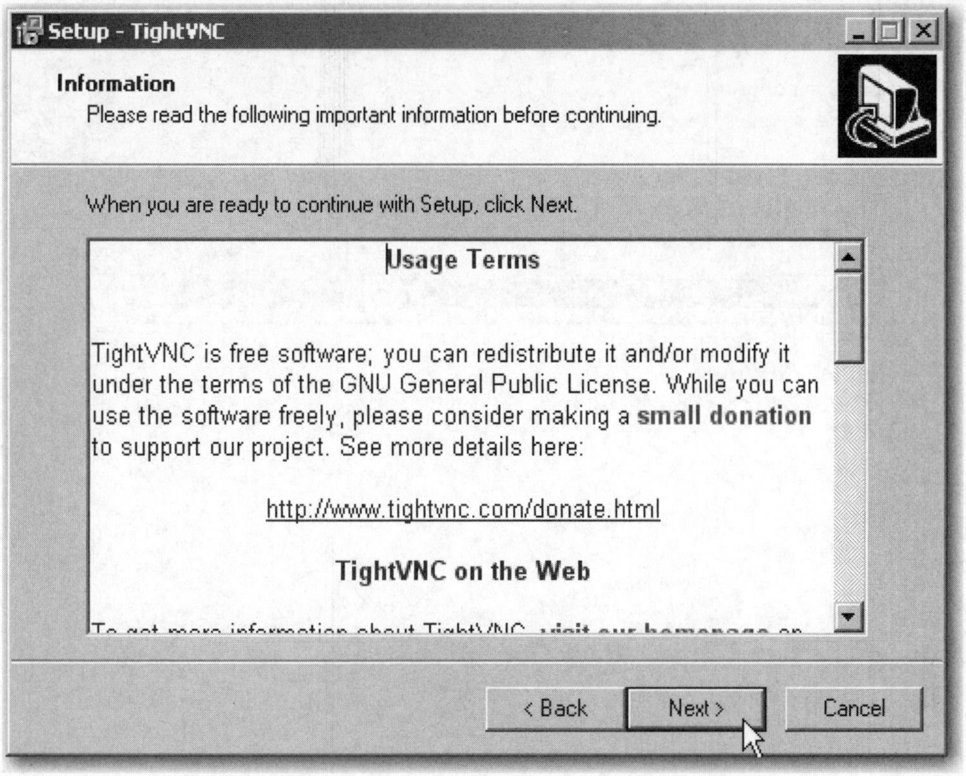

Figure 22: A *Terms of Usage* dialog box for TightVNC

15. A dialog box displaying the terms of usage for the TightVNC software appears (Figure 22). Read the information displayed in this dialog box and click the **Next** button to continue.

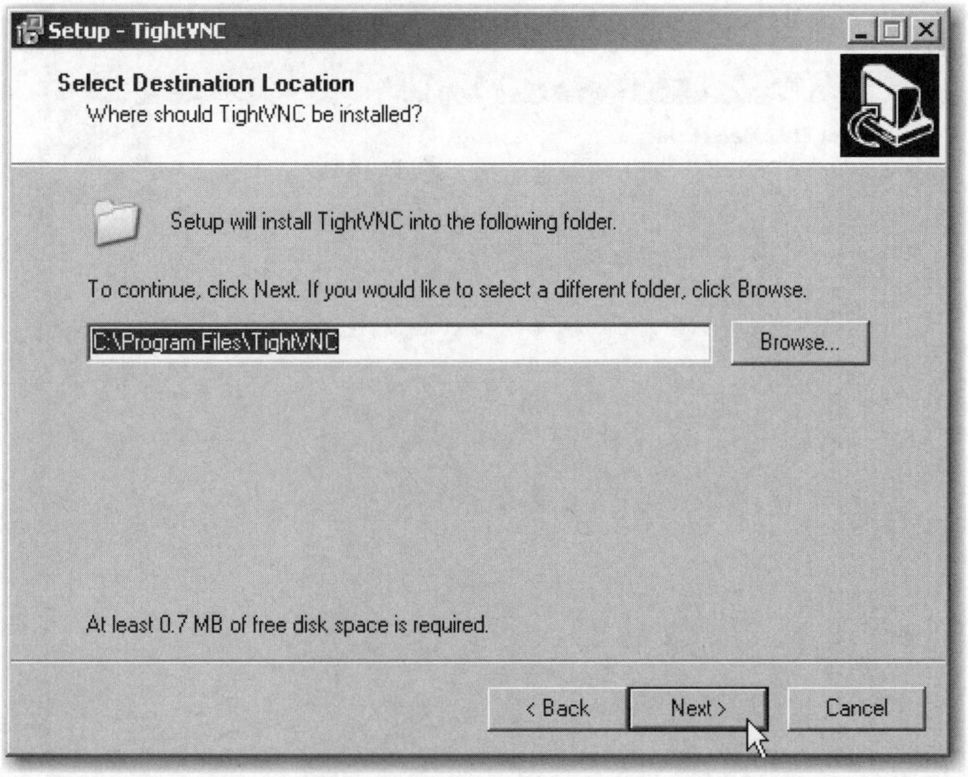

Figure 23: The TightVNC *Select Destination Location* dialog box

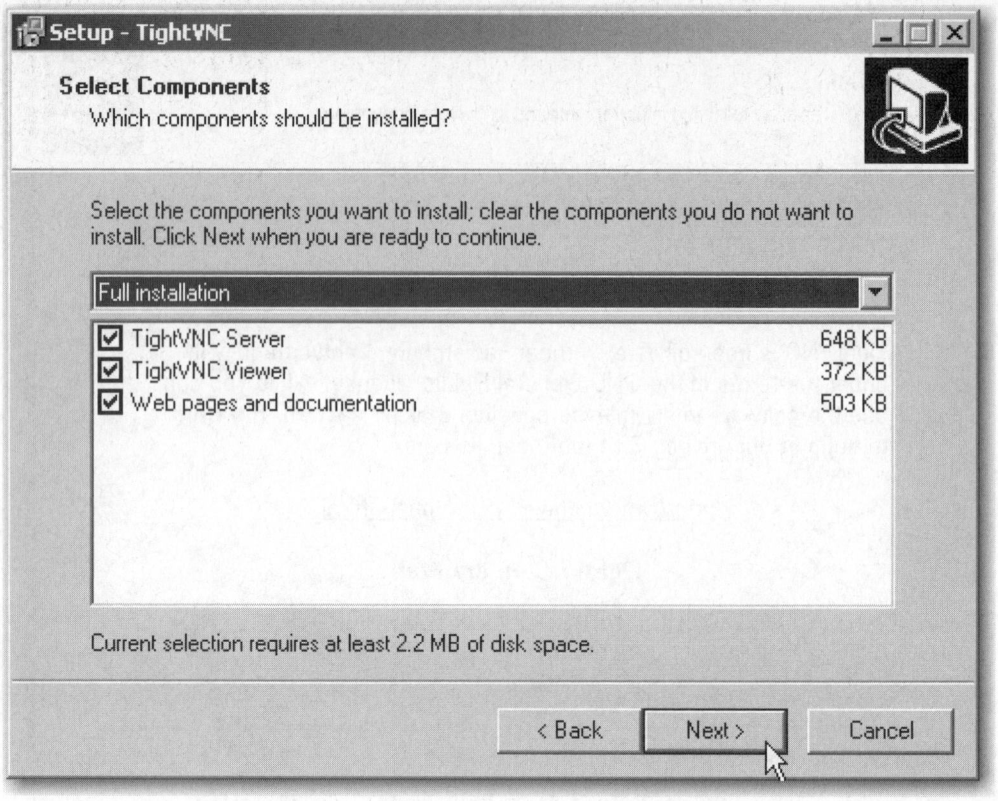

Figure 24: The *Select Components* dialog box

16. A dialog box that allows you to select the destination folder for the TightVNC software appears (Figure 23). Click the **Browse** button to select a different location than that displayed. It is recommended that you select the default location. Click the **Next** button to continue.

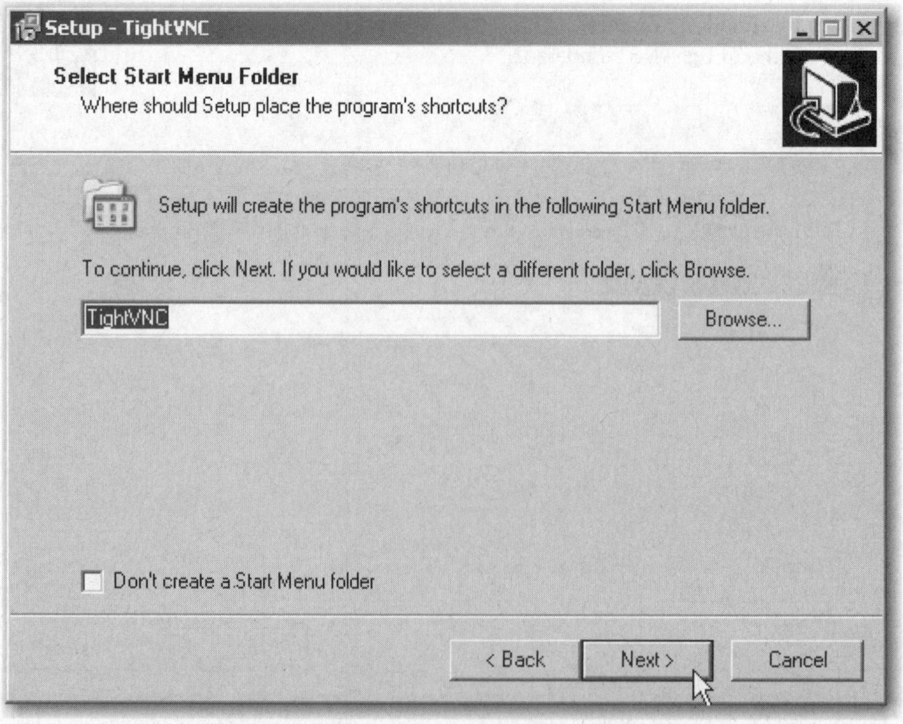

Figure 25: The TightVNC *Select Start Menu Folder* dialog box

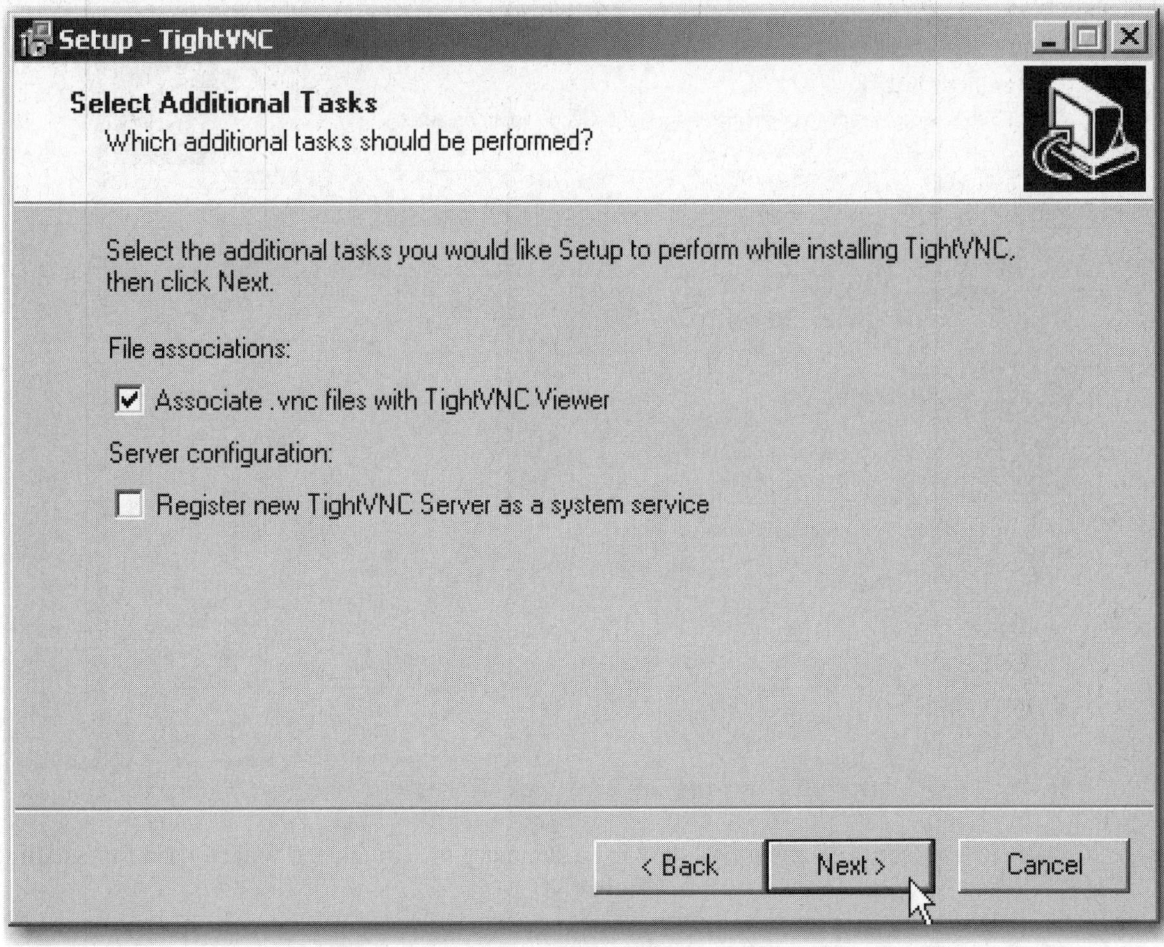

Figure 26: The TightVNC *Select Additional Tasks* dialog box

17. A dialog box displaying which components will be installed on your computer appears (Figure 24). It is recommended that you select the default settings. Click the **Next** button to continue.

18. A dialog box displaying the folder that will be created to save the *TightVNC shortcuts* appears (Figure 25). You can click the *Browse* button to select another location, but it is recommended that you select the default setting. If you do not want to create the folder click the checkbox displayed in the lower left-hand corner of the dialog box. Click the **Next** button to continue.

19. A dialog box asking if you would like to perform additional tasks is displayed (Figure 26). It is recommended that you accept the default settings. Click the **Next** button to continue.

20. A dialog box that summarizes all of the information gathered in the previous dialog boxes appears (Figure 27). To make changes to these settings you will need to click the **Back** button until the appropriate dialog box or boxes reappears. After making changes, click the **Next** button to return to the summary dialog box. Click the **Install** button to continue.

21. A progress dialog box will appear for a few seconds while the software is being installed. When installation is complete a dialog box indicating that the Setup Wizard has finished installing TightVNC appears. Click the **Finish** button to close this dialog box.

22. The TightVNC viewer is now ready to use.

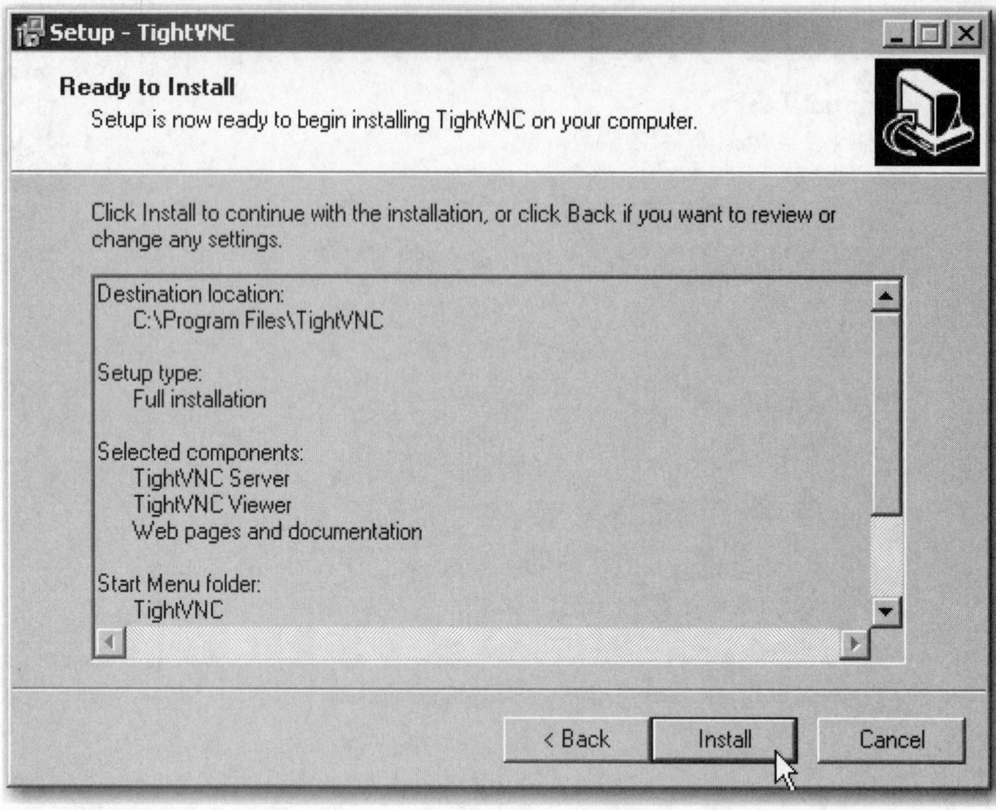

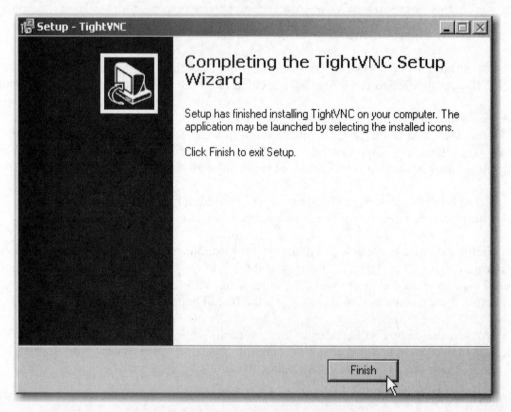

Figure 27: The *Ready to Install* dialog box showing a summary of settings that will be used for installing TightVNC

Figure 28: The *Setup Completed* dialog box

APPENDIX G

INSTALLING THE IT GURU ACADEMIC EDITION SIMULATION SOFTWARE

Introduction

Lab 15 requires the use of the IT Guru simulation software. The academic edition of this software is available as a free download. This appendix provides you with the information you will need to register, download, and install the software on your computer.

Part One: Creating a User Account

1. From the Windows Desktop open *Internet Explorer (IE)* and enter the following URL, **http://www.opnet.com/university_program/itguru_academic_edition/,** into IE's *Locator* text box. Click the **Go to** button. The *IT Guru Academic Edition* home page appears. Click the **Register and Download** button.

2. The *OPNET User Account Signup* page appears.

3. Enter the information requested. To complete the registration form you will need to enter

   - your name and address

   - your email address

   - your employer's name

   - the name of your academic institution

   - your year in school

   - your Course Name

   - your Instructor's name

   - how you learned about the IT Guru Academic Edition (a drop down list is provided so you can select *the name of your text book*, if listed)

   - a *username* that will be easy to remember

4. Click the **Submit** button after completing the form. Your username and password will be sent to the email address you listed on the registration form.

5. Click the **Close** button on Internet Explorer's title bar to close it.

Part Two: Downloading the IT Guru Software

1. Check your email to obtain the password sent to you after you completed the registration process. You will use this password along with the username you specified to download and install the IT Guru software.

2. If necessary, double-click the **Internet Explorer** icon on the Windows Desktop, enter the URL, **http://www.opnet.com/university_program/itguru_academic_edition/** into the *Locator* text box and click the **Go to** button to display the *IT Guru Academic Edition* home page.

3. Click the **Login** button for *Existing Users*. A login dialog box requesting your *user name* and *password* appears. Enter your **username** and **password** in their respective text boxes and click the **OK** button.

4. An OPNET Technologies *download* page appears. Read the notice to users. Click the **http://enterprise37.opnet.com/4dcgi/DOWNLOAD_HOME** link.

5. A login dialog box requesting your *user name* and *password* may appear. If it does enter your **username** and **password** in their respective text boxes and click the **OK** button.

6. The *Software Download* page appears displaying system requirements for the software. Scroll down the page until you see the **Download** button. Click the **Download** button.

7. The *License Agreement* page appears. Scroll down this page to read the remainder of the agreement. Click the **I have read this SOFTWARE AGREEMENT...** button to agree to the terms of the license and continue with the download. If you click the **I Do Not Accept** button the download procedure will be terminated.

8. A *Software Download* page appears. Within a few seconds the *Information Bar* dialog box (Figure 1) is displayed in front of the *Software Download* page.

9. Read the message in the dialog box and click the **Close** button to continue.

Figure 1: The *Information Bar* dialog box and security warning

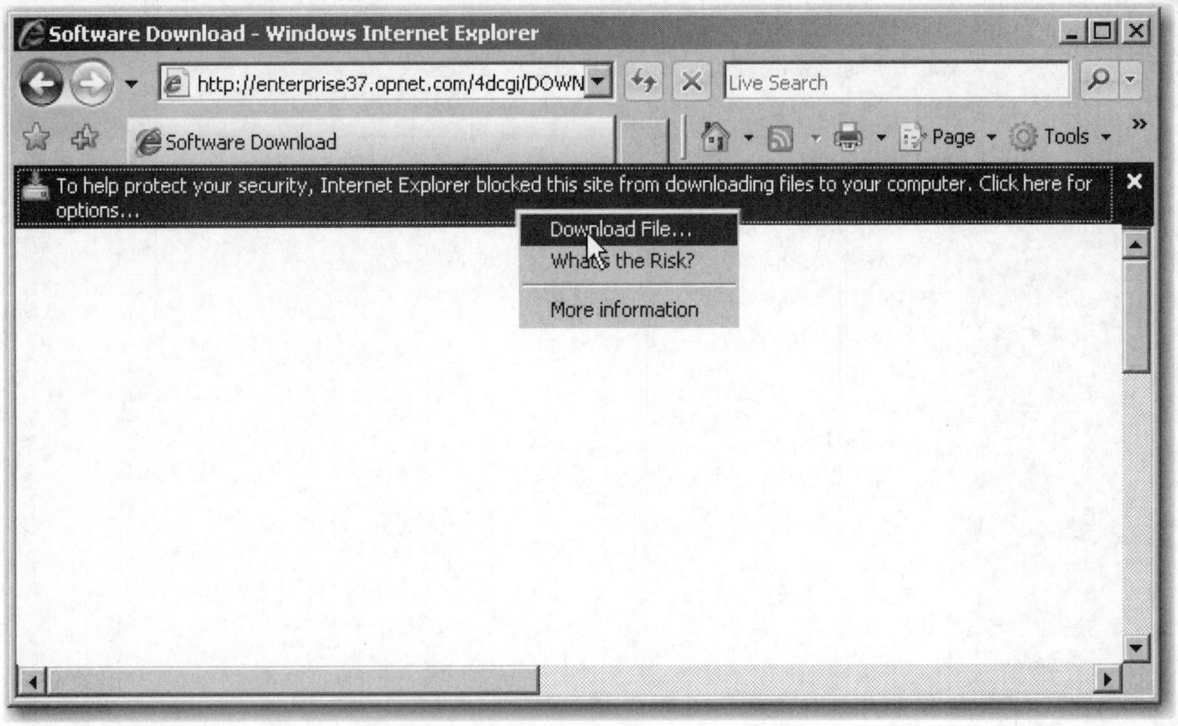

Figure 2: The *Software Download* page, *Information Bar*, and *pop-up* menu showing the *Download File* choice

10. The dialog box disappears revealing the underlying web page. The *Information Bar* is displayed towards the top of the page. Clicking the **Information Bar** displays a *pop-up* menu (Figure 2). Click the **Download File** choice to continue.

11. The *File Download* dialog box appears (Figure 3). Click the **Save** button to continue.

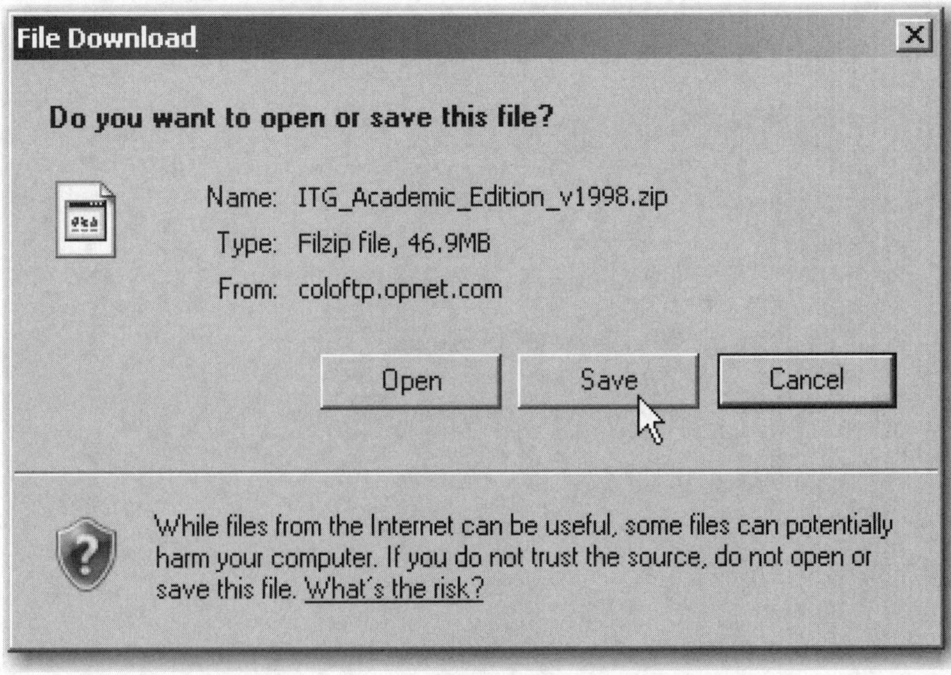

Figure 3: The *File Download* dialog box

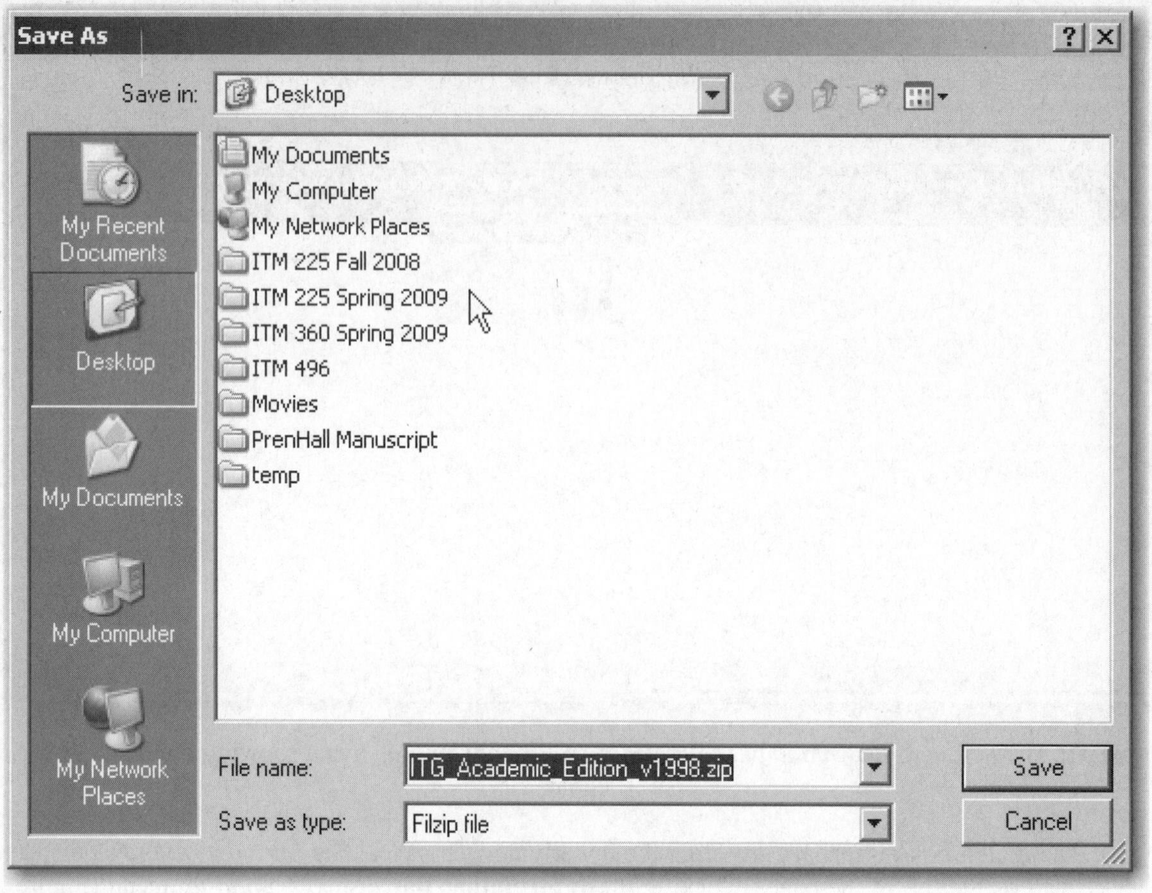

Figure 4: A Windows *Save As* dialog box

15. A Windows *Save As* dialog box appears (Figure 4). You can select a different location to save the file if you wish, but the default location is recommended. Click the **Save** button to continue.

16. A dialog box displaying the progress of the download appears (Figure 5).

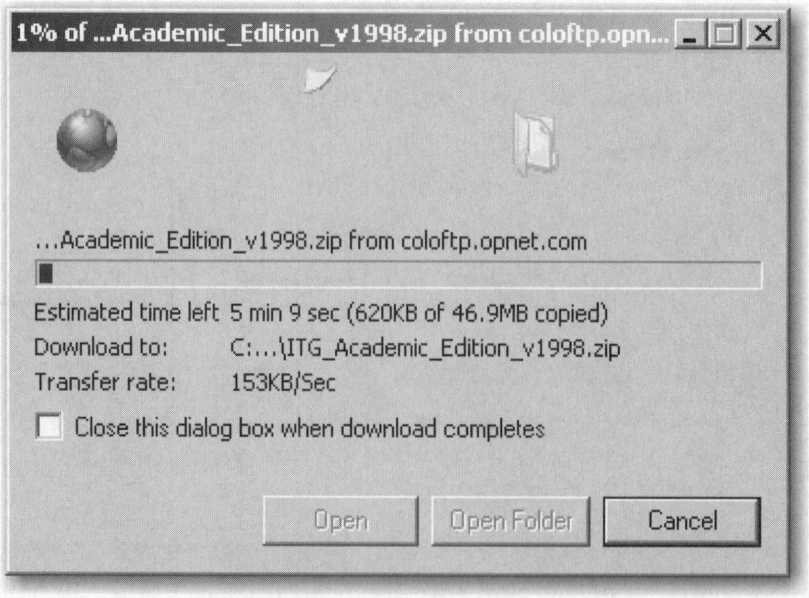

Figure 5: A dialog box showing *file download* progress

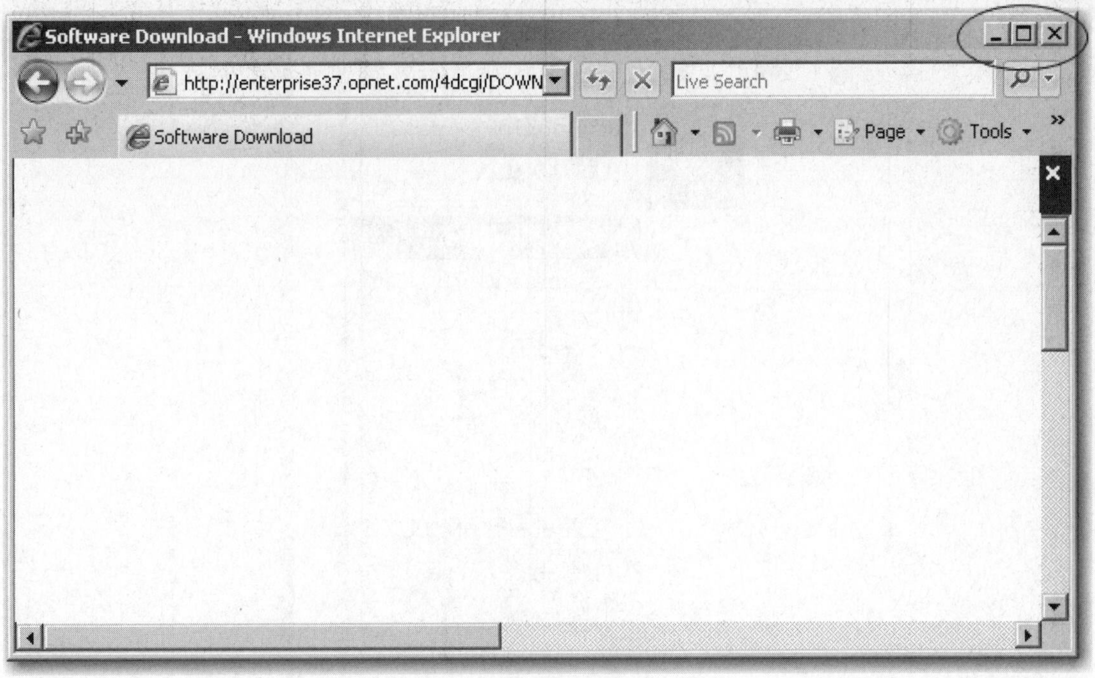

![Software Download - Windows Internet Explorer window with the Minimize, Maximize, and Close buttons circled in the top right corner, the address bar showing http://enterprise37.opnet.com/4dcgi/DOWN, and a blank content area]

Figure 6: The *Minimize*, *Maximize*, and *Close* buttons (from left to right, circled) on the title bar of an Internet Explorer dialog box

17. The file is fairly large (about 50 MB) and it will take about 5 minutes on a 1.5 Mbps DSL broadband connection to download the file. When the transfer is complete the *Cancel* button shown in Figure 5 changes to a *Close* button. Click the **Close** button to close the dialog box and continue.

18. Close the *Software Download* dialog box by clicking the **Close** button on the Internet Explorer *title* bar (Figure 6). You are now ready to install the IT Guru Academic Edition software.

Part Three: Installing the IT Guru Academic Edition Software

ITG_Academic
_Edition_v199
8.zip

Figure 7: The IT Guru installation file icon

1. Locate **IT Guru ITG_Academic_Edition_v1998.zip file** icon (Figure 7) on the Windows Desktop. This icon was created when the software was downloaded to your desktop and will be used to initiate the process for installing the software on your computer.

2. The installation file must be extracted (decompressed) before it can be installed. Right-click on the **ITG_Academic_Edition_v1998.zip** icon. A *pop-up* menu appears (Figure 8). Click on the **Extract All** choice.

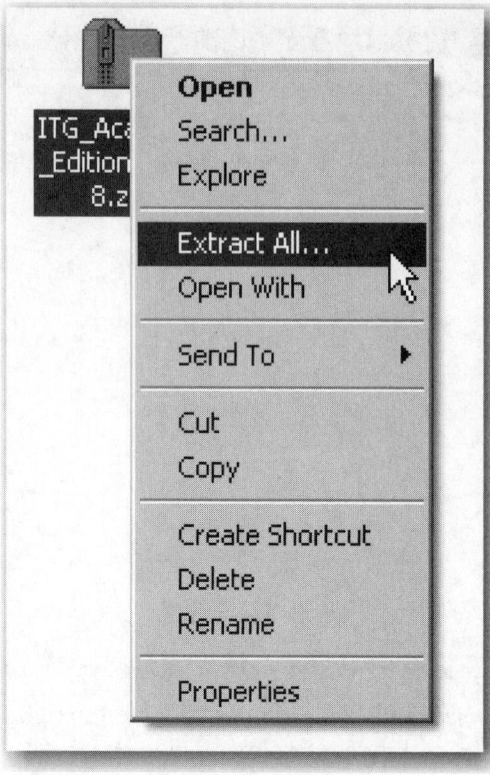

Figure 8: The pop-up menu displayed after right-clicking the *ITG_Academic_Edition zip file* icon

3. The *Extraction Wizard* dialog box appears (Figure 9). Click the **Next** button to continue.

Welcome to the Compressed (zipped) Folders Extraction Wizard

The extraction wizard helps you copy files from inside a ZIP archive.

To continue, click Next.

< Back   Next >   Cancel

Figure 9: The *Extraction Wizard* dialog box

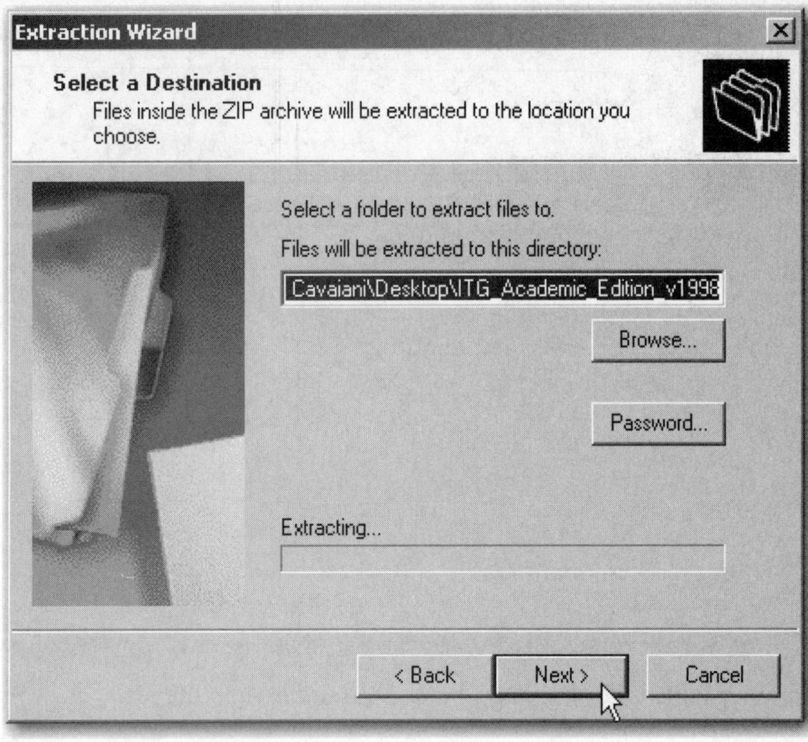

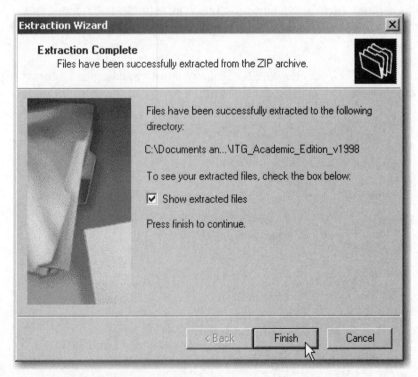

Figure 10: The *Select a Destination* dialog box

4. The *Select a Destination* dialog box appears (Figure 10). Click the **Next** button to create a folder on your desktop that contains the extracted file. The *Extraction Complete* dialog box appears (Figure 11). Click the *Finish* button to continue.

Figure 11: The *Extraction Complete* dialog box

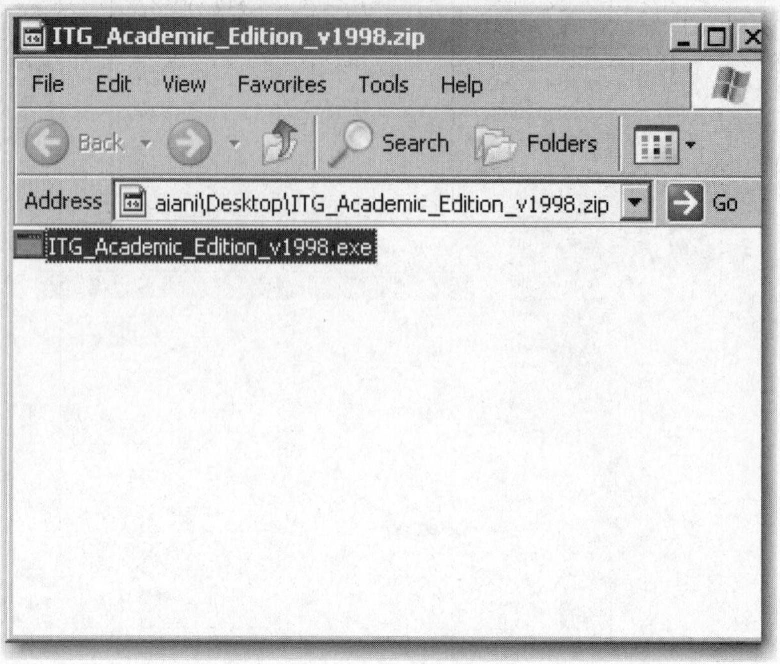

Figure 12: The ITG *Academic Edition setup* file icon

5. A dialog box showing the extracted setup file appears (Figure 12). Double-click the **ITG_Academic_Edition_v1998.exe file icon** shown in this dialog box to begin installing the application. **Note**: If you are installing the ITG Academic Edition software on a Vista computer you need to change the compatibility settings as follows: Right-click the **IT Guru setup** icon. Click the **Properties** choice. In *Properties* dialog box that appears click the **Compatibility** tab and set *Compatibility* Mode to *Windows XP (Service Pack 2)*. *Also* click the ***Run this program as an administrator*** check box. Click the **OK** button to close the dialog box. After completing these steps you can double-click the setup icon shown in the above dialog box to install the software.

6. After a short pause the *File Download – Security Warning* dialog box appears (Figure 13). Click the **Run** button to begin installing the software.

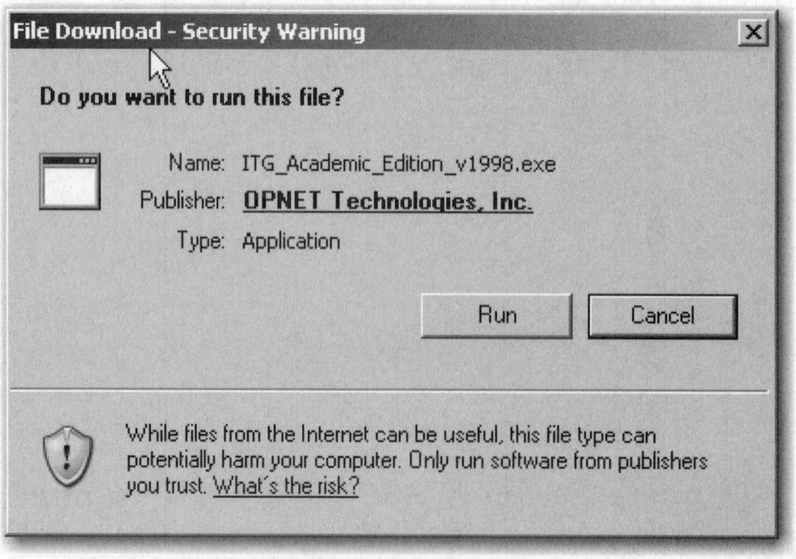

Figure 13: The *File Download – Security Warning* dialog box

7. After a longer pause the OPNET IT Guru *Academic Edition Setup* dialog box appears.

8. Click the **Next** button to continue. The *Choose Destination Location* dialog box appears.

9. Click **Next** button to continue. The *Start Copying Files* dialog box appears.

10. The settings that will be used to install the software are listed. Click **Next** button to continue. A *Setup Status* dialog box appears.

11. You may need to wait up to approximately 2 minutes for this phase of the installation to complete depending upon the memory capacity and speed of your computer. Eventually you will see a message box indicating that additional components are being installed.

12. In some cases this process may take up to approximately 2 minutes to complete. The *Setup Status* dialog box will disappear automatically. After a short pause a dialog box displaying a message about *Adobe Acrobat Reader* appears.

13. Click **OK** button to continue. A dialog box indicating that software installation has been completed appears.

14. Click the **Finish** button. Close Internet Explorer by clicking the **Close** button on its title bar.

Part Four: Activating the Software License

After you have installed the software it must be activated. To activate the software you must obtain a *License Approval Code* from the OPNET site. The process is somewhat involved. The following section guides you through this process.

1. Click the **Start** button on the Windows *Task Bar* to open the *Start* menu. Click the **All Programs** choice. An option for *OPNET IT Guru Academic Edition 9.1* will be displayed (Figure 14). Click the *OPNET IT Guru Academic Edition* choice on the right to launch the program.

2. An empty command window appears briefly then disappears. An OPNET splash screen also appears briefly. The *IT Guru Academic Edition 9.1* main window appears.

3. Almost immediately the *License Not Obtained* dialog box overlays the IT Guru main window.

4. You must obtain a *License Approval Code* before you can use the IT Guru software. Click the **License Management** button to begin the activation process.

5. The *Perform License Transaction* dialog box appears. Click the **Next** button. A dialog box containing a *License Request Code* appears.

Figure 14: The OPNET IT Guru choices displayed in the *All Programs* menu

6. Here's the tricky part. Almost immediately a browser window and a login dialog box appear and cover this dialog box up. Click on the **Performance License Transaction** dialog box or its **icon** on the *Windows Task Bar* to make it the active window. Click the **Copy to Clipboard** button to copy the *License Request Code* to the Windows Clipboard. Click the **Next** button.

7. Activate the **login** dialog box by clicking on it or its **icon** in the *Windows Task Bar*. Enter your OPNET **username** and **password** and click the **OK** button.

8. The *OPNET License Activation* page appears.

9. Press **CTRL** and **v** keys simultaneously to paste the *License Request Code* into the text box.

10. Click the **Submit** button. The OPNET *License Activation Confirmation* dialog box appears.

11. A *License Approval Code* is displayed on this page.

12. Drag your mouse pointer across the **License Approval Code** to highlight it.

13. Press the **CTRL** and **c** keys simultaneously to copy the code to the clipboard.

14. If necessary scroll down the page to display the *Next* button. Click the **Next** button to continue.

15. The *License Transaction-Enter License Approval Code* dialog box appears. Click the **Paste from Clipboard** button to paste the *License Approval Code* into the *License Approval Code* text box. Click the **Next** button.

16. The *Success* dialog box appears. Your license has been activated. Click the **Close** button. Also close Internet Explorer by clicking the **Close** button on its title bar. You are now ready to use the IT Guru software.

Part Five: Using the IT Guru Software

1. Click the **Start** button on the Windows *Task Bar* to open the *Start* menu. Click the **All Programs** choice. An option for *OPNET IT Guru Academic Edition 9.1* will be displayed (Figure 14). Click the **OPNET IT Guru Academic Edition** choice on the right to launch the program.

2. An empty command window appears briefly then disappears. An OPNET splash screen may also briefly appear. After a few seconds the *Restricted Use Agreement* dialog box appears.

3. Click the **I have read this SOFTWARE AGREEMENT...** button to accept the software agreement. The *IT Guru Academic Edition 9.1* application window appears. You are now ready to begin working with existing simulations or creating your own.

4. To begin working with an existing scenario click the **File** menu in the IT Guru application window and then click the **Open** choice. The *File-Open* dialog box appears.

5. Select a choice by clicking on it. For purposes of this discussion the Frame Relay choice has been selected. Click the **OK** button to continue. A *Project* window for the *Frame Relay Scenarios* appears.

6. To learn more about using existing scenarios and creating your own, refer to Lab 15. Lab 15 discusses the *IT Guru Tutorials*, which will provide a good starting point for learning more about the IT Guru software.

APPENDIX H

CREATING A GMAIL ACCOUNT

Introduction

The labs in this manual require that you have a Gmail account. Your will use this account to create a Google site and for posting your homework assignments to the site so that your instructor can review them. Gmail accounts are free and are easy to create. To create your own account, proceed as follows:

1. From your Windows Desktop or the Windows *Start* menu double-click the **Internet Explorer** icon. Enter **http://www.Google.com** in IE's *Locator* text box and click the **Go to** button or press the **Enter** key.

2. The Google *home page* appears (Figure 1). Click the **Gmail** link directly above the *Google* logo.

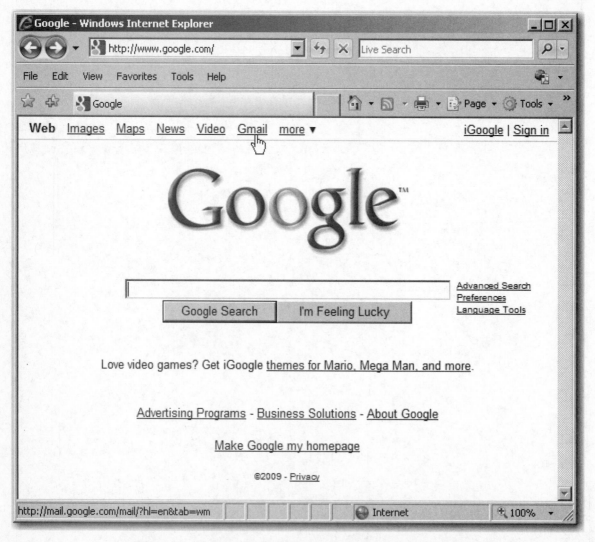

Figure 1: The Google home page showing the *Gmail* link

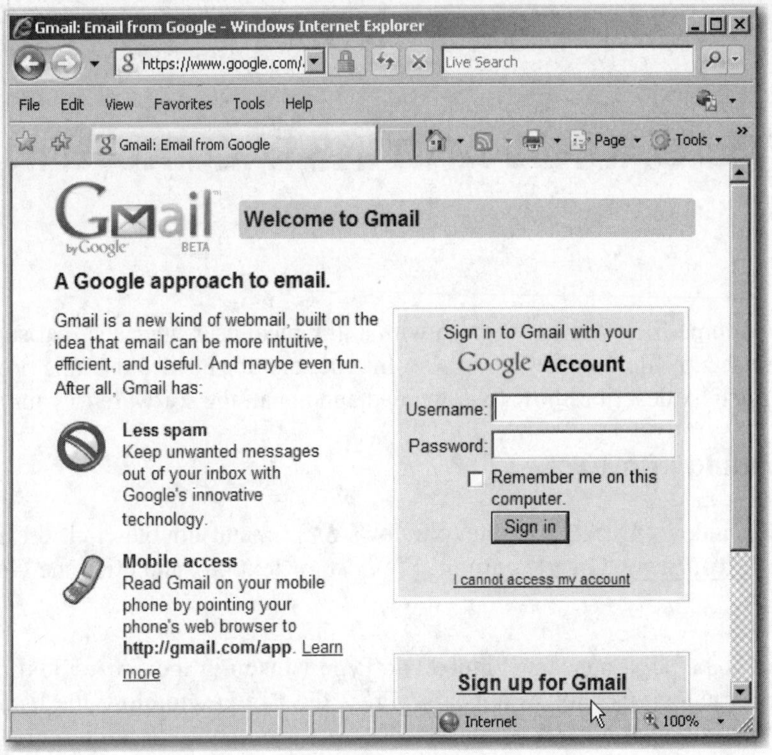

Figure 2: The *Welcome to Gmail* web page

3. The *Welcome to Gmail page* appears (Figure 2). Click the **Sign up for Gmail** link.

4. The *Create a Google Account – Gmail* page appears. Complete the signup form by entering the required information. Click the **I accept. Create my account** button to create your account.

Figure 3: The Create a *Google Account – Gmail* page

APPENDIX I

DOWNLOADING AND INSTALLING WINSCP

Introduction

WinSCP is an open-source file transfer program with a graphical user interface that supports a number of both secure and non-secure file transfer protocols. Instructions for how to use this program are provided in Lab two. This appendix describes how to download and install the software to your computer.

Part 1: Downloading WinSCP

1. From your Windows Desktop or the Windows *Start* menu double-click the **Internet Explorer** icon. Enter **http://www.Google.com** in IE's *Locator* text box and click the **Go to** button or press the **Enter** key.

2. The Google *home page* appears (Figure 1). Type **winscp** in the *Search* text box. A drop down list displaying numerous choices appears. Press the **Esc** key to close the list. Click the **Google Search** button or the **Enter** key to continue.

Figure 1: The Google home page showing the keyword *winscp* in the Google *Search* text box

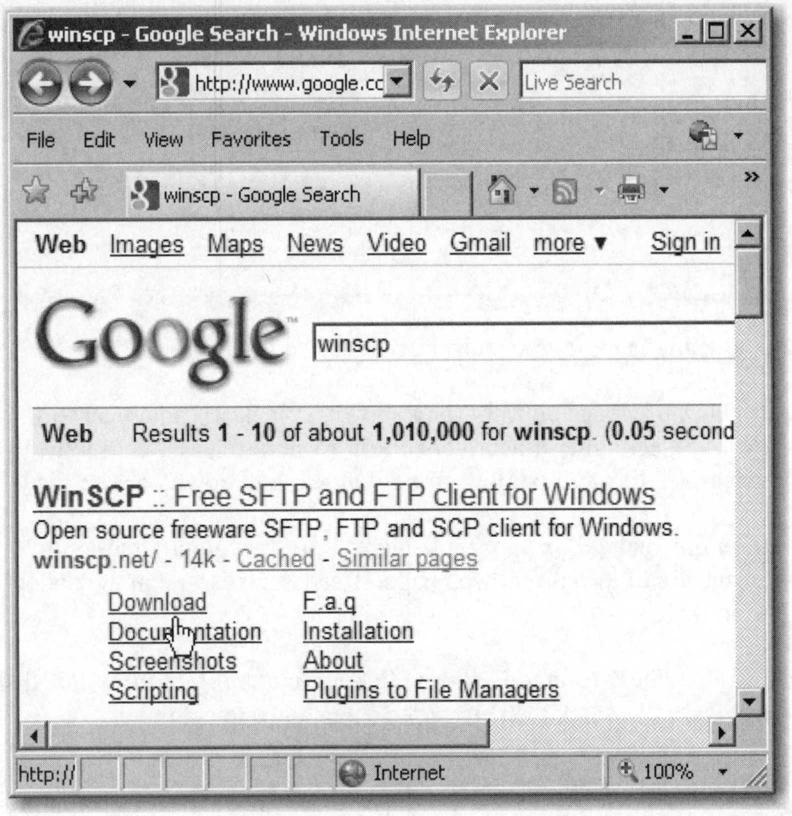

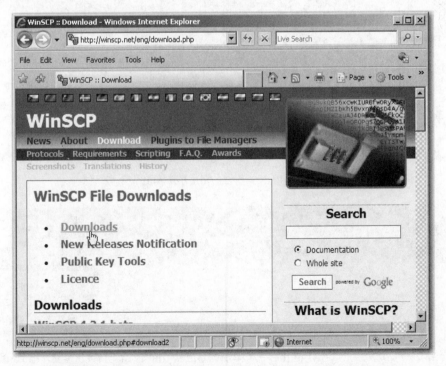

Figure 2: The *Results* page for a Google search for *WinSCP*

3. The Google Results page displays numerous links that meet the search criteria. Figure 2 shows a WinSCP Download link. Click this **link** to continue. The WinSCP *home* page appears (Figure 3). A *Download* link is displayed. Double-click this link to open the WinSCP *download* page.

Figure 3: The WinSCP *home* page showing a *Download* link

WinSCP 4.1.8

Installation package   Released: 2008-12-01

(2,483,799 ytes; 1,510,210 downloads to date)

Figure 4: The download link for the latest stable release of the WinSCP *Installation* package

4.   The WinSCP *Download* page appears (Not shown. It is nearly identical to Figure 3). Download links are shown.   Select either a beta version or a stable release. Currently WinSCP 4.1.8 is the latest stable release.   Click an **Installation package** link to download the file (Figure 4).

5.   The *Information Bar* dialog box appears (Figure 5) to draw your attention to the *Information Bar* displayed near the top of the current web page.   Read the message in the dialog box and then click the **Close** button.

6.   Read the message in the *Information Bar*.   Clicking on the *Information Bar* displays a menu with three choices (Figure 7).   Click the **Download** File choice to continue.

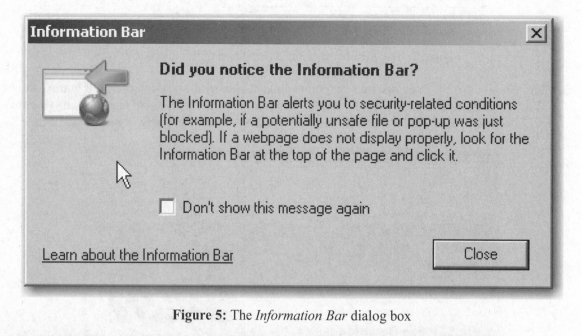

Figure 5: The *Information Bar* dialog box

Figure 6: The *Information Bar* showing the *drop-down menu* that is displayed when the Information Bar is clicked

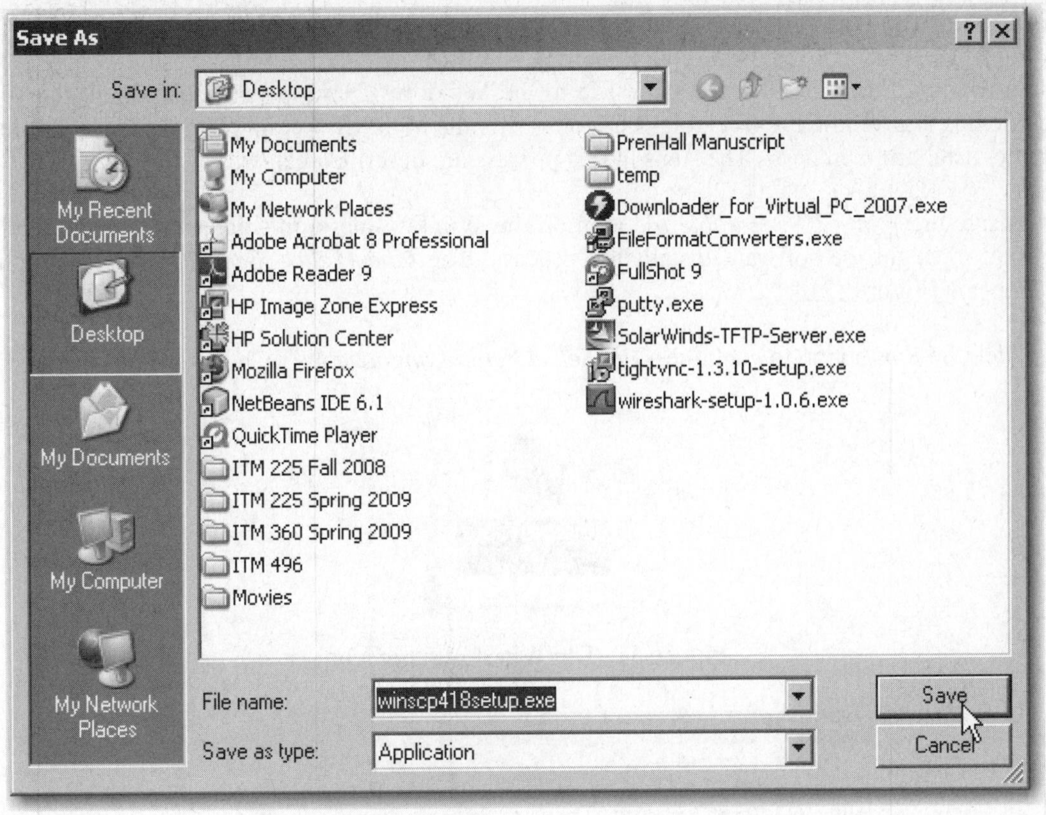

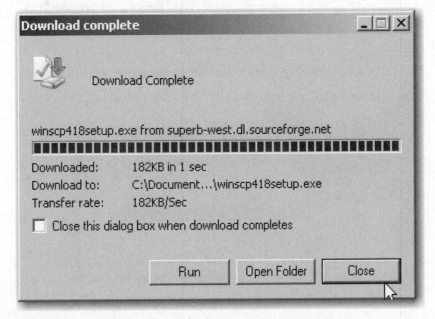

Figure 9: A Windows *Save As* dialog box

7. A Windows *Save As* dialog box appears. Click the **Save** button to save the file to your Windows Desktop. A dialog box displaying the progress of the download appears (Figure 10). The WinSCP setup file is quite small so the download will take just a few seconds. When the download is complete, the progress dialog is replaced with a *Download complete* dialog box. Click the **Close** button. Also close Internet Explorer by clicking the **Close** button on its title bar. You are now ready to install WinSCP.

Figure 10: The *Download complete* dialog box

Part 2: Installing the WinSCP Software

After downloading the WinSCP executable file to the Windows Desktop you must install the software. Double-clicking the WinSCP executable file icon opens the WinSCP Setup Wizard which will lead you through the installation process. The steps in this process are described below.

1. Locate the *WinSCP executable file* icon on the Windows desktop (Figure 11). Double-click the icon to begin the software installation process. The *Open File – Security Warning* dialog box appears (Figure 12).

2. Click the *Run* button to continue. The *Select Setup Language* dialog box appears (Figure 13).

Figure 11: The WinSCP *setup* icon

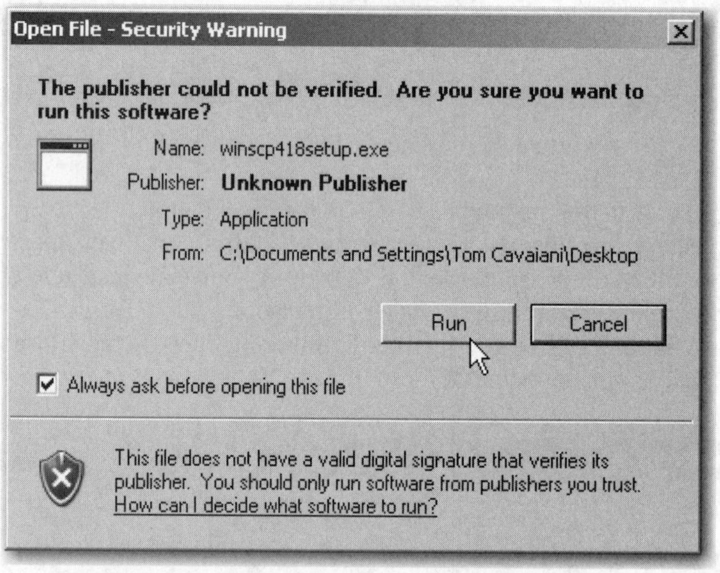

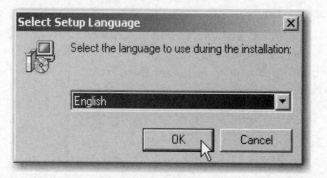

Figure 12: The *Open File – Security Warning* dialog box

Figure 13: The WinSCP *Language Selection* dialog box

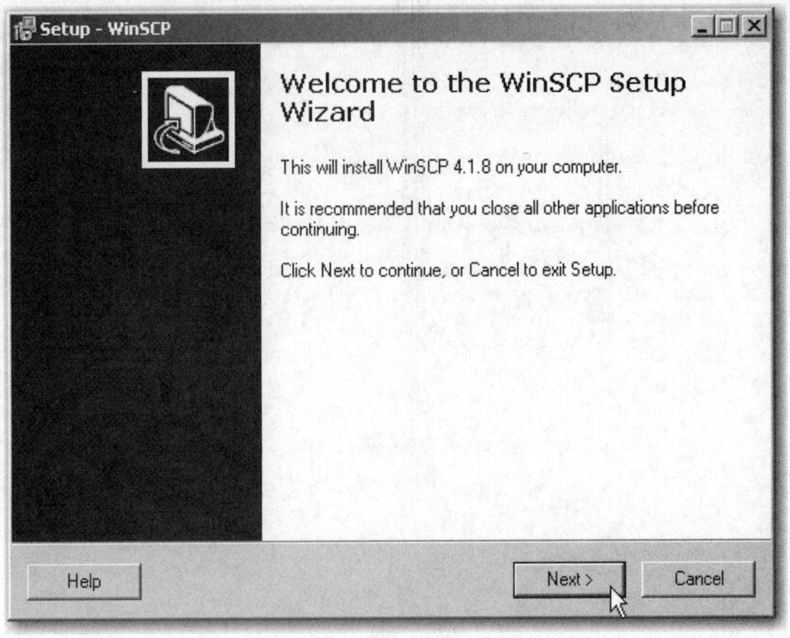

Figure 14: The WinSCP *Setup* dialog

3. Click the **down arrow** to select another language. Click the **OK** button to continue. The *Setup – WinSCP* dialog box appears (Figure 14).

4. Close any applications that may be open. Click the **Next** button to continue. A *License Agreement* dialog box appears (Figure 15).

5. Read the agreement. If you do not agree to its terms click the **Cancel** button. The installation process will be terminated. Otherwise, click the **Next** button. The *Initial user settings* dialog box appears (Figure 16).

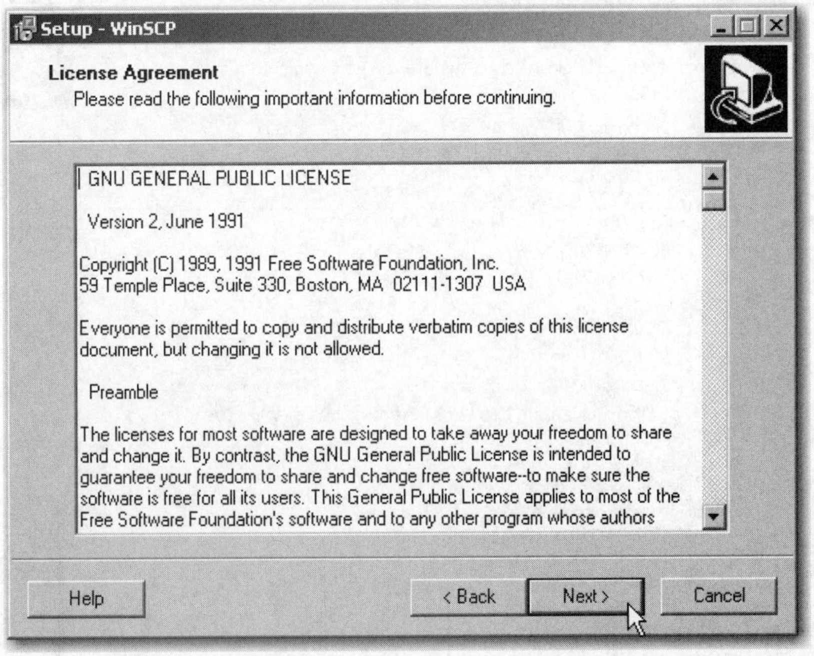

Figure 15: The WinSCP *License Agreement* dialog box

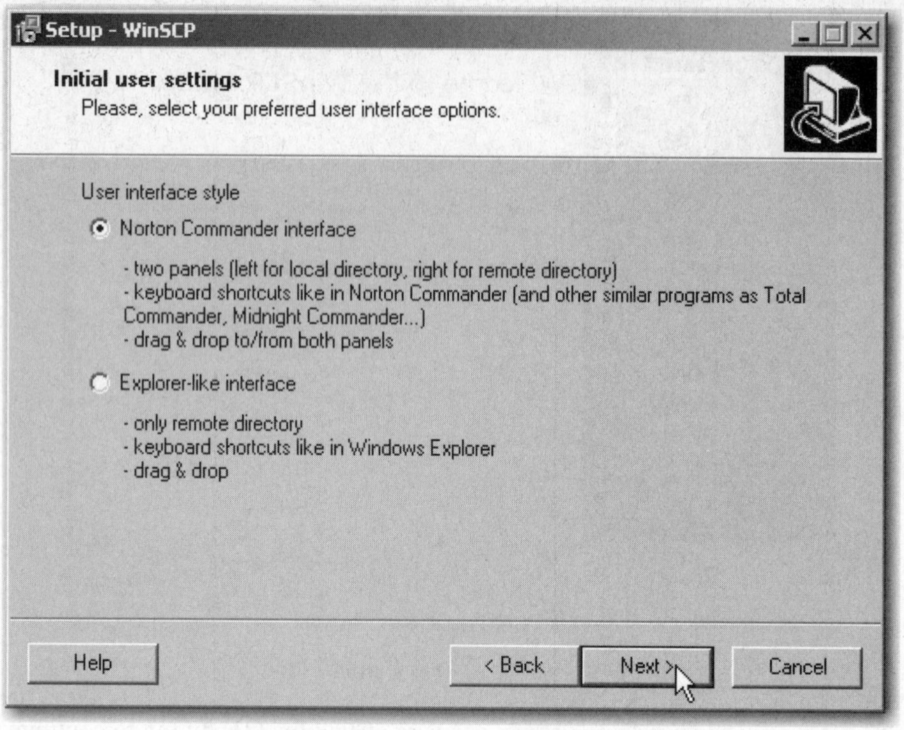

Figure 16: The *Initial user settings* dialog box

6. The default choice is the *Norton Commander* interface. If you prefer an *Explorer-like* interface click the **option button** for that choice. Click the **Next** button to continue.

7. The *Ready to install* dialog box appears (Figure 17). This dialog box summarizes the settings that will be used to install the software on your computer. Click the **Install** button to continue.

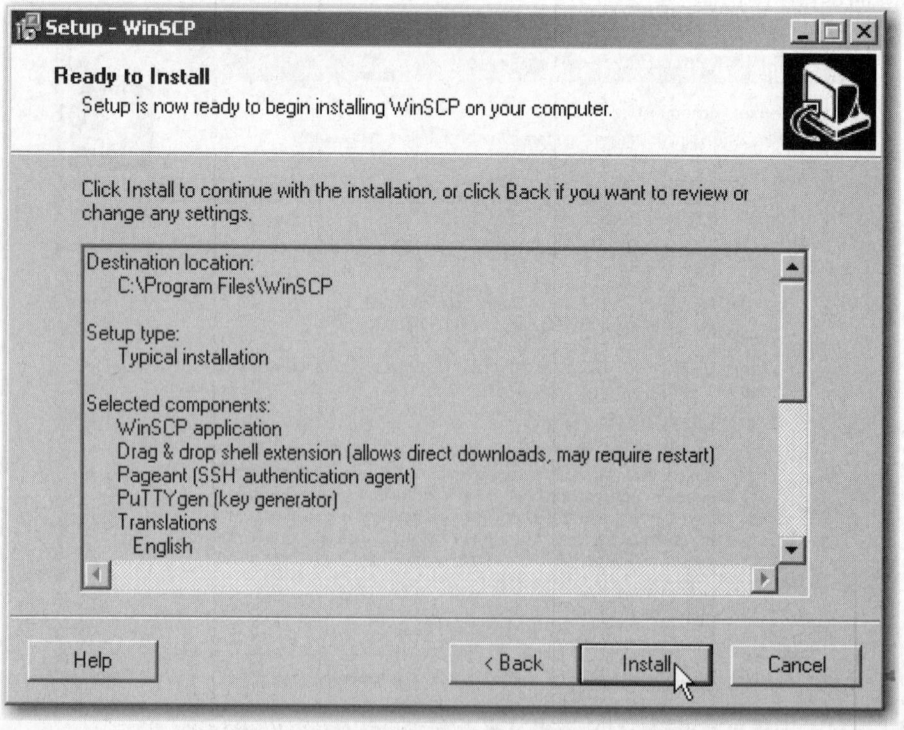

Figure 17: The *Ready to Install* dialog box

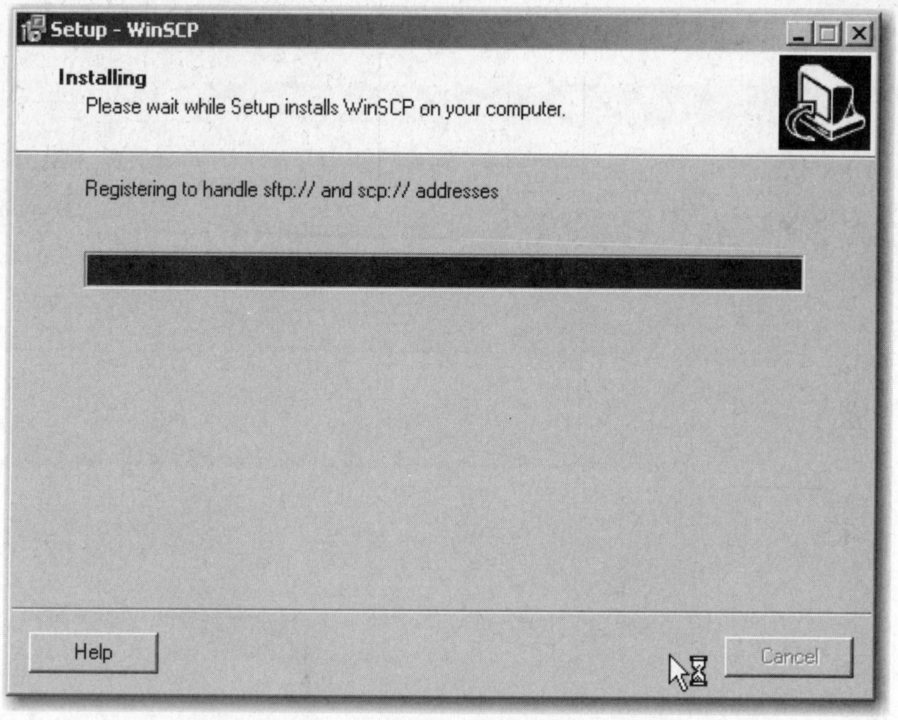

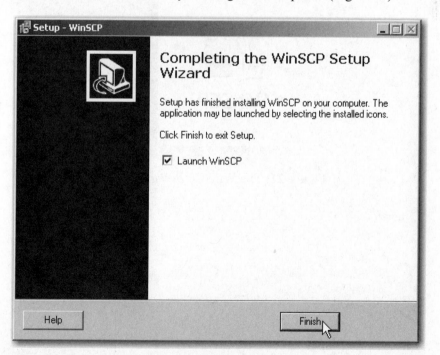

Figure 18: The *Installing* dialog box showing setup progress

8. A dialog box displaying installation progress appears (Figure 18). This dialog box disappears automatically when the installation process is complete and is replaced by a dialog box indicating that WinSCP has been installed on your computer (Figure 19).

9. Click the **Finish** button to close this dialog box. The *WinSCP login screen* (Figure 20) appears on your desktop unless you cleared the *Launch WinSCP* checkbox in the *Setup – WinSCP* dialog box. You can also launch WinSCP by clicking its desktop icon (Figure 21).

Figure 19: The *Setup – WinSCP* dialog box indicating that the installation process is complete

WinSCP Login

Session
    ⌐ Stored sessions
Environment
    ⌐ Directories
SSH
Preferences

┌ Session ─────────────────────────────────
  Host name: Port number:

  | | | 22 ↕|

  User name: Password:

  | | | |

  Private key file:

  | | ... |

┌ Protocol ─────────────────────────────────
  File protocol: | SFTP ▼ | ☑ Allow SCP fallback

                                           Select color

☐ Advanced options

| About... | | Languages | | Login | | Save... | | Close |

Figure 20: The WinSCP *Login* dialog box

Figure 21: The WinSCP *desktop* icon

GLOSSARY

802.x: The set of IEEE standards used for defining LAN protocols.

10BaseT: The technical designation used for Ethernet (IEEE 802.3) LANs, indicating that unshielded twisted pair cabling is being used to transmit data at a maximum rate of 10 Mbps over a maximum distance of 100 meters per segment.

Access method: In general a protocol by which hosts connect to a network for purposes of transmitting data.

ACK: An acknowledgment. A type of message sent to indicate that a block of data arrived at its destination without error. A negative acknowledgement is called a NAK.

Authentication: The requirement for users to prove their identity when requesting to use a network resource.

Authorization: Permission granted to a person or program to take certain actions on a resource.

bps: Stands for bits per second and represents the rate at which data can be transmitted across a network. See bit rate.

Backbone: A network of high-speed communication lines that carries the bulk of the traffic between major segments of the networks.

bandwidth: The range of frequencies over which a signal is spread.

baseline: A measure of network performance that is used as a basis for providing an understanding of the current system to help isolate and identify network performance problems

Bit: Short for "Binary digit". This is the unit of measure for the binary number system. A bit can be either 0 or 1. Typically, a sequence of 8 bits is used to represent one binary character (byte).

Bit rate: The speed at which bits are transmitted, usually expressed in bits per second (bps).

Blu-Ray: Also known as Blu-ray Disc (BD). The next-generation optical disc format developed by the Blu-ray Disc Association to enable recording, rewriting and playback of high-definition video (HD), as well as storing large amounts of data. The format can hold up to 25GB on a single-layer disc and 50GB on a dual-layer disc.

Broadband: A transmission type that employs several transmission channels on a single physical medium. Thus, more than one node can transmit at a time.

BSD: Berkeley Software Distribution. Term used when describing different versions of the Berkeley UNIX software, as in "4.3 BSD UNIX."

bus: a system of pathways on a computer motherboard over which data is transmitted from primary to secondary storage and to peripheral device interfaces.

Bus topology: A LAN architecture in which all computers are attached to a shared medium – commonly a hub or a single coaxial cable terminated at each end. One computer transmits at a time; the signal travels along the bus (both ways) and is received by all other stations.

Byte: A group of eight bits that are processed as a unit.

Cache: A store of information typically located in primary memory that is used to hold data that are frequently needed for processing purposes.

Capture filter: a rule that is used to eliminate extraneous data stored in files that pertain to traffic flow on a network

Cat 5e: An extension of the UTP Cat 5 cable standard that supports transmission rates above 100 Mbps.

Client: A computer system or process that requests a service from another computer system or process. A workstation requesting the contents of a file from a file server is an example of a client of a file server.

Client\server model: The processes or programs used by hosts to obtain network services. Examples include the *name server/name resolver* paradigm of DNS and *file server/file client* relationships.

Client\server application - an application in which a client program requests services that are provided by another computer or process called a server.

Cloud computing: Using multiple computers connected to the Internet to provide common applications, processing power, and file storage capabilities to end users.

Coaxial cable: A type of cable used on older computer networks and cable television, consisting of a central core that carries the signal, an insulating layer, a layer of shielding, and an outer insulation jacket. The shielding protects the signal transmitted on the inner wire from electrical-magnetic interference.

Collision: An event that occurs on a CSMA/CD network when two stations attempt to transmit simultaneously. The signals interfere with each other, forcing the two stations to back off and try again.

Collision detection: A network management technique that allows each computer to transmit whenever it chooses. If a collision is detected, the messages are retransmitted.

Command-line interface: A simple interface that provides a command prompt for entering commands that can be used to manage a computer's file system or run programs by name.

Communications hardware: Hardware that allows a workstation to access and transmit data over a network.

CSMA: Stands for *Carrier Sense Multiple Access*. Stations using this access method "listen to" the channel before sending a packet to determine if another station is attempting to send a signal at the same time.

CSMA/CD: Stands for *Carrier Sense Multiple Access with Collision Detection*. This is a popular access method used on Ethernet LANs. Under this scheme, a computer senses the channel and transmits data if the channel is idle. If the channel is busy, the station waits until the channel is idle, and then transmits immediately. If a collision occurs the station waits a randomly determined amount of time, and then attempts to re-transmit the data.

Delay: an attribute of a network that impedes the flow of data between source and destination nodes.

Directory: a file system location used for organizing and storing files that may have similar characteristics based upon some criteria.

DHCP: Stands for Dynamic Host Configuration Protocol, the protocol used by DHCP servers to provide IP addresses to workstations requesting a network address. These addresses are "leased" to the workstations so that they can be recovered by the DHCP server when the lease expires and then assigned to other workstations requesting an IP address.

DNS: See *Domain Name System*.

Domain: Part of a network naming hierarchy. An Internet domain name, for example, consists of a sequence of names separated by periods such as *tundra.mpk.ca.us*.

Domain Name System: An application layer protocol in the TCP/IP protocol stack that resolves host computer domain names to IP addresses and vice-versa.

Driver: Software that enables a computer to communicate with devices like NICs, printers, monitors, and hard drives. Each driver has a specific purpose, such as handling Ethernet network communications.

EIA: Stands for the Electronic Industries Alliance, which is an alliance of trade associations for electronics manufacturers in the United States.

Ethernet: A popular LAN technology (invented by Xerox Corporation and developed jointly by Xerox, Intel, and Digital Equipment Corporation) that uses a shared channel and the CSMA/CD access method. Basic Ethernet operates at 10 Mbps, Fast Ethernet operates at 100 Mbps, and Gigabit Ethernet operates at 1000 Mbps.

Fast Ethernet: A class of Ethernet technology that operates at the rate of 100 Mbps.

FDDI: Stands for *Fiber Distributed Data Interface*. A token passing network operating at 100 Mbps using dual counter-rotating rings of fiber-optic cable. Typically used as a backbone network in metropolitan areas to link LANs to WANs.

File: a collection of zero or more data items.

File server: A network computer that makes software applications, data files, and network utilities available to other network client computers.

Frame: A data link layer "packet" containing header and trailer information used for transmission purposes over the physical network media.

FTP: Stands for *File Transfer Protocol*. The Internet protocol (and program) used to transfer files between hosts.

Full Duplex: A transmission mode where data are transmitted between a sender and a receiver at the same time. Multiple channels are required for this type of communication.

Gbps: Stands for Giga bits per second. A unit of data transfer equal to 1000 Mbps or 10^9 bps.

Gigabit Ethernet: An Ethernet specification that supports data transmission rates up to 1000 Mbps (1 Gbps).

Graphical User Interface or **GUI**: a computer interface that provides menus and dialog boxes so that users can use a pointing device, such as a computer mouse, to access and modify data as well as configure the computer system.

Guided media: Different types of cabling such as fiber optic, coaxial, and twisted-pair that physically connect network node together for data transmission purposes.

Half duplex: A mode of data transmission in which data can be sent in both directions, but only in one direction at a time. A walkie-talkie is an example of a device that transmits data in this fashion.

Hertz (Hz): The unit of measure associated with the frequency of a signal, where the signal is modeled as a continuous sine wave. The number of Hertz is equivalent to the number of cycles per second made by the signal.

Host: A term used to describe any device attached to a network that allows a user to log into the network and do useful work.

HTML: Stands for the *Hyper Text Markup Language*, which is the language used on the World-Wide Web to create web pages.

HTTP: Stands for *Hyper Text Transport Protocol*, which is the protocol used for transmitting hypertext files over the Internet. HTTP allows a client program, such as a browser, to request pages from a server program, commonly called a web server.

Hypertext: In general, document text that contains virtual links to other documents accessible on the network that when chosen by a reader causes another document to be retrieved and displayed. See HTML.

Hub: A device, often called a multi-port repeater that interconnects two or more workstations using a physical star topology. Incoming data are broadcast onto all outgoing connections.

Institute of Electrical and Electronic Engineers (IEEE): A professional non-profit organization that defines network standards, such as IEEE 802.3.

IEEE: See Institute of Electrical and Electronics Engineers

IEEE 802.3: The IEEE standard for Ethernet LANs that use the CSMA/CD media access protocol.

Internet: When spelled with a capital "I" this term refers to a collection of networks connected by routers to form a world-wide network that allows any network host to communicate with any other network host.

Internetwork: A collection of networks connected by routers that allows any network host to communicate with any other network host.

IP address: A 32-bit (IP version 4) or 128-bit (IP version 6) long address assigned to hosts using the TCP/IP protocol. The dotted decimal format of an IP address is written as four octets separated with periods. A portion of an IP addresses is used to designate the network address and the remainder is used to identify a host on the network.

ipconfig: a DOS utility program that provides feedback for determining if a path from one host to another exists on the network.

Kbps: Stands for *kilo bits per second*. A unit of data transfer equal to 1000 bps.

LAN: See *Local Area Network*.

Local Area Network: A class of computer network that covers a small geographic area, such as a room, a building, or a campus. A LAN is usually owned by a single organization and physically located on the organization's premises.

Linux: An operating system developed by Linux Torvalds that is based upon UNIX and designed to be used on personal computers. Numerous distributions of Linux exist including Suse, Knoppix, Red Hat, Fedora, FreeBSD, and others.

Local computer: A computer that is physically accessible to an end-user.

Logical topology: Refers to the methods used to send data from one computer (or device) to another. For example, Ethernet uses a logical bus topology in which data are sent to a repeater and then broadcast out to all hosts connected to the repeater.

MHz: Stands for *Megahertz* which is a measure of frequency equivalent to 1 million cycles per second.

MAC: Stands for *Medium Access Control Protocol*. See access method.

Motherboard: The main circuit board in a computer. The motherboard contains sockets for the CPU, RAM, peripheral devices.

Network: Two or more computers connected together so that they can share resources. The computers can be connected with wires or send signals using wireless methods and devices.

Network traffic: Denotes the number, size, and the frequency of packets transmitted across a network in a given amount of time.

Network interface card (NIC): A printed circuit board that plugs into a slot on the motherboard of a computer, file server, printer, or other device to connect it to a network and allow communication with other network nodes. A NIC can transmit and a receive data and can be described as a transceiver.

Netstat: A DOS command-line utility program that displays network protocol statistics and current TCP/IP network connections.

NSLookup: A DOS command-line utility program that displays DNS host name to IP address mappings.

Node: Any device connected to a network such as a personal computer (PC), a mainframe computer, a router, a printer, or other network equipment.

NOS: Stands for *Network Operating System*. A large, complex program that manages the common resources of a local area network, as well as providing standard operating system services. Examples include NetWare, Linux, and MS Windows Server.

Optical fiber: A type of cable consisting of one or more hollow glass or plastic cores covered by protective cladding. Optical signals (pulses of light) are transmitted through the fibers. The optical fiber cable can transmit extremely large amounts of data. Optical fiber is used for undersea cables, and also for country-wide telecommunications backbones.

OSI model: Stands for *Open Systems Interconnection* model. This model defines a network architecture that provides a basis for developing network protocol standards so that different manufacturers can develop equipment that can interconnect with equipment made by other manufacturers. The OSI model formally defines and codifies the concept of a network architecture composed of multiple layers that communicate with each other. The OSI model consists of the following seven layers: (1) physical; (2) data link; (3) network; (4) transport; (5) session; (6) presentation; and (7) application.

Packet: A unit of data formatted for transmission over a network. A packet normally includes control information, the packet's source and destination addresses, the data to be transmitted and error-checking information.

Packet analyzer: A program that can capture and display the contents of all packets transmitted on the network to a workstation's NIC for the purpose of determining if problems exist on the network or one of its nodes. A packet analyzer also includes filtering tools that facilitate the analysis of the data captured by hiding irrelevant packets.

Peer-to-peer network: A class of networks in which all computers on the network are consider equals and are capable of sharing resources with each other.

Physical topology: The way computers and other networking devices are physically connected to each other. Common physical topologies are star, bus, and ring.

ping: Supposedly short for *packet internet groper*. A program used to test if one station can communicate with another on a network. Ping sends an ICMP echo request from a source to a destination computer and waits for a reply. If the destination machine is running and connected to the source, it will send a reply to the requesting computer.

Port: An identifier used by transport layer protocols to distinguish among multiple simultaneous connections to a single destination host.

Protocol: A set of rules for formatting, ordering, and error-checking data sent across a network.

Protocol Analyzer: See packet analyzer.

PuTTY: An open-source program with a graphical user interface that is used primarily for connecting to a remote computer.

RAID: Stands for *Redundant Array of Independent Devices*. RAID defines different combinations of multiple hard drives for replicating data.

RAM: Stands for *Random Access Memory*. The primary storage media used by a computer. RAM is volatile, i.e. if power is lost so is all data stored in RAM.

ROM: Stands for *Read Only Memory*. A permanent type of memory that is typically used to hold instructions for starting up or "booting" a computer.

Remote computer: A networked computer that cannot be physically accessed by end users. From a local computer an end user must use a terminal emulation program, perhaps over a virtual private network (VPN) to access the remote computer and its resources.

Repeater: A hardware device used to either strengthen and/or retransmit network signals without making routing decisions. Repeaters are considered to be physical layer devices. See hub.

RJ 45: A connector used on unshielded twisted-pair (UTP) cable.

Router: A computer or dedicated device that forwards packets from one LAN to another by comparing data stored in its routing table with the destination address stored in a packet's header.

Security policy: A set of guidelines established by an organization that have been developed to protect valuable company data from threats, disasters, and security breaches.

Sector: a subdivision of a track on a hard disk drive platter.

Server: A provider of services, such as file services, print services, mail services, and web services.

Signal: Electrical or electromagnetic impulses that represent data transmitted over a network medium.

SMTP Stands for *Simple Mail Transport Protocol*. SMTP is an electronic mail protocol used on the Internet. It is the protocol that sends messages from one server to another. End users must use another protocol, such as IMAP to access and read their messages.

Software: Program instructions used to direct computer hardware.

Star topology: A physical network configuration where computers are connected to a hub or switch by cables. A hub redirects messages sent to it either to all connected workstations. A switch sets up a dedicated connection between sender and receiver.

Switch: A connectivity device that is capable of setting up short-term dedicated connections between senders and receivers so that multiple users can communicate simultaneously.

TCP: Stands for *Transmission Control Protocol*. TCP is the primary transport protocol in the Internet suite of protocols. It provides reliable, connection-oriented, full-duplex data transmission. TCP uses IP for delivery of packets over the network.

TCP/IP Protocol Suite: Sometimes called the Internet suite. A collection of communications protocols divided into layers. Each layer solves a set of problems involving the transmission of data, and provides a well-defined service to the upper layers based on using services available at the lower layers.

Telnet: The virtual terminal protocol in the Internet suite of protocols. Allows users of a local host to log onto a remote host and interact as it they were accessing the host locally.

Terminal Emulation Software: A program that allows a computer to behave like a terminal so that it can access a remote host.

Terminator: A device that is connected to the end of network cable. For coaxial cable used on a LAN a terminator absorbs signals "down the line" and keeps them from "echoing back" to their source and causing interference or a collision. UTP cable has RJ-45 connectors connected to its ends. Sometimes these connectors are called terminators or are said to terminate the cable.

TFTP: Stands for Trivial File Transport Protocol, which is a variation on FTP. TFTP uses UDP instead of TCP as its transport layer protocol and does not require authentication, like FTP does.

TIA: Stands for Telecommunications Industry Association, which is a global trade association that represents about 600 telecommunications companies. TIA helps create universal networking standards that have been used worldwide.

Topology: The physical layout or configuration of a local or a wide area network.

Tracert or traceroute: A DOS command-line utility program that provides a count of the number of hops (routers traversed) between two communicating network hosts.

Track: Concentric circles on the surface of a hard disk platter that are used for storing data.

Twisted pair: For network applications, typically four pairs of insulated copper wires that are twisted together to eliminate electromagnetic interference between the wires. Twisted pair wiring is either unshielded (UTP) or shielded (STP). A variety of categories are available. The lower categories are used in telephone lines, while the higher categories are used in LANs.

UDP: Stands for *User Datagram Protocol*. UDP is a transport layer protocol in the Internet suite of protocols. UDP, like TCP, uses IP for delivery; unlike TCP, UDP does not establish a connection between sender and receiver nor does it provide for reliable transmission of packets. UDP is a lightweight "best effort" type protocol.

UNIX: A multi-user computer operating system designed to be used by many people at the same time. It is the most common operating system used on servers on the Internet.

URL: Stands for *Uniform Resource Locator*. A URL provides a format for specifying host addresses used to locate pages on the World Wide Web (WWW). **HTTP://www.boisestate.edu/** is an example of the URL that can be used to locate and display home page for Boise State University. URLs are typically entered into the Locator text box of a browser program, such as Firefox or Internet Explorer.

USB: Stands for Universal Serial Bus, which is a modern standard for connecting peripheral devices to personal computers.

VLAN: Stands for *Virtual Local Area Network*. A VLAN uses software to configure a network into subnetworks of logical workgroups, independent of the physical network topology.

WAN: Stands for *Wide Area Network*. A WAN covers a large geographical area (e.g. a country, a continent). Telephone networks and the Internet are examples of WANs.

Wireless Access Point: A device, based upon one of the IEEE 802.11x standards, that receives data packets sent over radio waves from a computer and then transmits the packets to a wired network. Wireless access points can be configured to communicate among themselves in what is called an *ad hoc* network.

Wireless communications: Sending signals through the air by using radio waves, microwaves, and satellites for transmission of data in telephone and computer networks. In most all cases the wireless signal is eventually send to a wired network for delivery to its final destination.

Web Server: A computer that has been configured to respond to network browser requests from clients for information stored on the web server in the form of web pages.

Web Space: The storage space located on a web server connected to the Internet. The purpose of this storage space is to provide a location for users to store web pages that they want to make accessible by other Internet users. Web space can be leased from vendors who provide web hosting services on their computers.

WinSCP: An open source file transfer application with a graphical user interface. WinSCP provides both secure (encrypted) and non-secure (unencrypted) file transfer options.

World Wide Web (WWW): A collection of resources that form a global information system on the Internet. The HTTP protocol is used to access these resources.

Workgroup: a collection of network computers that share common resources and services. Many organizations create departmental workgroups so that members of the department have access to the information they need to do their jobs.

Workstation: An end-user computer that can be used as either a standalone computer or as a client for accessing network services or other computers connected to the network.

INDEX